Hate Mail

Hate Mail
Mr Bingo

MICHAEL JOSEPH
an imprint of
PENGUIN BOOKS

MICHAEL JOSEPH

Published by the Penguin Group

Penguin Books Ltd, 80 Strand,
London WC2R 0RL, England

Penguin Group (USA) Inc., 375 Hudson Street,
New York, New York 10014, USA

Penguin Group (Canada), 90 Eglinton Avenue East,
Suite 700, Toronto, Ontario, Canada M4P 2Y3
(a division of Pearson Penguin Canada Inc.)

Penguin Ireland, 25 St Stephen's Green, Dublin 2,
Ireland (a division of Penguin Books Ltd)

Penguin Group (Australia), 250 Camberwell Road,
Camberwell, Victoria 3124, Australia
(a division of Pearson Australia Group Pty Ltd)

Penguin Books India Pvt Ltd, 11 Community Centre,
Panchsheel Park, New Delhi – 110 017, India

Penguin Group (NZ), 67 Apollo Drive, Rosedale,
North Shore 0632, New Zealand
(a division of Pearson New Zealand Ltd)

Penguin Books (South Africa) (Pty) Ltd,
Block D, Rosebank Office Park, Parktown North,
Gauteng 2193, South Africa

Penguin Books Ltd, Registered Offices:
80 Strand, London WC2R 0RL, England

www.penguin.com

First published 2012
1

Printed in China
Colour reproduction by Altaimage Ltd

A CIP catalogue record for this book is available from the British Library

ISBN: 978–0–718–15903–0

ALWAYS LEARNING PEARSON

Dedication:

To the business studies teacher who said to me:
'Get used to failing, you'll be doing a lot of it in life.'

This book is dedicated to you, sir.

Introduction

I love post.

With the majority of modern post consisting mainly of bills and junk mail, I'm worried that people don't get enough fun post these days.
So I set up Hate Mail.
It's a simple concept. I invited strangers to pay me £10 and in return I'd send them an offensive postcard with an original drawing on. It was a late-night drunk idea (naturally) but it really took off. So much so that I had to close the service after six days because it proved too popular.
This book is a collection of 100 of my favourite Hate Mails.

Please enjoy – oh, and go fuck yourself.

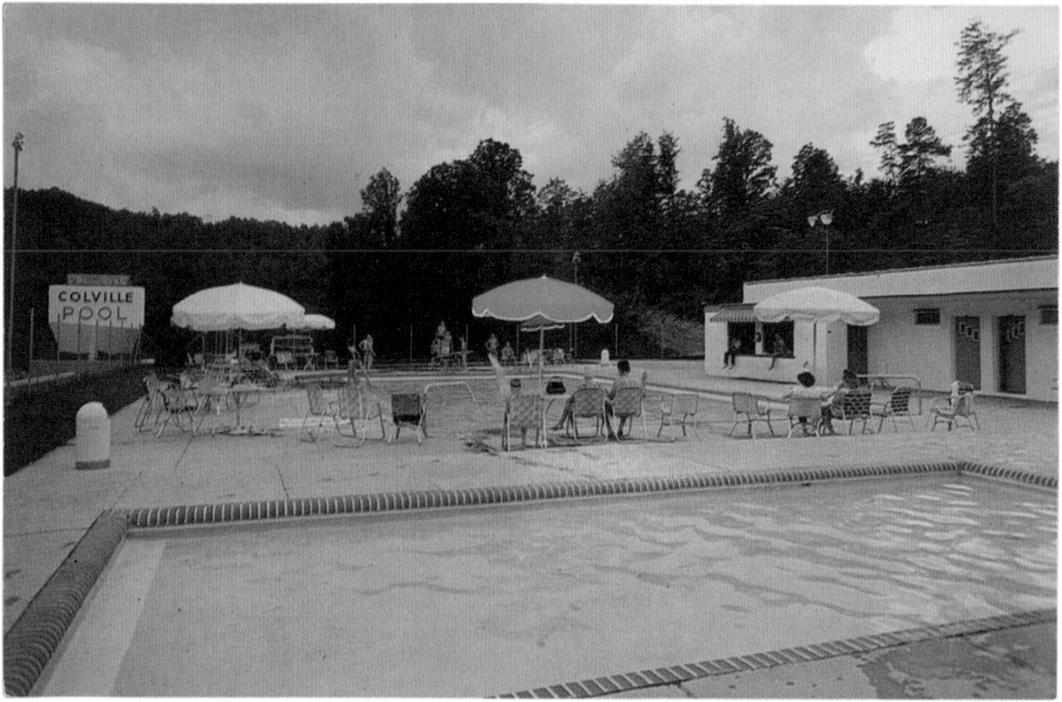
COLVILLE
POOL

COLVILLE POOL
(Open to the Public)
ELA, NORTH CAROLINA

Dear MARK

FUCK YOU

AND FUCK YOUR CAT

MR Bingo

Published by Thomas B. Kehoe, P. O. Box 192, Asheville, N.C.

POST CARD

Address

Mark FERGUSON

21B RICHARDSON Road
HOVE
East SUSSEX
BN3 5RB

S3921

PLACE
STAMP
HERE

IDK-2172

SLY. 151.   WEST BEACH. SELSEY.   Copyright FUS

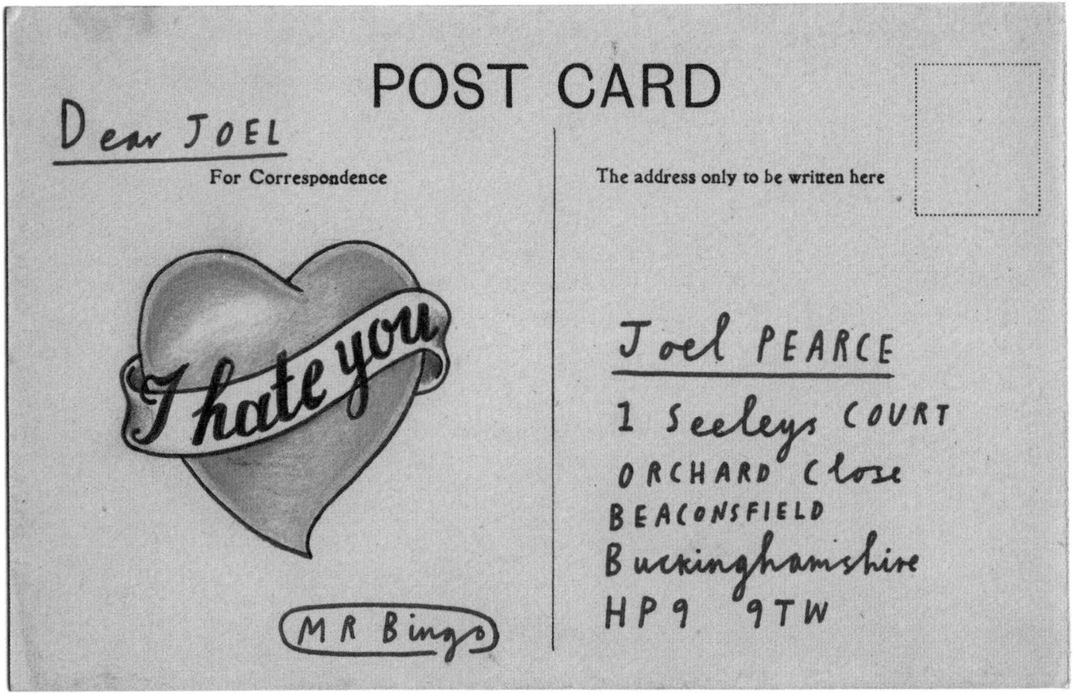

POST CARD

Dear JOEL

For Correspondence

The address only to be written here

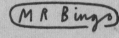

MR Bingo

Joel PEARCE
1 Seeleys COURT
ORCHARD Close
BEACONSFIELD
Buckinghamshire
HP9 9TW

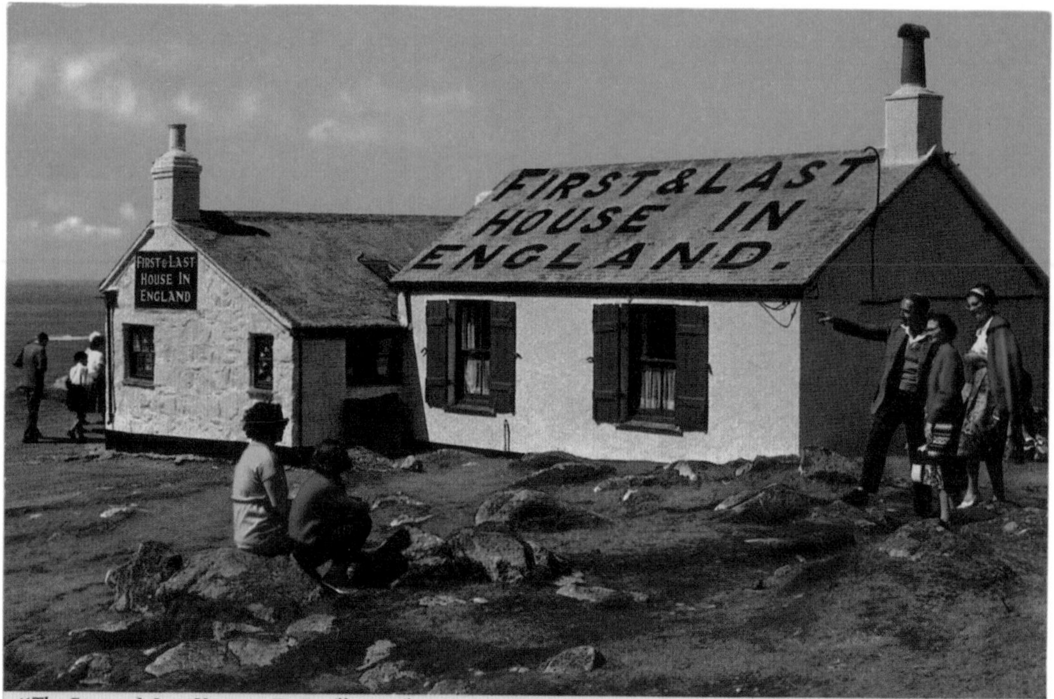
FIRST & LAST HOUSE IN ENGLAND
FIRST & LAST HOUSE IN ENGLAND.
"The First and Last House in England", Land's End, Cornwall.

Photo: E. Ludwig, John Hinde Studios.

Dear CHRIS

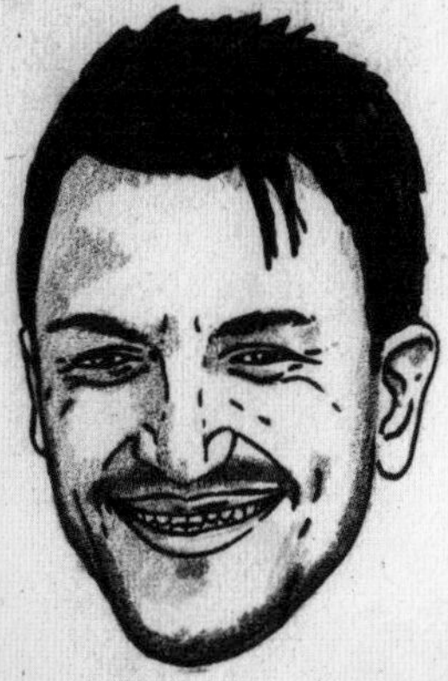

YOU WILL NEVER BE AS GOOD AS PETER ANDRE

MR Bingo

JOHN HINDE ORIGINAL

Published by John Hinde (Distributors) Ltd., 3/5, Dunn Street, London. E.8. Printed in the Republic of Ireland.

CHRIS Leaning
15 MOORFIELD Road
NEW HAW
ADDLESTONE
Surrey
KT13 5LB
UK

SPRINGFIELDS SPALDING

BY SPRING PHOTOGRAPHIC LTD SPALDING

Printed by Jarrold & Sons Ltd Norwich, England

POST OFFICE PREFERRED
*
AFFIX STAMP HERE

ALL BRITISH PRODUCTION

Dear KEVIN

You're a COCK JOCKEY

MR Bingo

KEVIN Lynn

22 BARET Road

WALKERGATE

Newcastle Upon TYNE

TYNE & WEAR

NE6 4HY

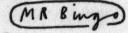

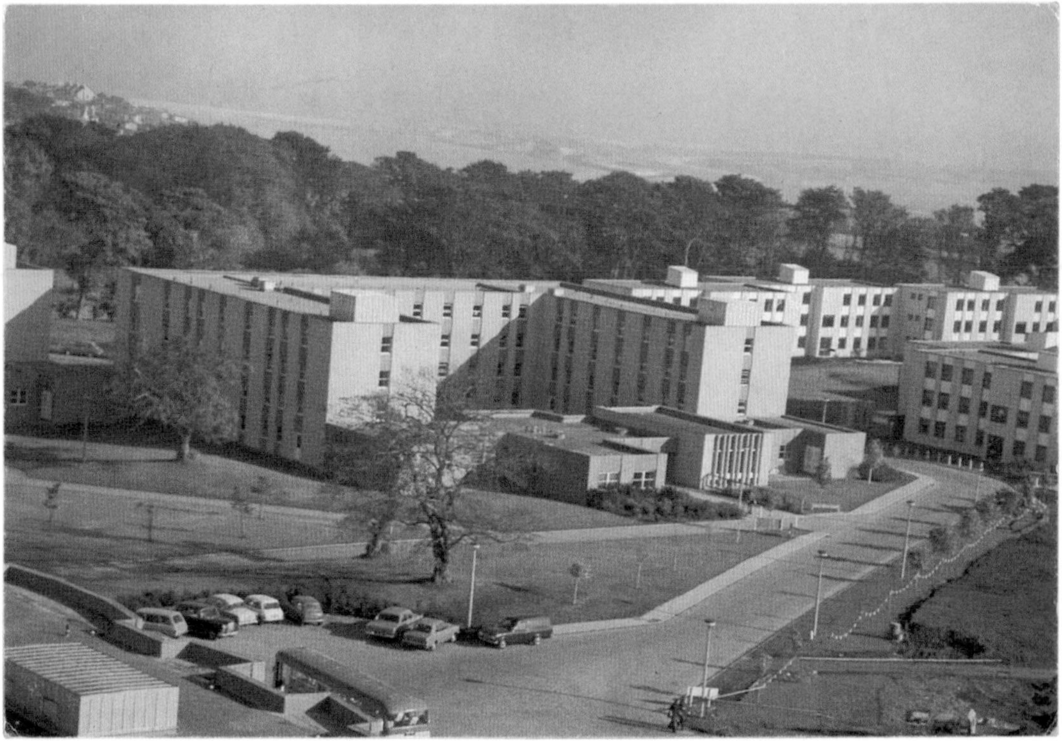

Dear TIM

YOU'RE A MASSIVE

NATURAL COLOUR
J. Arthur Dixon
PHOTOGRAVURE
POST CARD

TIM Diacon

2 HURST Road

WALTHAMSTOW

London

E17 3BL

MR Bingo

Printed and Published by J. Arth

S.A. VAAL
(Tonnage 32,697)

SS. 6295

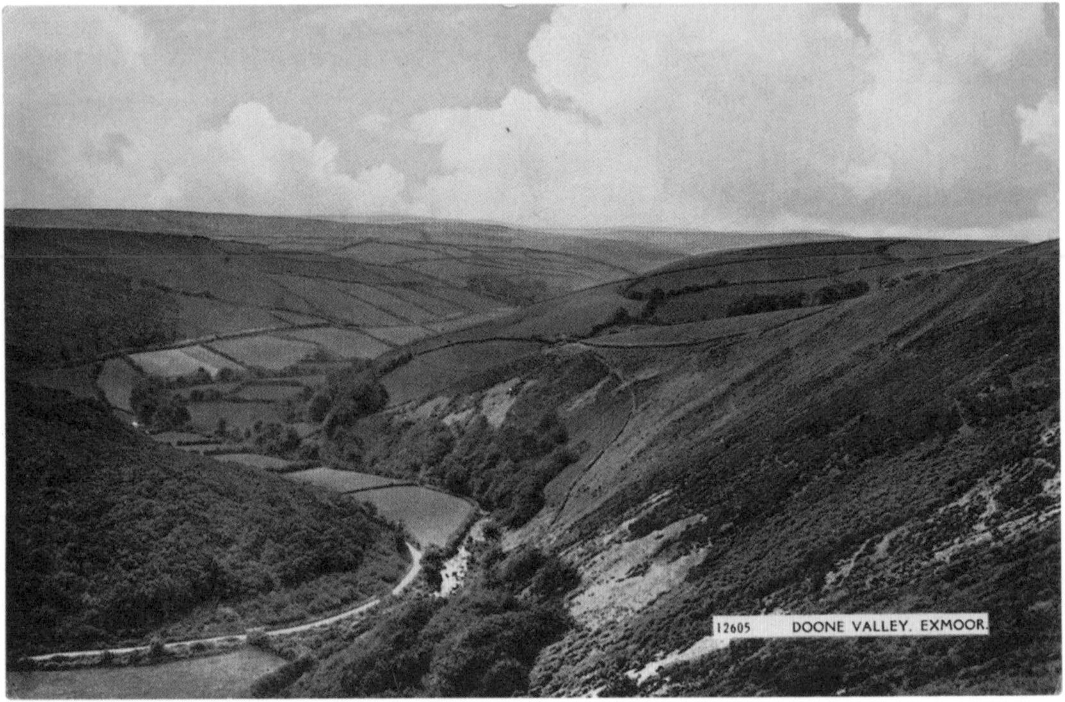
12605 DOONE VALLEY. EXMOOR.

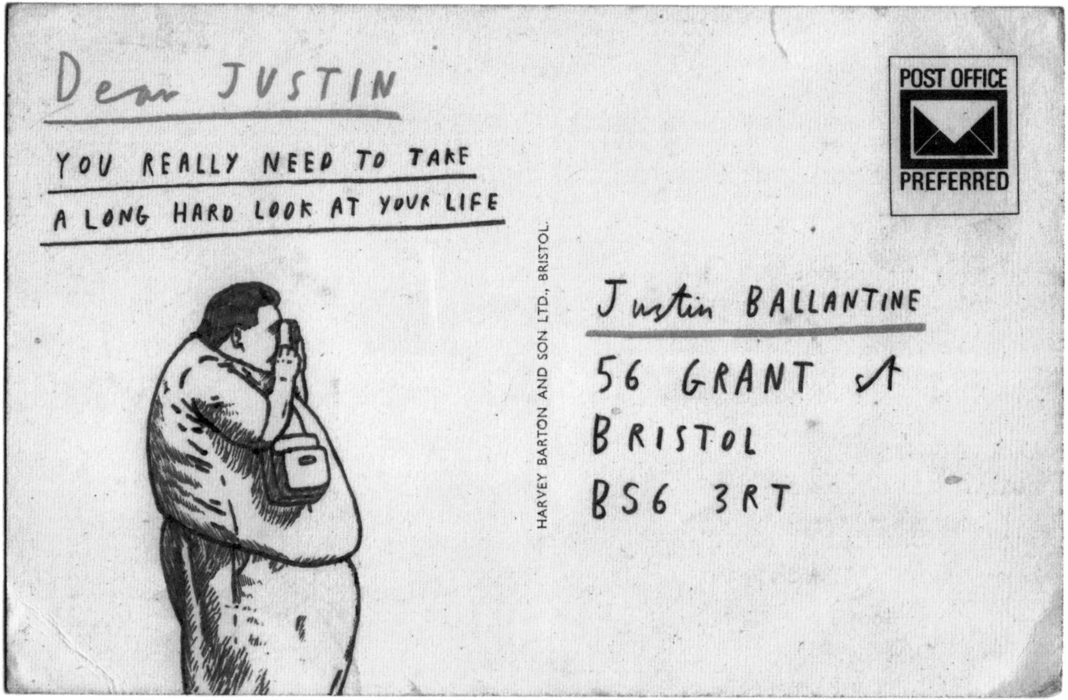
Dear JUSTIN
YOU REALLY NEED TO TAKE
A LONG HARD LOOK AT YOUR LIFE
HARVEY BARTON AND SON LTD., BRISTOL.
POST OFFICE
PREFERRED
Justin BALLANTINE
56 GRANT St
BRISTOL
BS6 3RT

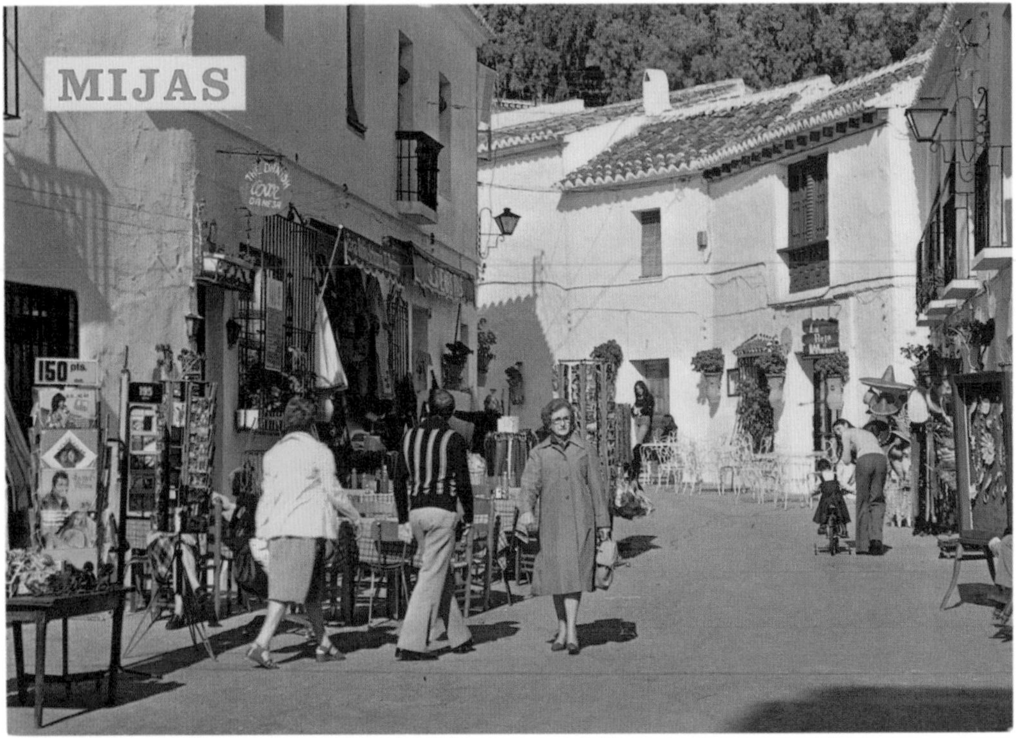
MIJAS
150 pts.

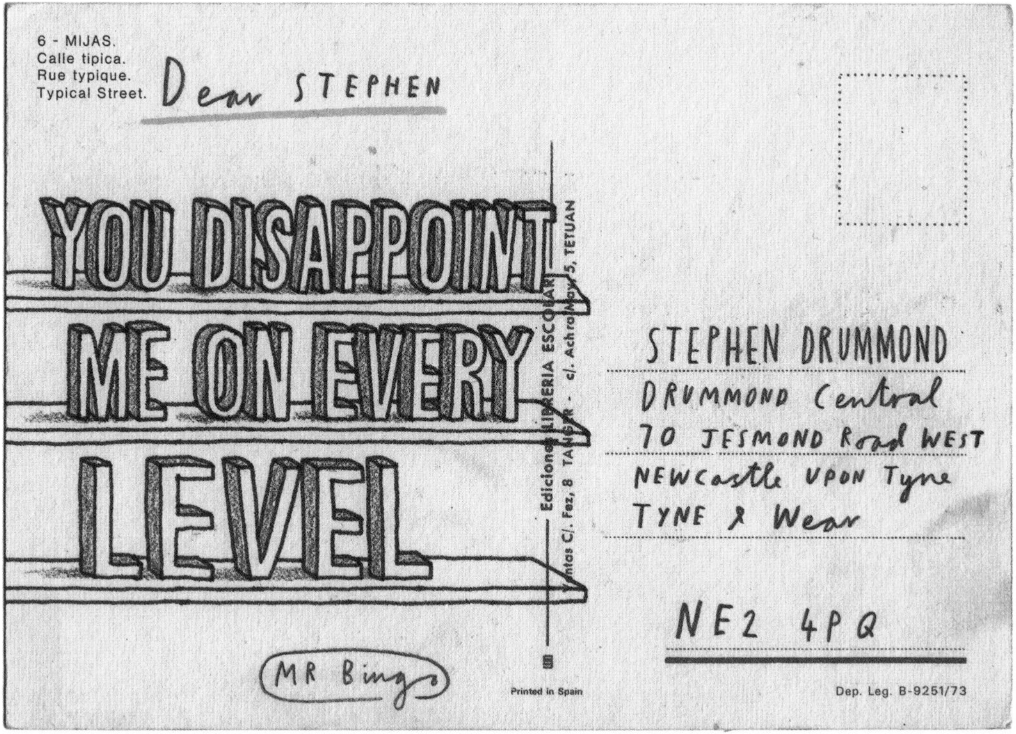
6 - MIJAS.
Calle tipica.
Rue typique.
Typical Street.
Dear STEPHEN
YOU DISAPPOINT ME ON EVERY LEVEL
MR Bingo
Ediciones LIBRERIA ESCOLAR
Ventas C/. Fez, 8 TANGER - c/. Achra May 5, TETUAN
Printed in Spain
STEPHEN DRUMMOND
DRUMMOND Central
70 JESMOND Road WEST
NEWCastle UPON Tyne
TYNE & Wear
NE2 4PQ
Dep. Leg. B-9251/73

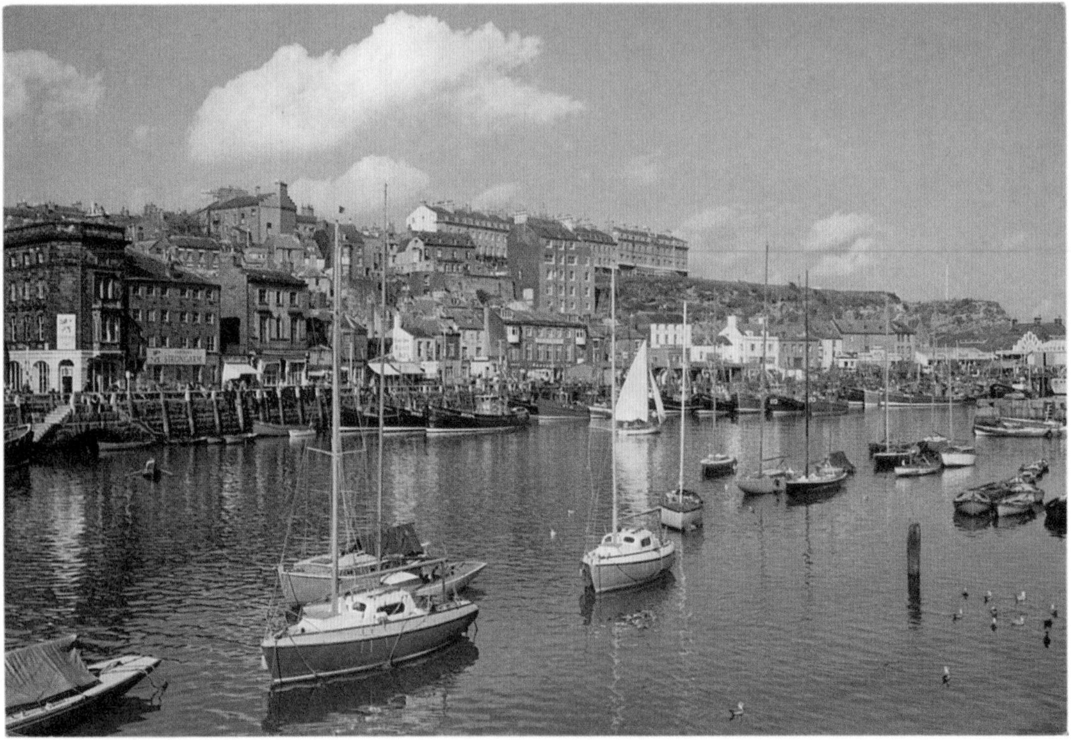

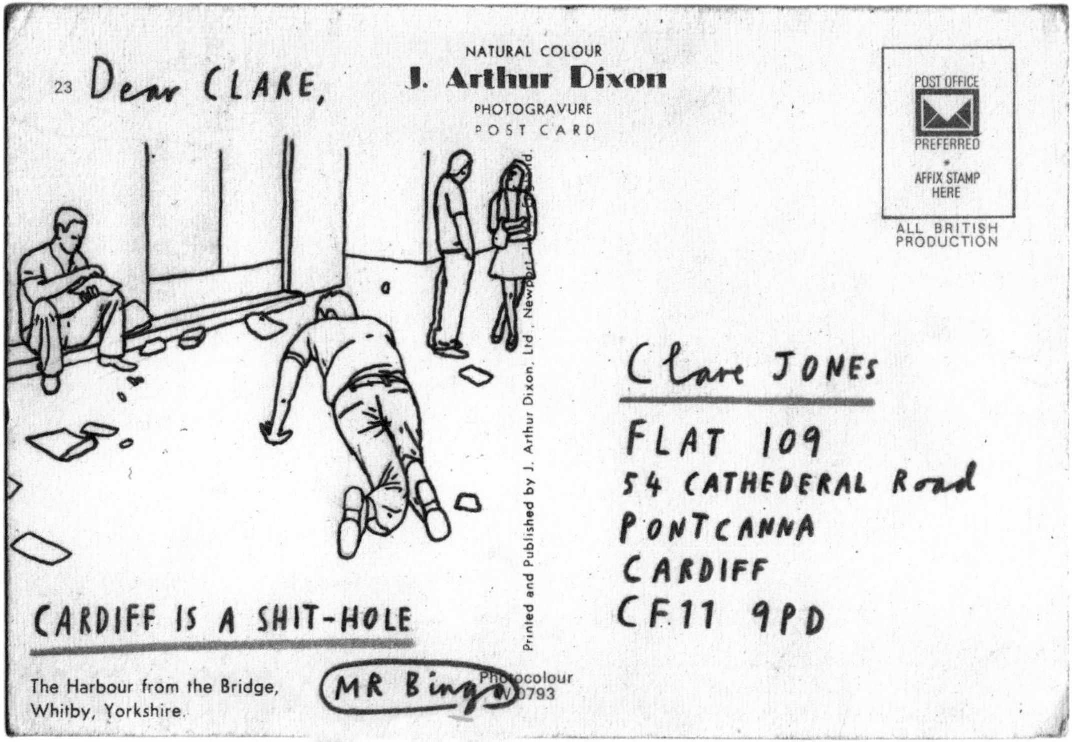
23 Dear CLARE,
NATURAL COLOUR
J. Arthur Dixon
PHOTOGRAVURE
POST CARD
POST OFFICE
PREFERRED
AFFIX STAMP HERE
ALL BRITISH PRODUCTION
Printed and Published by J. Arthur Dixon, Ltd., Newport
Clare JONES
FLAT 109
54 CATHEDERAL Road
PONTCANNA
CARDIFF
CF11 9PD
CARDIFF IS A SHIT-HOLE
The Harbour from the Bridge,
Whitby, Yorkshire.
MR Bingo
Photocolour
W.0793

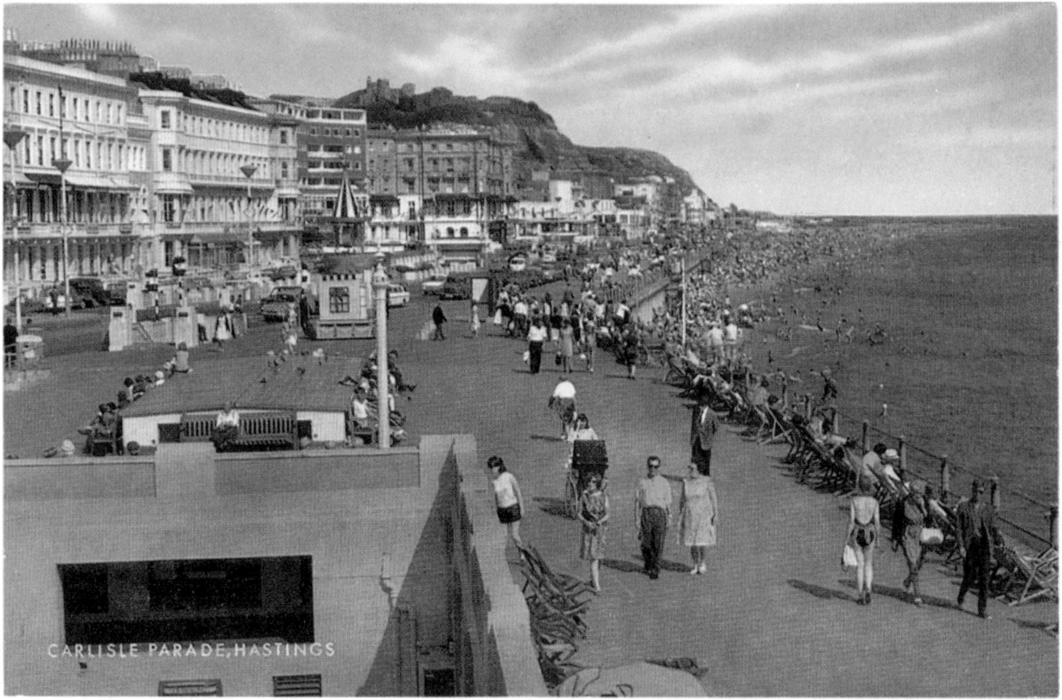
CARLISLE PARADE, HASTINGS

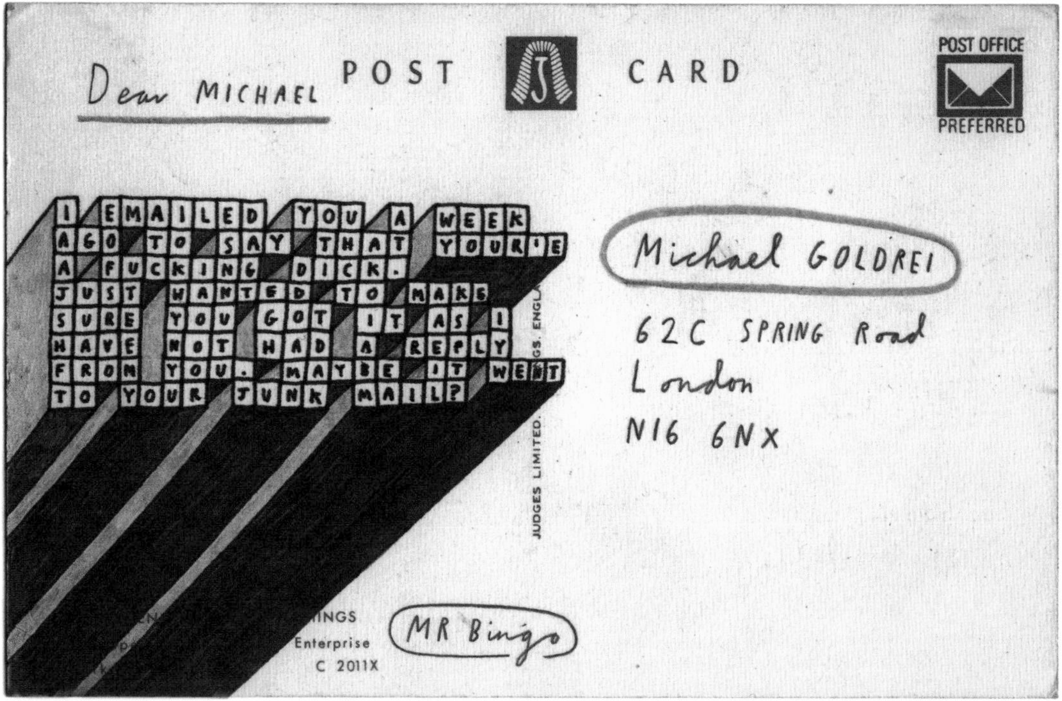

Dear MICHAEL

POST CARD

POST OFFICE PREFERRED

I EMAILED YOU A WEEK AGO TO SAY THAT YOUR'E A FUCKING DICK. JUST WANTED TO MAKE SURE YOU GOT IT AS I HAVE NOT HAD A REPLY FROM YOU. MAYBE IT WENT TO YOUR JUNK MAIL?

Michael GOLDREI
62C SPRING Road
London
N16 6NX

MR Bingo

JUDGES LIMITED. ...GS. ENGL...

...INGS
Enterprise
C 2011X

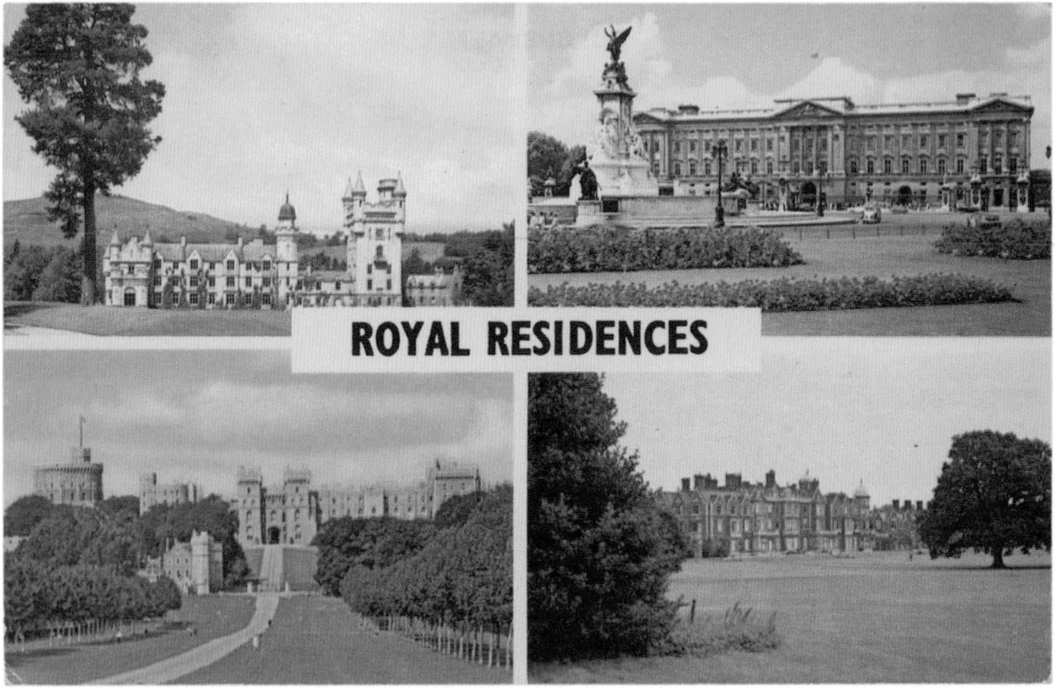
ROYAL RESIDENCES

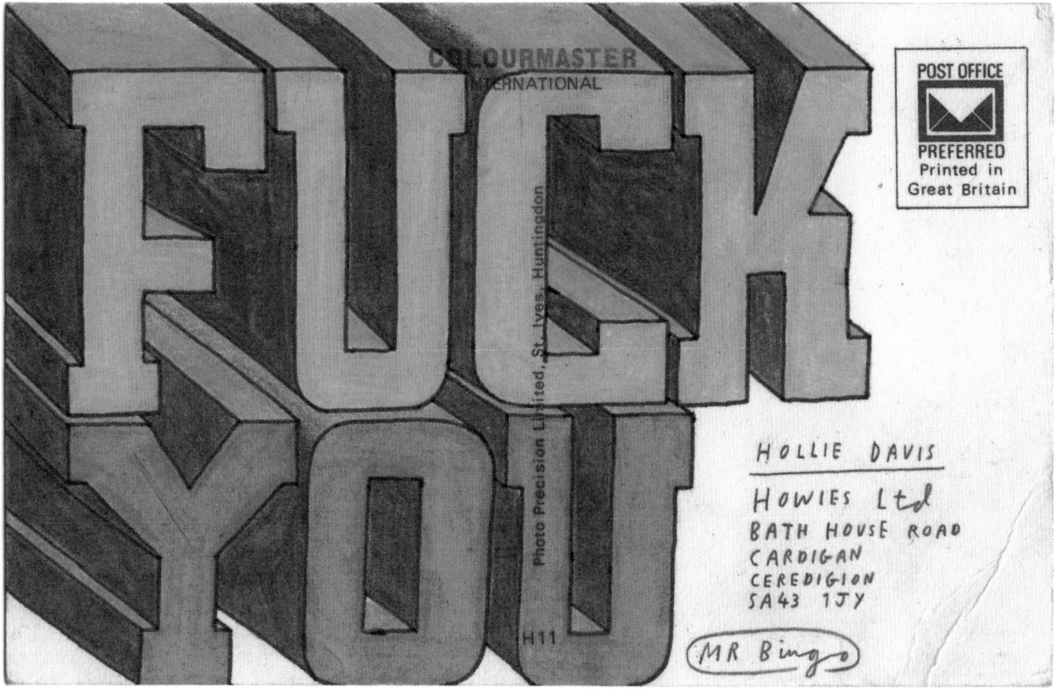
FUCK
YOU
COLOURMASTER
INTERNATIONAL
Photo Precision Limited, St. Ives, Huntingdon
H11
POST OFFICE
PREFERRED
Printed in
Great Britain
HOLLIE DAVIS
HOWIES Ltd
BATH HOUSE ROAD
CARDIGAN
CEREDIGION
SA43 1JY
MR Bingo

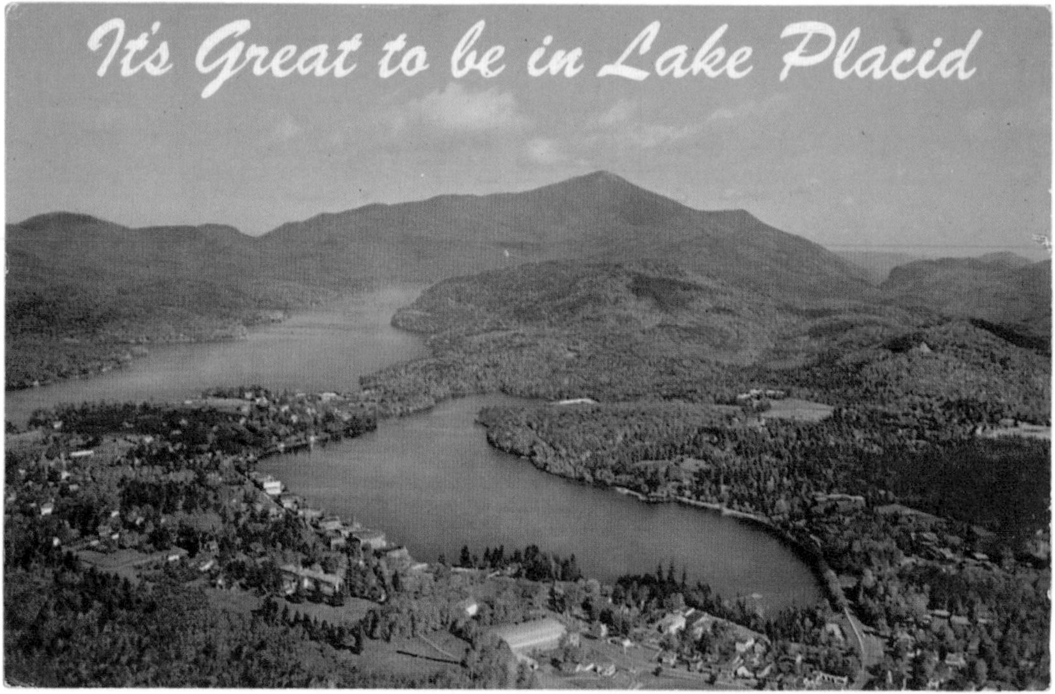
It's Great to be in Lake Placid

THE BEAUTIFUL ADIRONDACK MTS.
OF NEW YORK STATE

Dear DENNIS

Cheers for the party last weekend. Just to let you know, I DID A SHIT IN YOUR MICROWAVE.

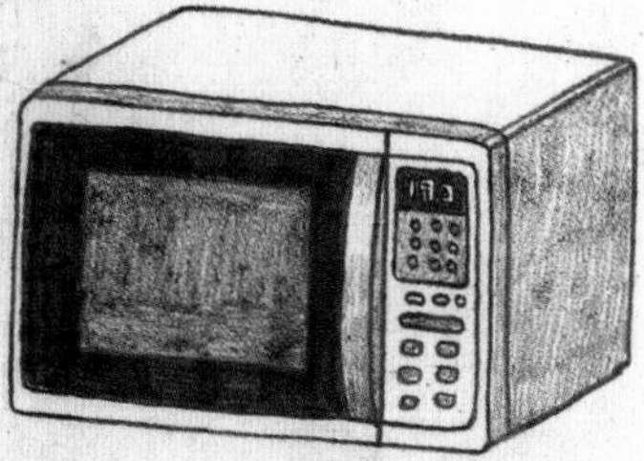

MR Bingo

267—DISTRIBUTED BY ADIRONDACK PHOTO SERVICE, LAKE PLACID, N. Y.

NATURAL COLOR REPRODUCTION—CURTEICHCOLOR ® ART-CREATION REG. U. S. PAT. OFF.

C7967

POST CARD

Dennis RICHARDS

Panton VRANE
PORTSCATHO
TRURO
Cornwall
TR2 SET

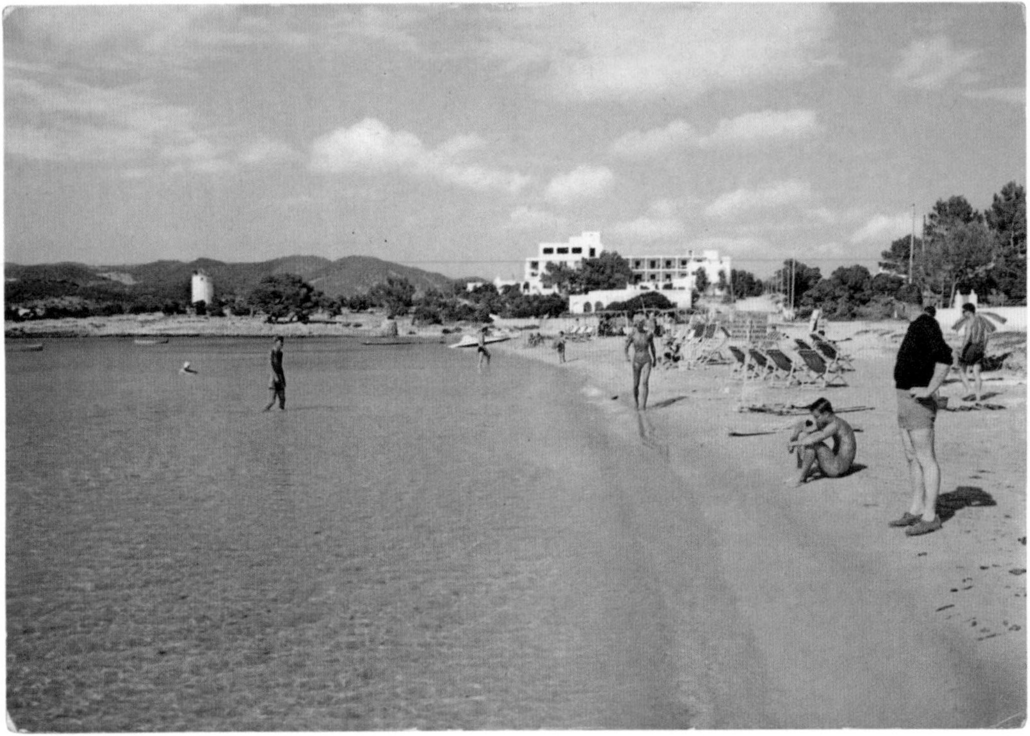

IBIZA (Baleares)
San Antonio Abad
Hotel San Antonio

Dear MARK

I HAVE HATED

YOU SINCE

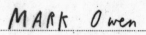

1987

MR Bingo

MARK Owen

73 CHURCH Walk

London

N16 8QR

Foto Balear - Edición de Vistas artísticas - J. Orsinger
Palma de Mallorca « Reproducción prohibida »

fotogr fía original

DEPÓSITO LEGAL. B. 5418. - IV

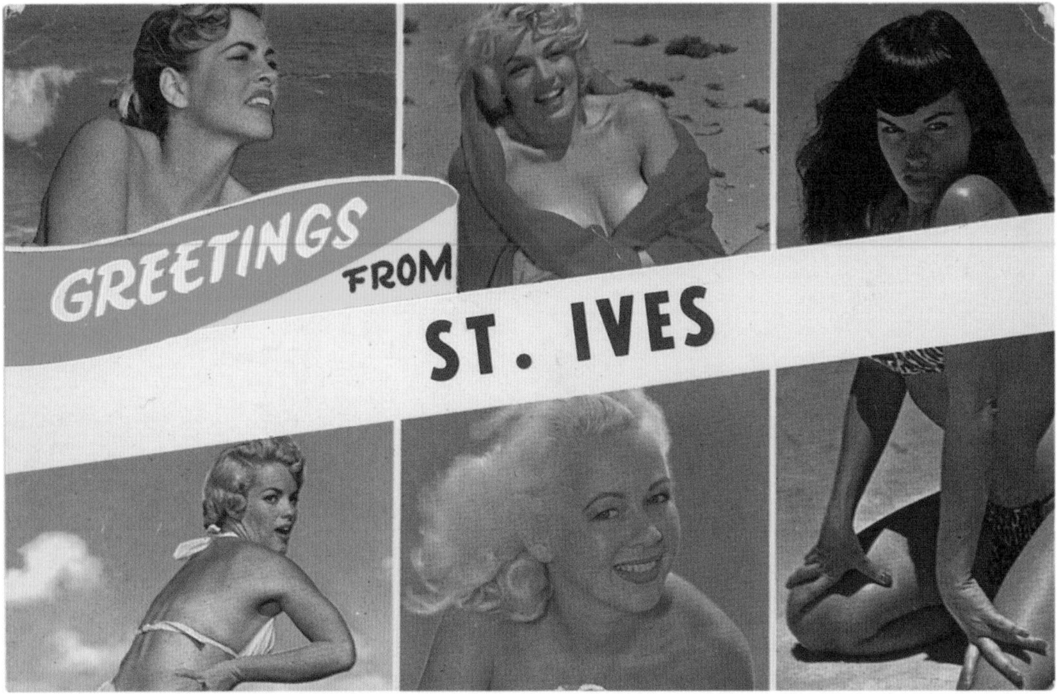
GREETINGS
FROM
ST. IVES

WHS 262

P41100

Post Card

Dear MARY

For Correspondence

Plastichrome ® by COLOURPICTURE PUBLISHERS, INC., NORWICH, NORFOLK

Address Only

YOU DON'T DO IT FOR ME ANYMORE

MR Bingo

MARY Lam

135 BATH RD

London

NW10 5JG

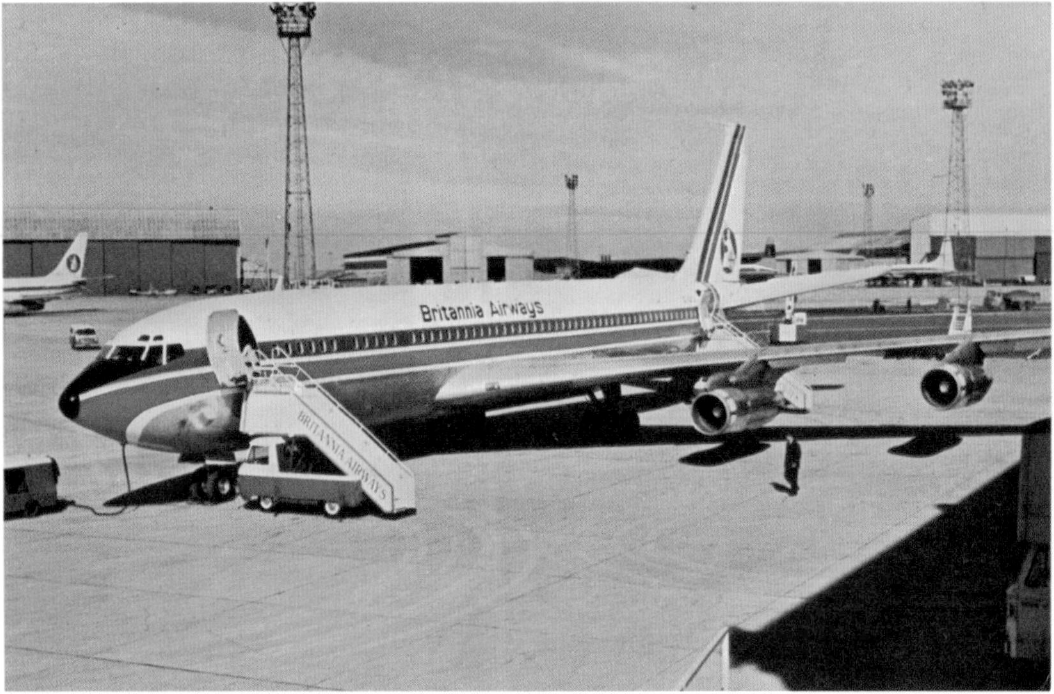
Britannia Airways
BRITANNIA AIRWAYS

POST CARD

Dear PAUL,

YOUR EYES ARE REALLY
FUCKING CREEPY

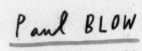

Paul BLOW
St. MICHAELS Studios
St. MICHAELS Trading ESTATE
BRIDPORT
Dorset
DT6 3RR

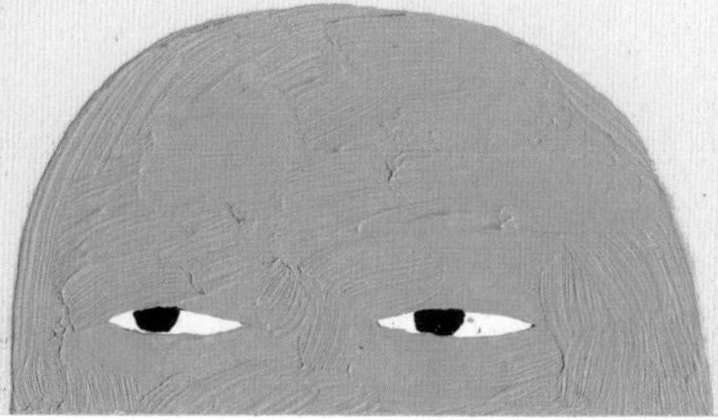

Printed in England by Aerad (IAL).

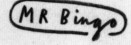

MR Bingo

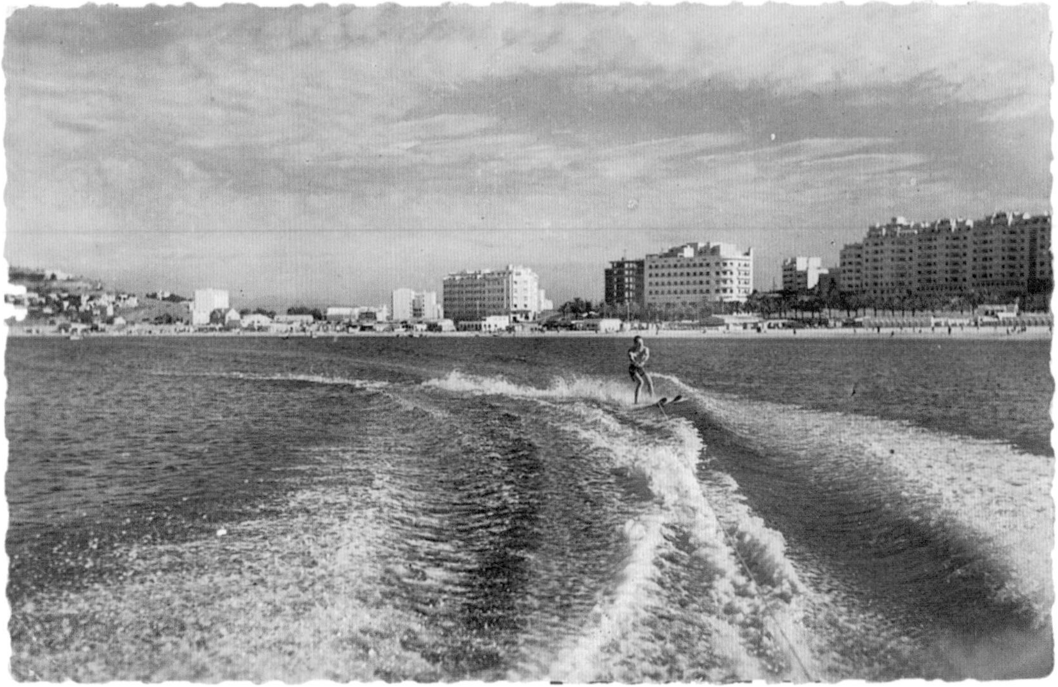

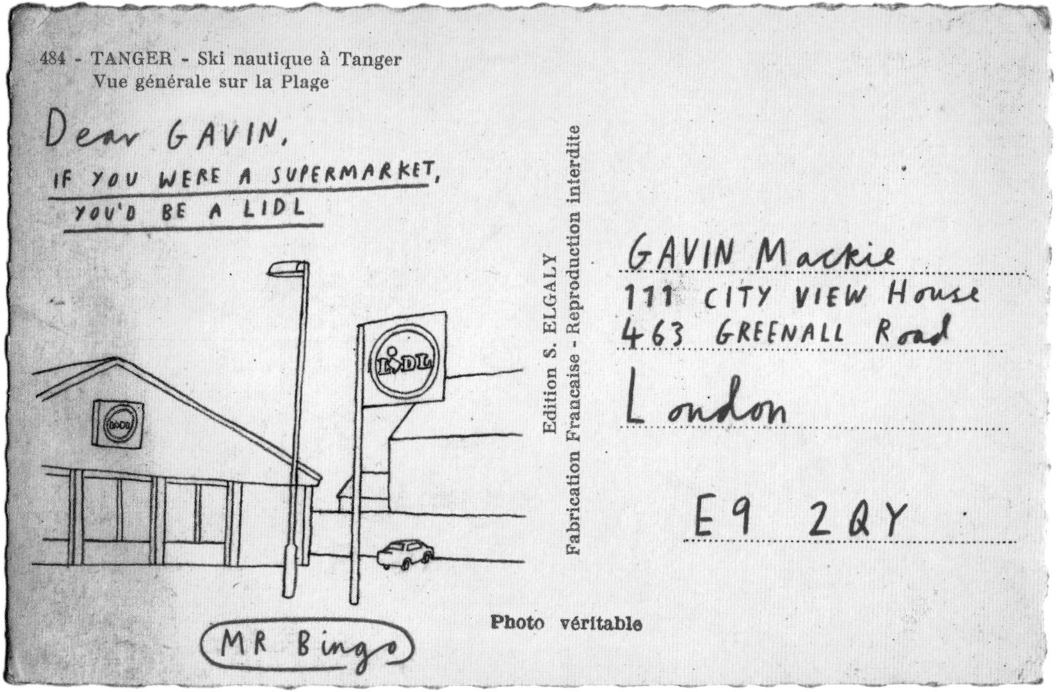
484 - TANGER - Ski nautique à Tanger
Vue générale sur la Plage

Dear GAVIN,
IF YOU WERE A SUPERMARKET,
YOU'D BE A LIDL

LIDL
LIDL

MR Bingo

Edition S. ELGALY
Fabrication Francaise - Reproduction interdite

GAVIN Mackie
111 CITY VIEW House
463 GREENALL Road
London
E9 2QY

Photo véritable

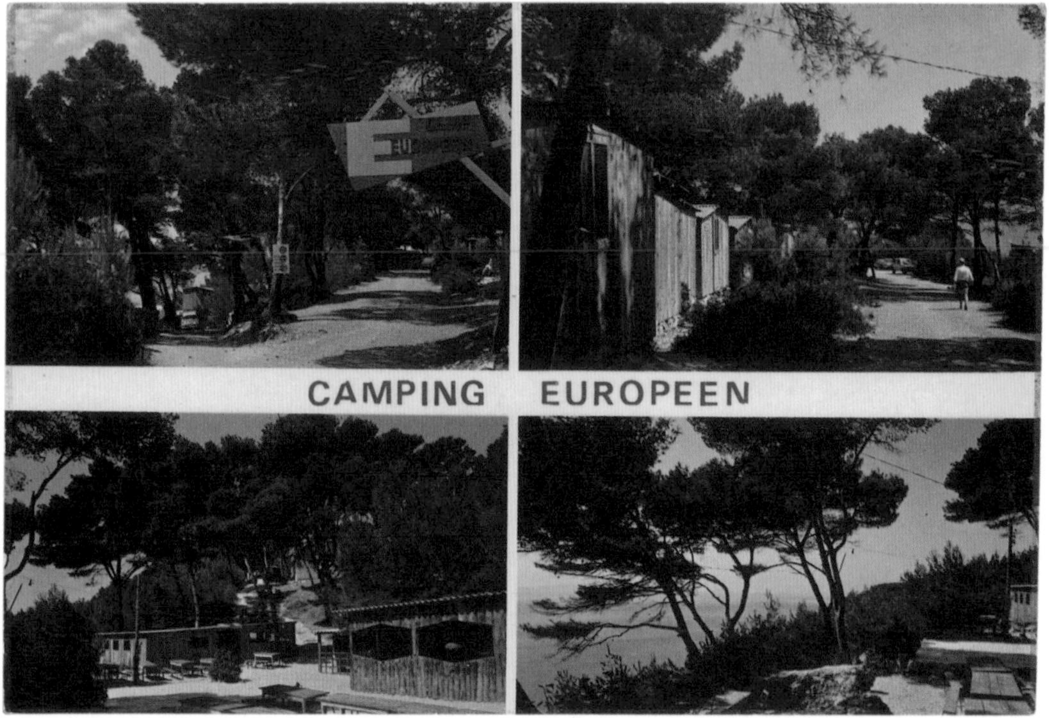
CAMPING EUROPEEN

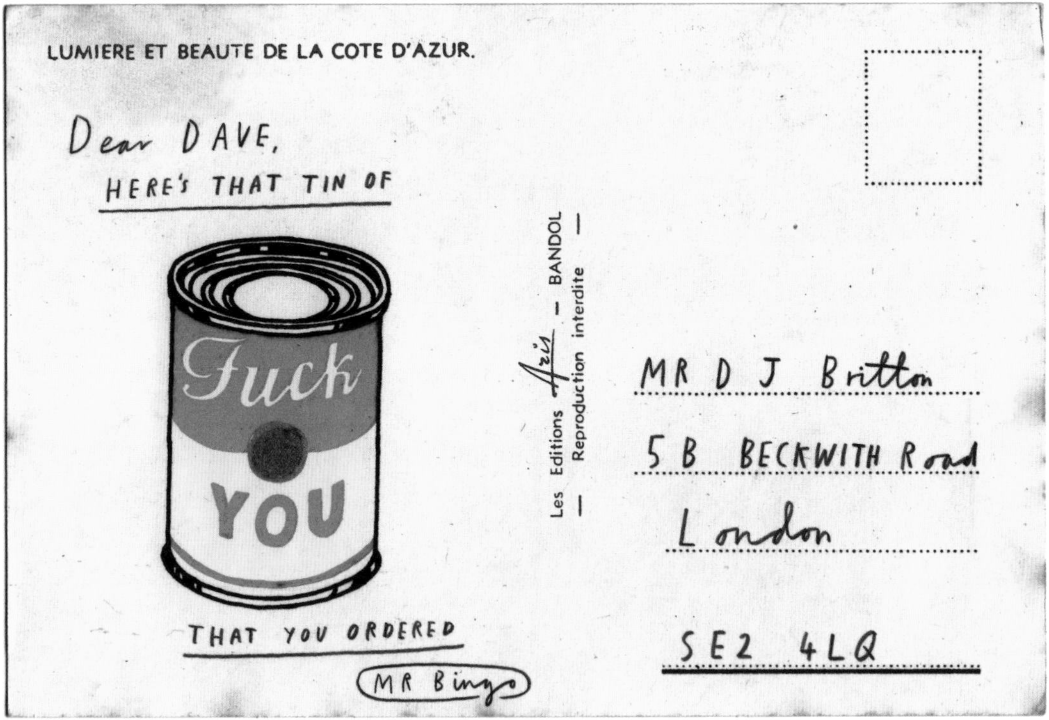
LUMIERE ET BEAUTE DE LA COTE D'AZUR.

Dear DAVE,

HERE'S THAT TIN OF

Fuck
YOU

THAT YOU ORDERED

MR Bingo

Les Editions Aris – BANDOL
– Reproduction interdite –

MR D J Britton
5 B BECKWITH Road
London
SE2 4LQ

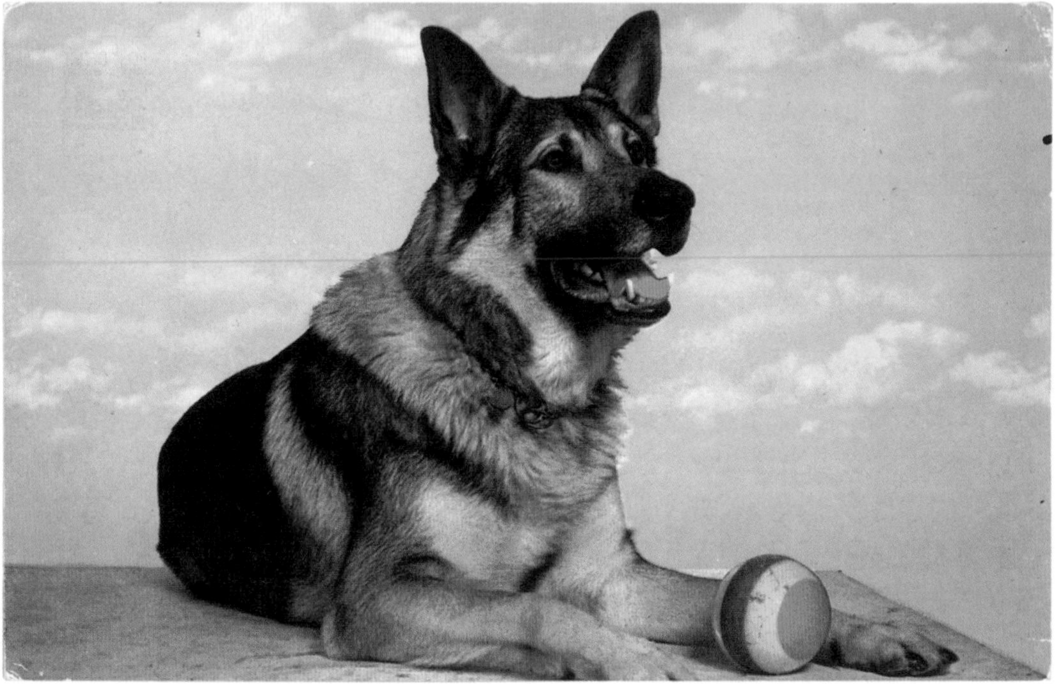

COLOURMASTER
INTERNATIONAL

Dear WILLIAM,

You're a DICK mate

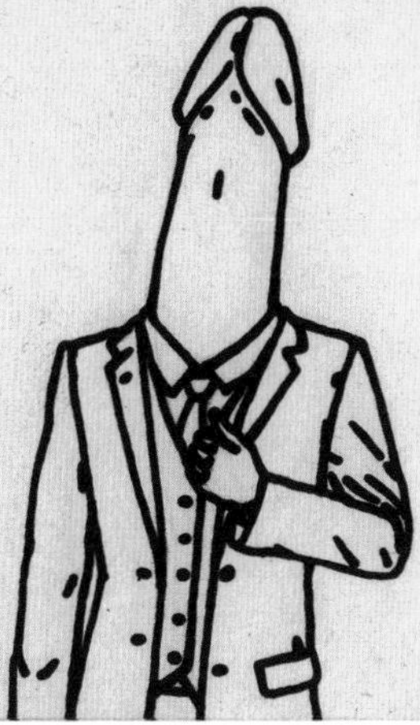

Photo Precision Limited, St. Ives, Huntingdon

MR Bingo

319fc

WILLIAM Shephard
2 GARDEN Avenue
Corringham
ESSEX
SS17 7ES

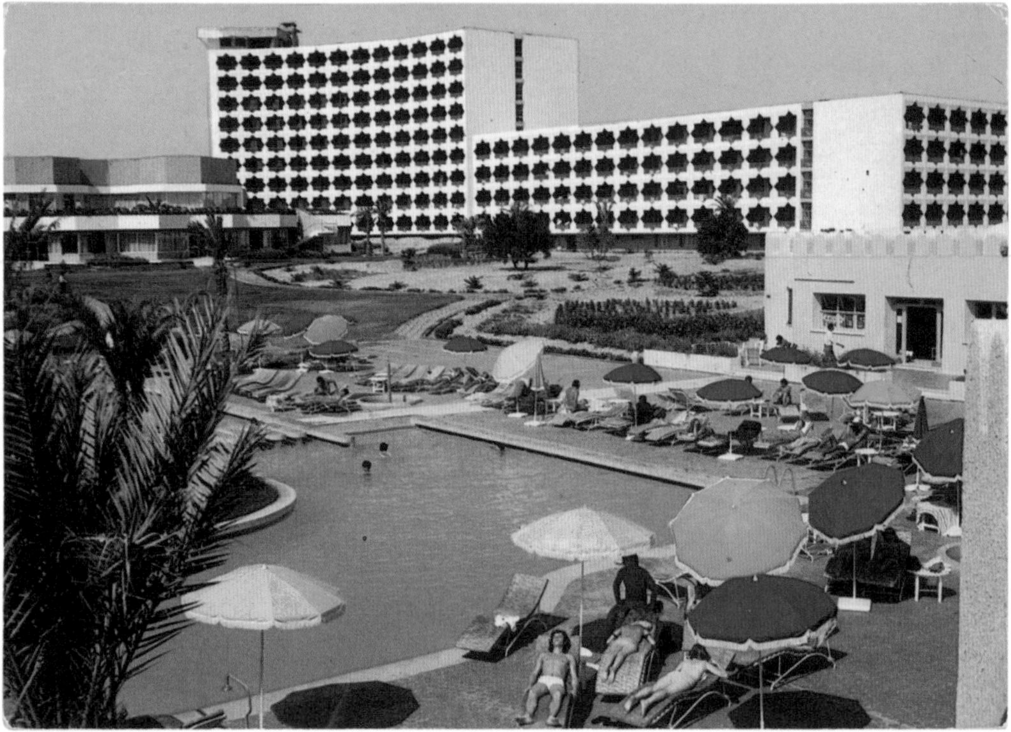

Hôtel TOUR KHALEF
Sousse, Tunisie

Dear GRAEME,

I SAW YOU
WERE ON THE
COVER OF

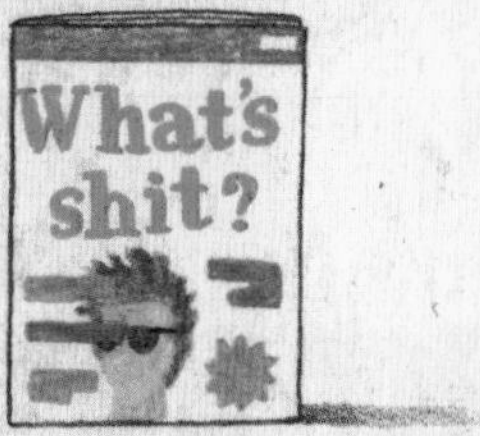
What's
shit?

MAGAZINE AGAIN.

MR Bingo

Couleurs
naturelles

CARTHAGE, Tunis - Reproduction interdite

H 114

MR Graeme DART
1 SHEER House
CHAUCER Road
Bath
SOMERSET

BA4 2QY

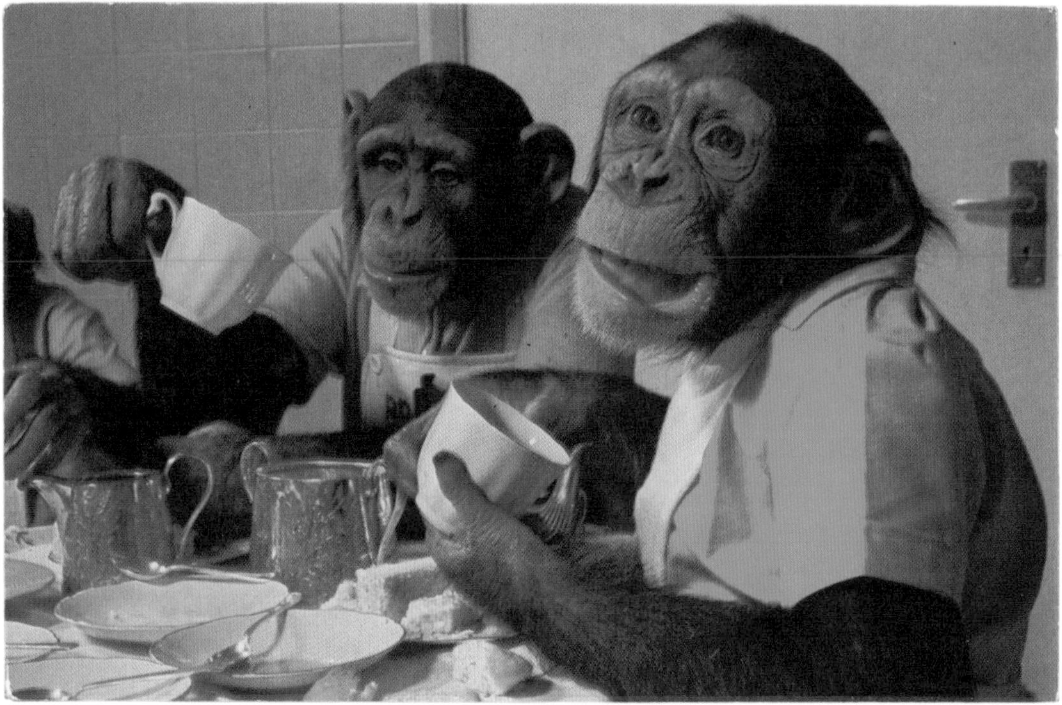

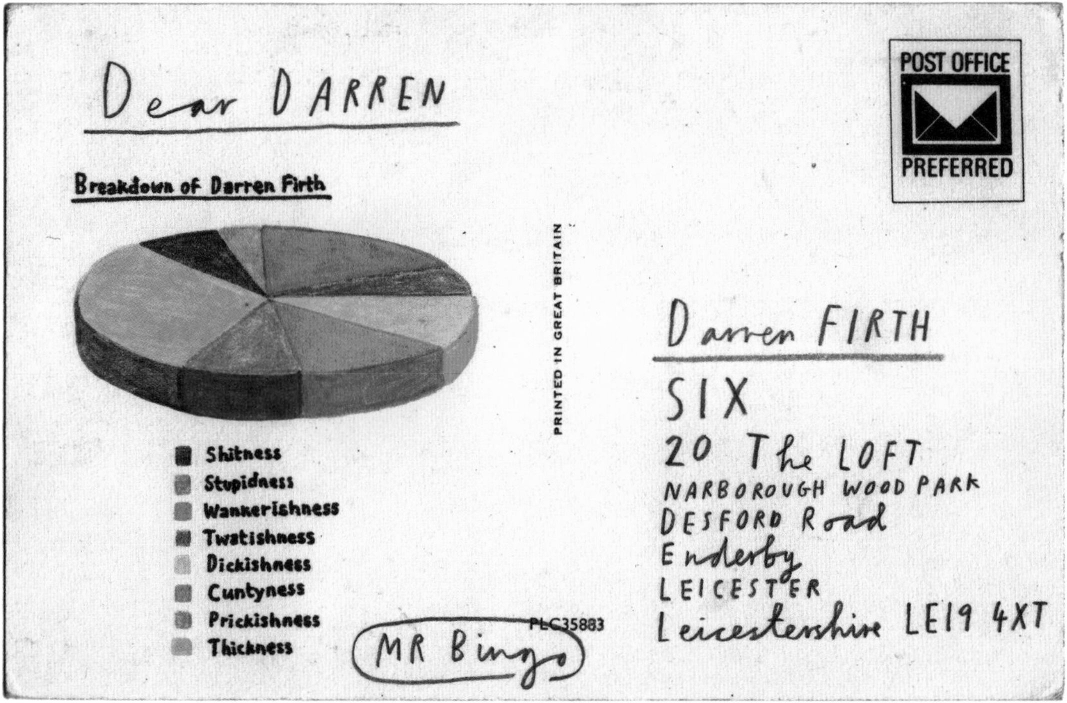

Dear DARREN

Breakdown of Darren Firth

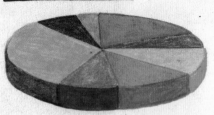

- ■ Shitness
- ■ Stupidness
- ■ Wankerishness
- ■ Twotishness
- ■ Dickishness
- ■ Cuntyness
- ■ Prickishness
- ■ Thickness

PRINTED IN GREAT BRITAIN

Darren FIRTH

SIX
20 The LOFT
NARBOROUGH WOOD PARK
DESFORD Road
Enderby
LEICESTER
Leicestershire LE19 4XT

PLC35883

MR Bingo

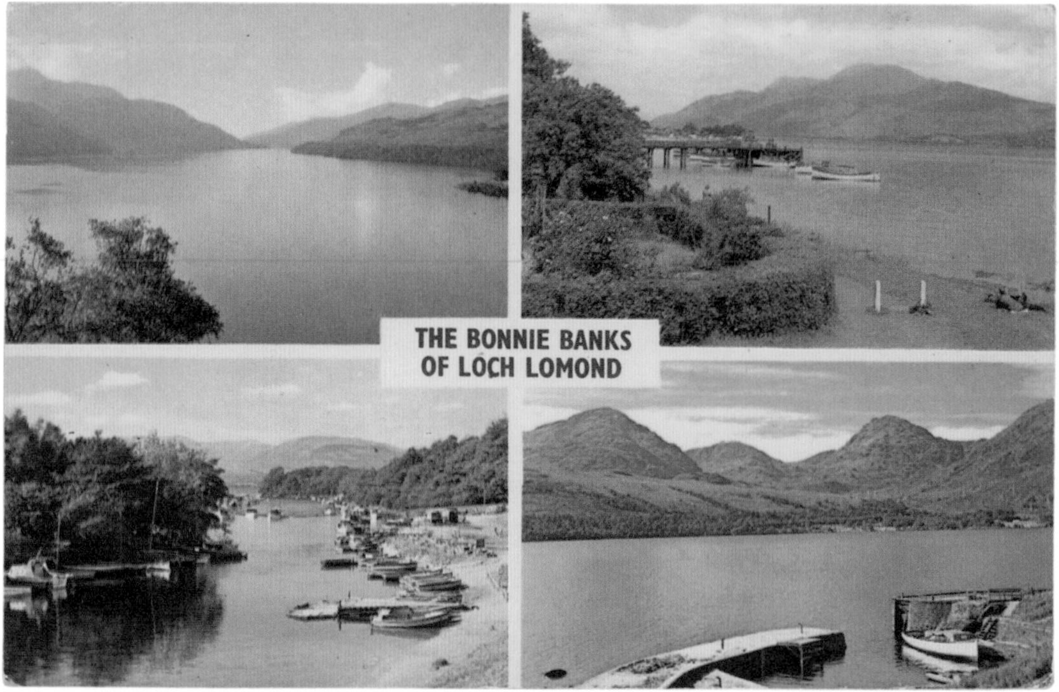
THE BONNIE BANKS
OF LOCH LOMOND

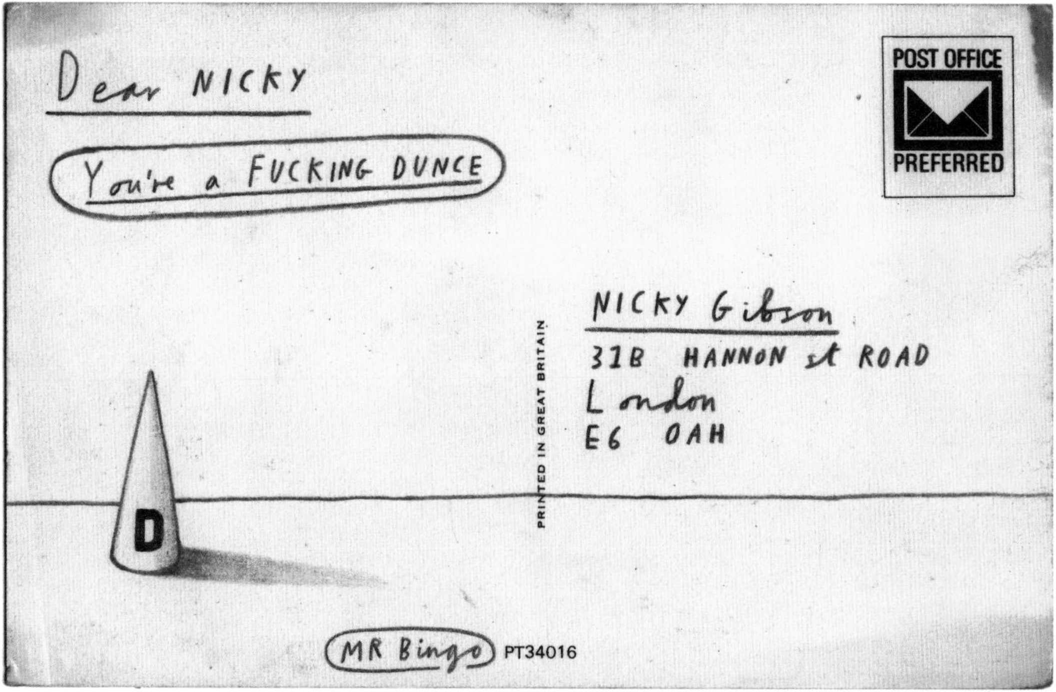

Dear NICKY

<u>You're a FUCKING DUNCE</u>

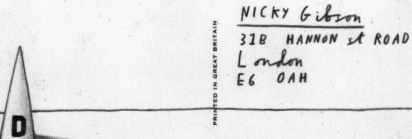

NICKY Gibson
31B HANNON st ROAD
London
E6 OAH

PRINTED IN GREAT BRITAIN

MR Bingo PT34016

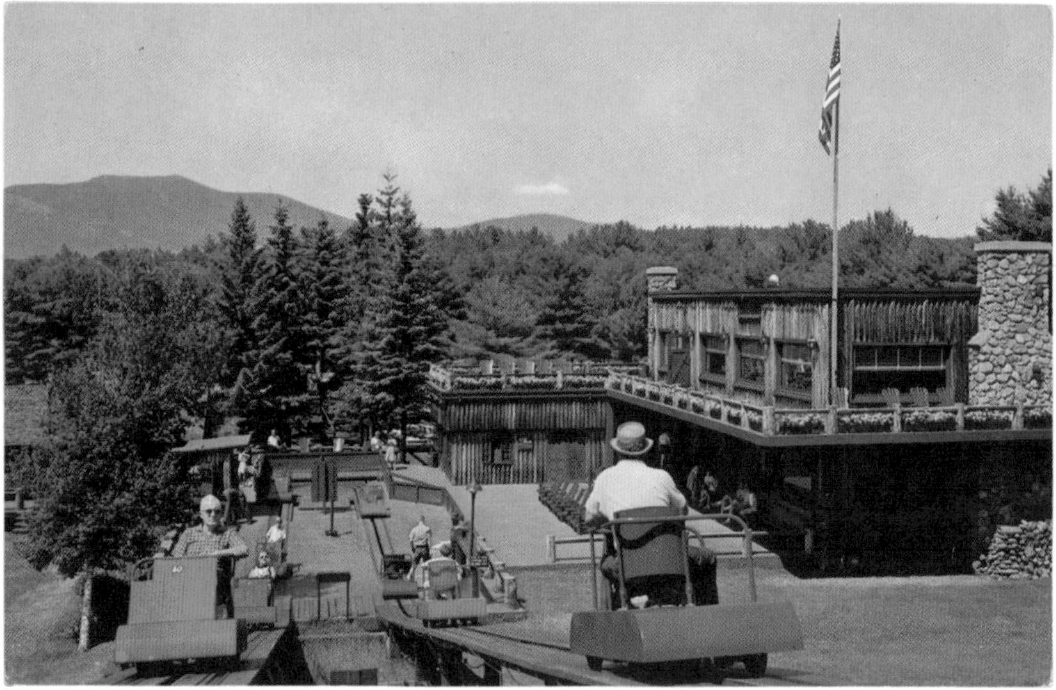

MT. CRANMORE SKIMOBILE BASE STATION AT
NORTH CONWAY, NEW HAMPSHIRE.
Moat Mountain Range in the background.

Mt. Cranmore Skimobile, No. Conway, N.H.
SUMMER-WINTER

Dear BRYONY

SHIT CHIN

MR Bingo

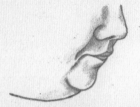

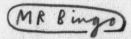

NC862

Published For Bromley & Company, Inc., Boston, Mass. 02210

COLOR BY MIKE ROBERTS
BERKELEY, CALIF. 94710

C16295
U.S.A.

BRYONY Raistrick

9 HAIL Road
Greengates
BRADFORD
West YORKSHIRE
BD10 9AW

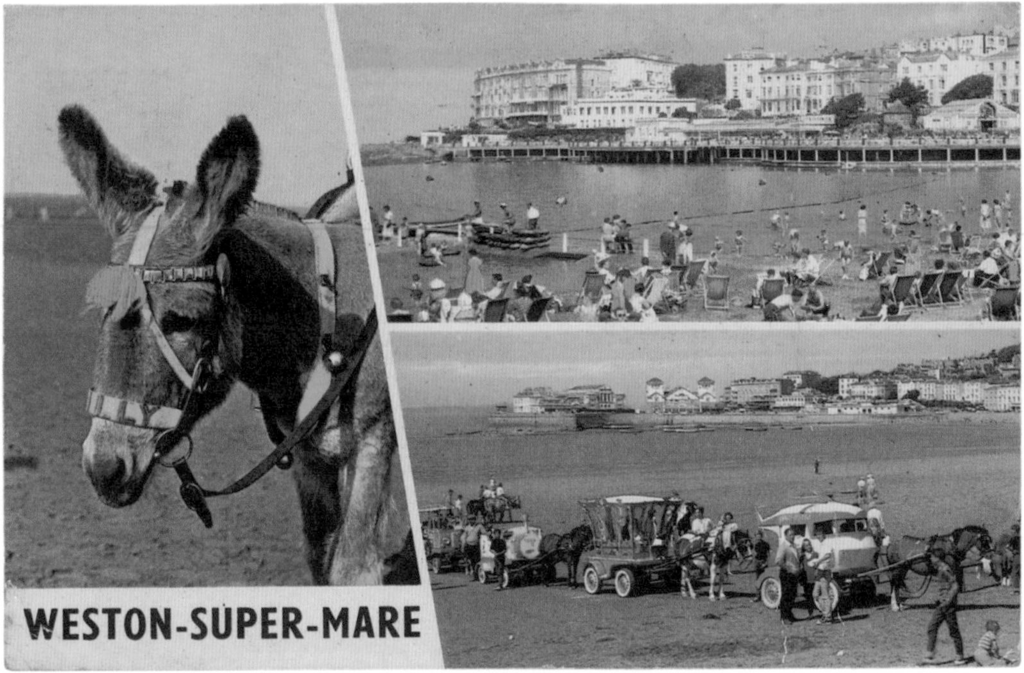
WESTON-SUPER-MARE

Dear DAVE

I SAW YOUR MUM COMING OUT OF

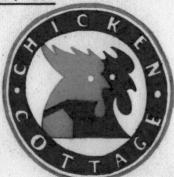

CHICKEN COTTAGE

MR Bingo

MARINE LAKE, MADEIRA COVE

THE SANDS AND KNIGHTSTONE PLC6564

PRINTED IN GREAT BRITAIN

POST OFFICE PREFERRED

DAVE Tweedle

2 Longfeild

MELLS

Frome

SOMERSET

BA13 1EY

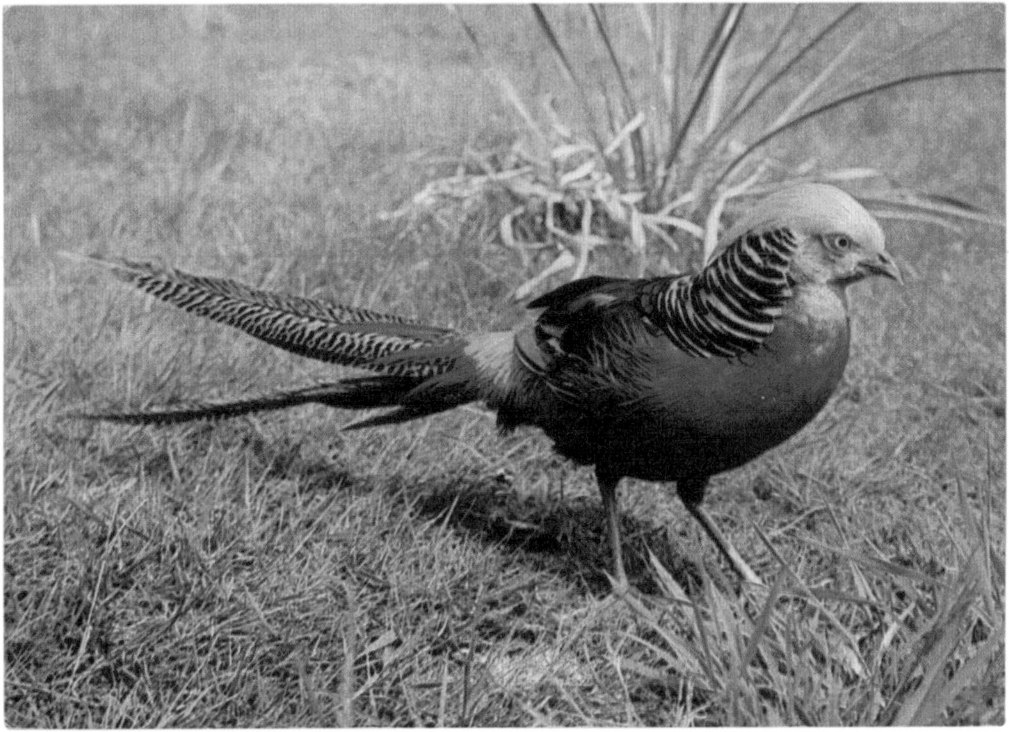

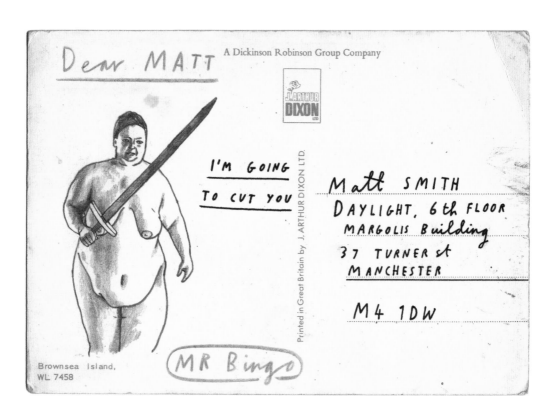

Dear MATT

A Dickinson Robinson Group Company

J. ARTHUR DIXON LTD

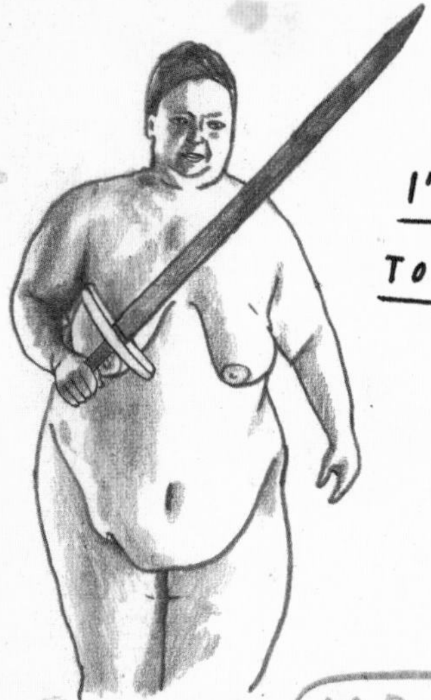

I'M GOING

TO CUT YOU

Printed in Great Britain by J. ARTHUR DIXON LTD.

Matt SMITH
DAYLIGHT, 6th FLOOR
MARGOLIS Building
37 TURNER st
MANCHESTER

M4 1DW

Brownsea Island,
WL 7458

MR Bingo

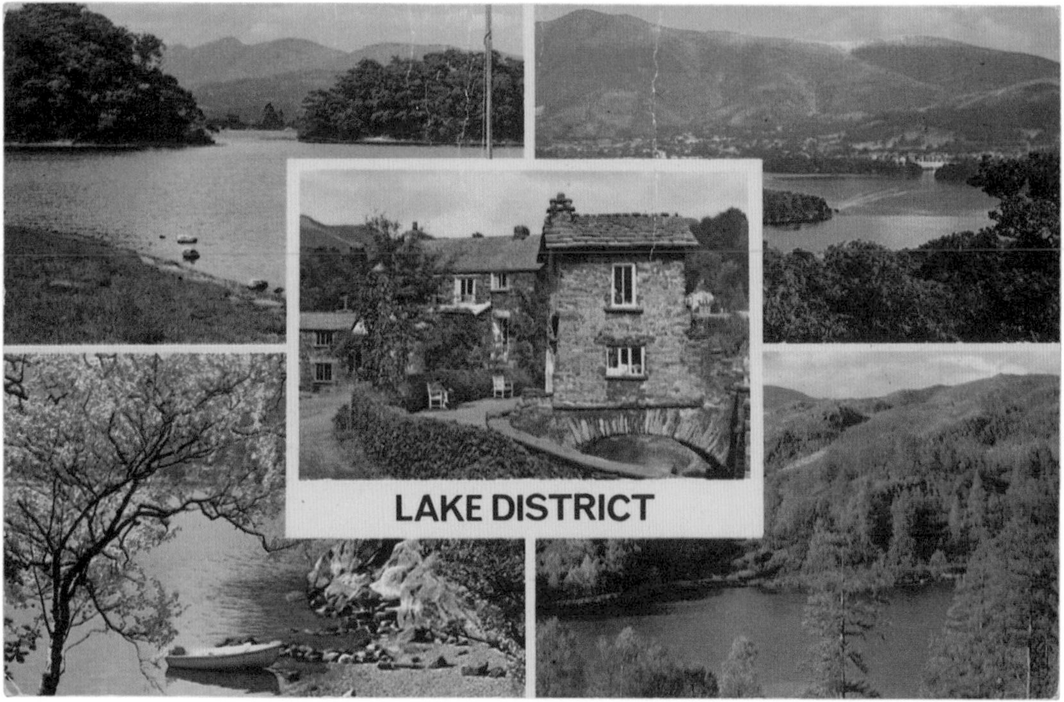
LAKE DISTRICT

COLOURMASTER
INTERNATIONAL

LK 363

Photo Precision Limited. St. Ives, Huntingdon

PLC21141

Dear BEN,

You make me:

MR Bingo

Ben COX

FLAT 4
ORWELL COURT
POLLEN Road
London
E8 2PS

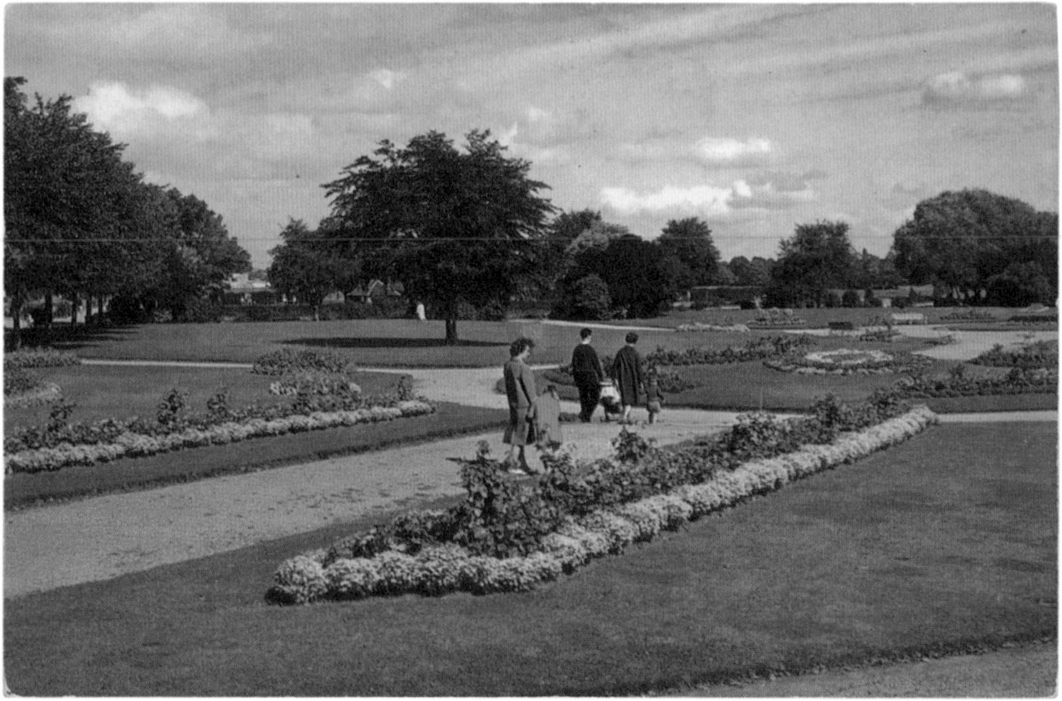

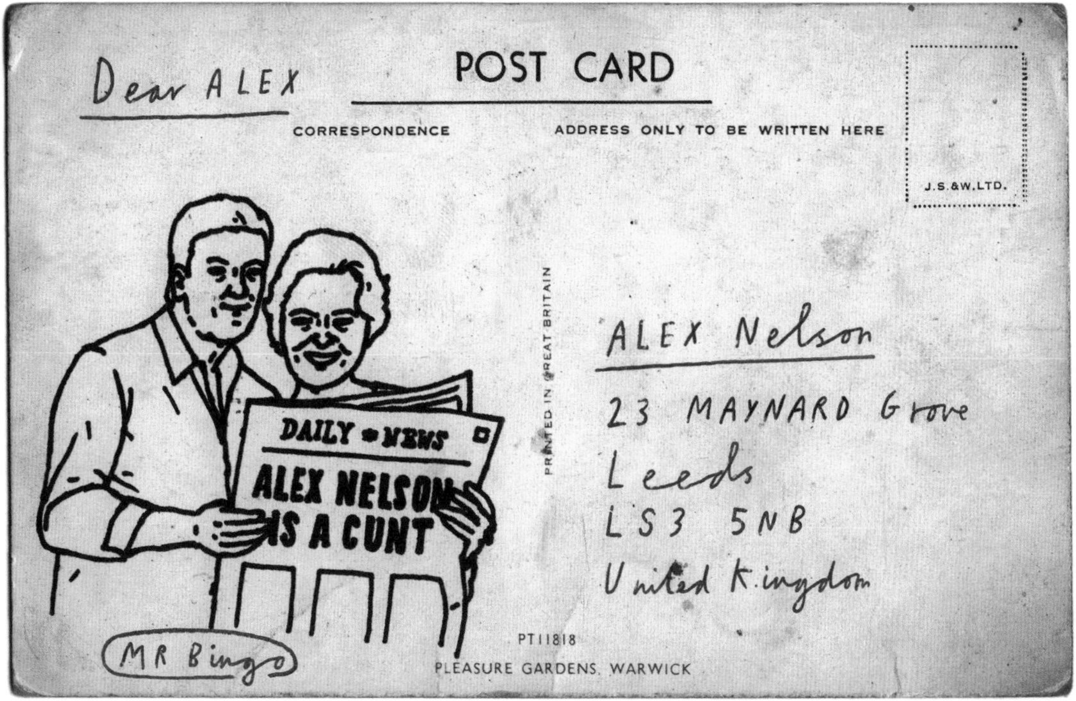

Dear ALEX

POST CARD

CORRESPONDENCE

ADDRESS ONLY TO BE WRITTEN HERE

J.S.&W.LTD.

DAILY NEWS

ALEX NELSON IS A CUNT

PRINTED IN GREAT BRITAIN

ALEX Nelson

23 MAYNARD Grove

Leeds

LS3 5NB

United Kingdom

MR Bingo

PT11818

PLEASURE GARDENS, WARWICK

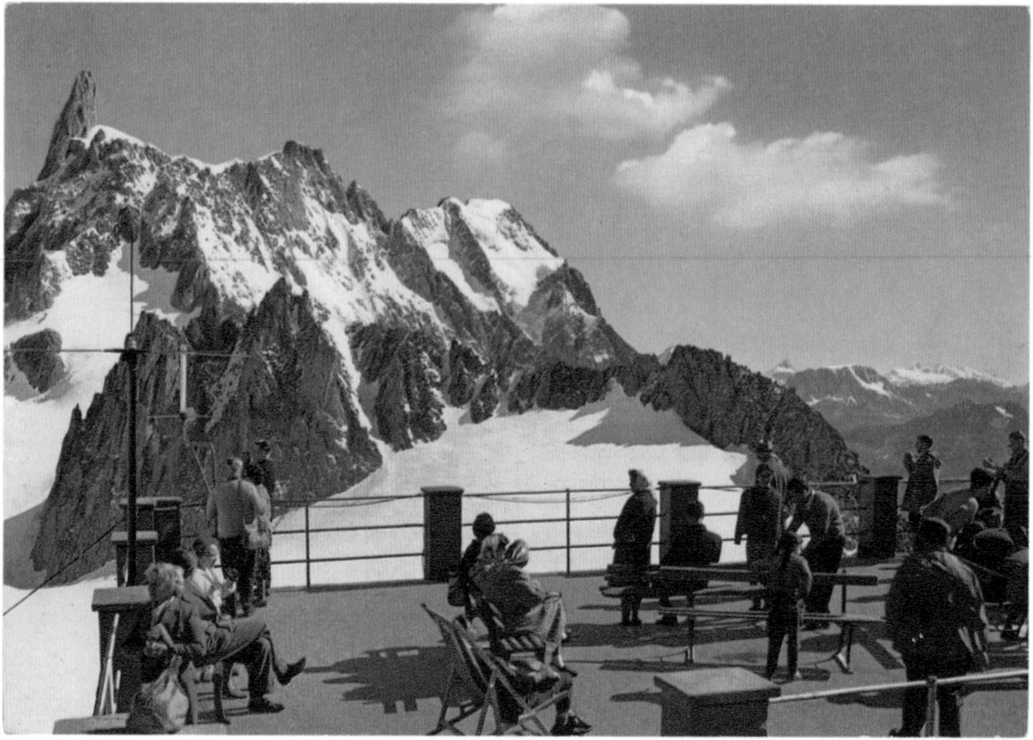

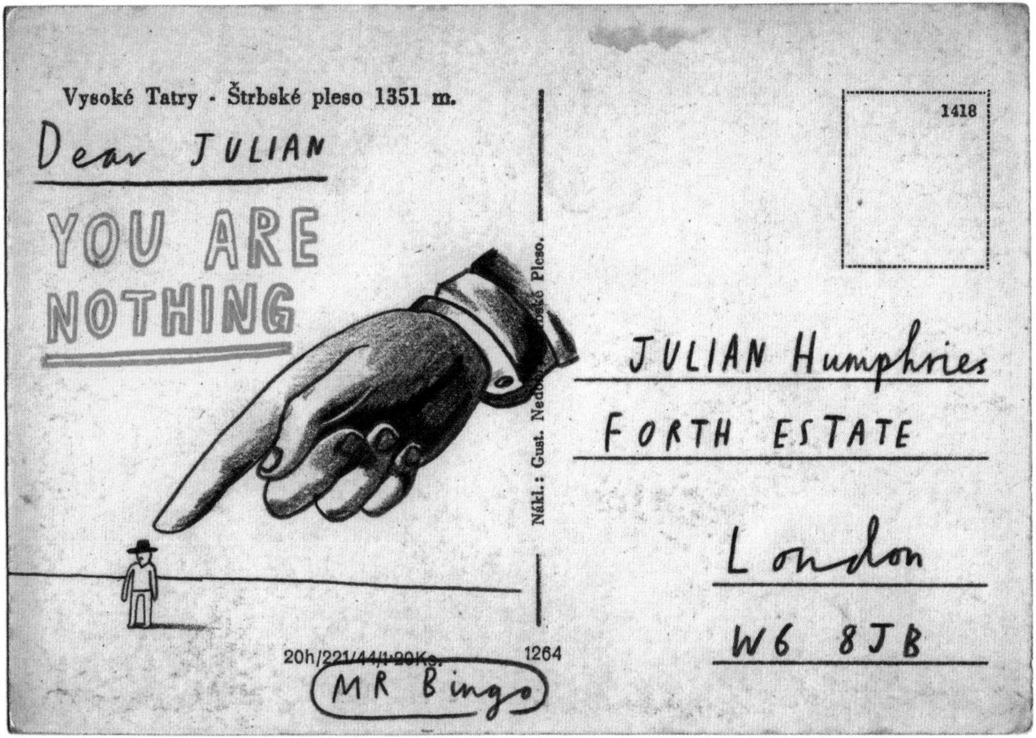

Vysoké Tatry · Štrbské pleso 1351 m.

Dear JULIAN

YOU ARE
NOTHING

NÁKL.: Gust. Nedo____ ____oské Pleso.

1418

JULIAN Humphries

FORTH ESTATE

London

W6 8JB

20h/221/44/1-20Kčs. 1264

MR Bingo

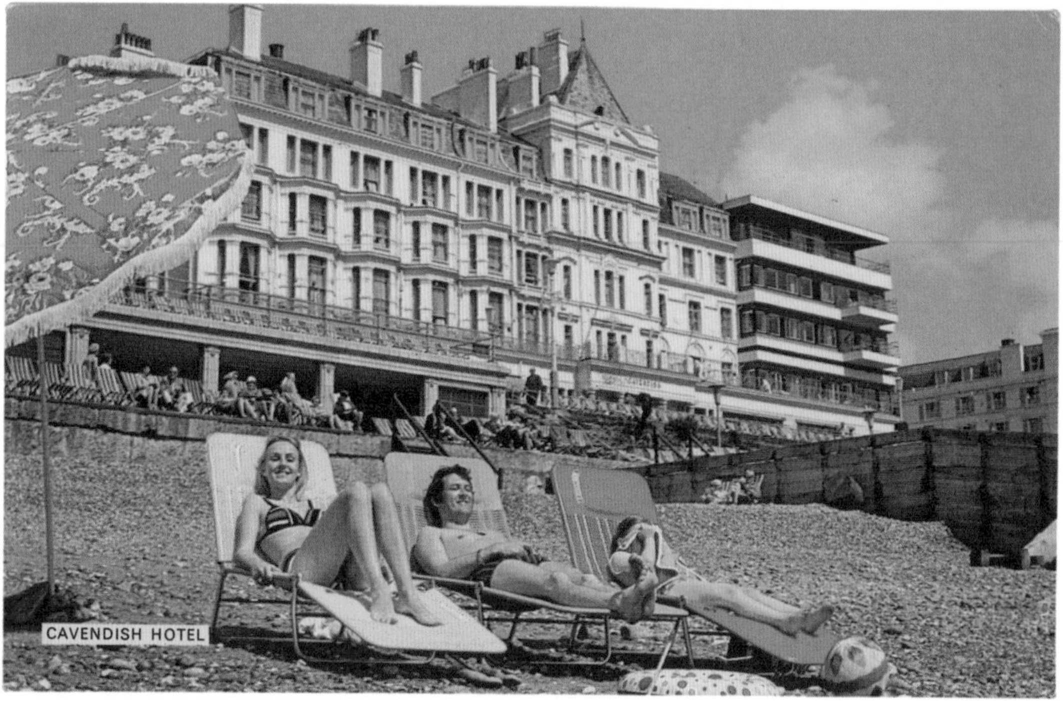
CAVENDISH HOTEL

Dear JAMES

Thanks for dinner
on Thursday night.

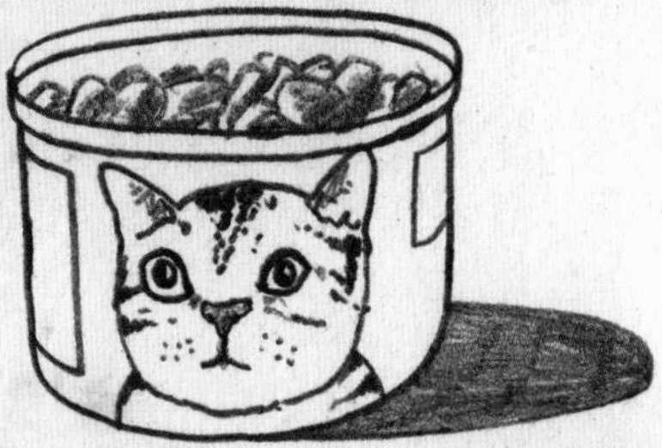

IT TASTED LIKE FUCKING
CAT FOOD

MR Bingo

185

PHOTO
GREETINGS

Printed by E. T. W. DENNIS & SONS LTD. SCARBOROUGH

AFFIX
STAMP
HERE

C11805

JAMES DENMAN
Flat 2
57 QUEENSBRIDGE Road
HACKNEY
London
E8 4AS

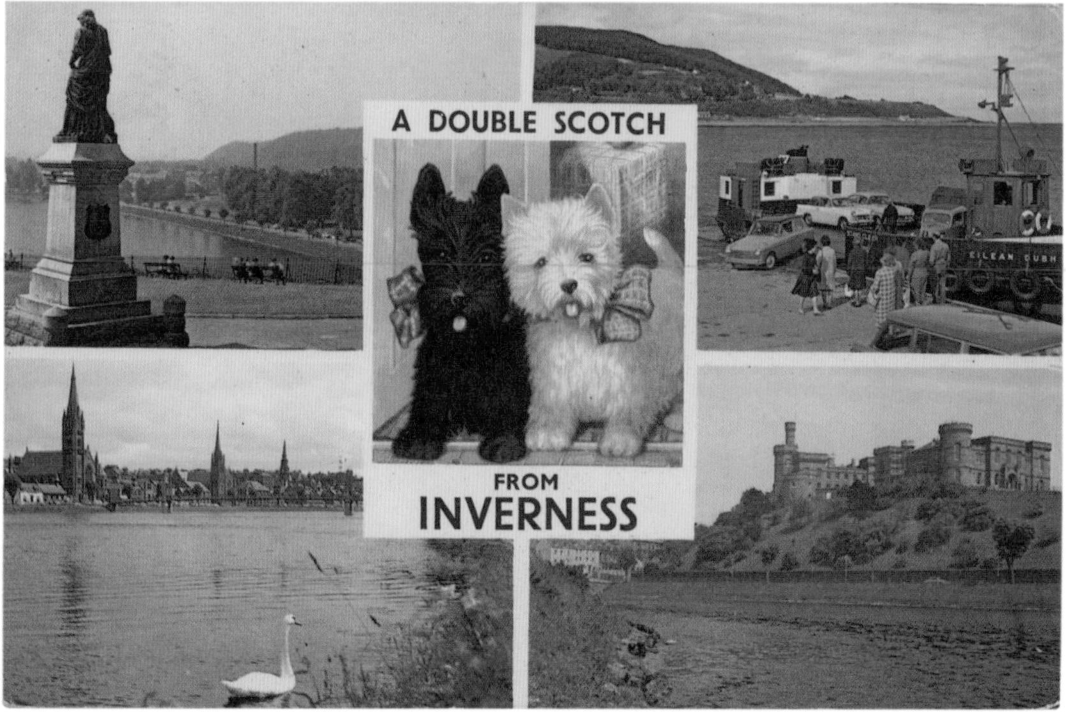
A DOUBLE SCOTCH
FROM
INVERNESS

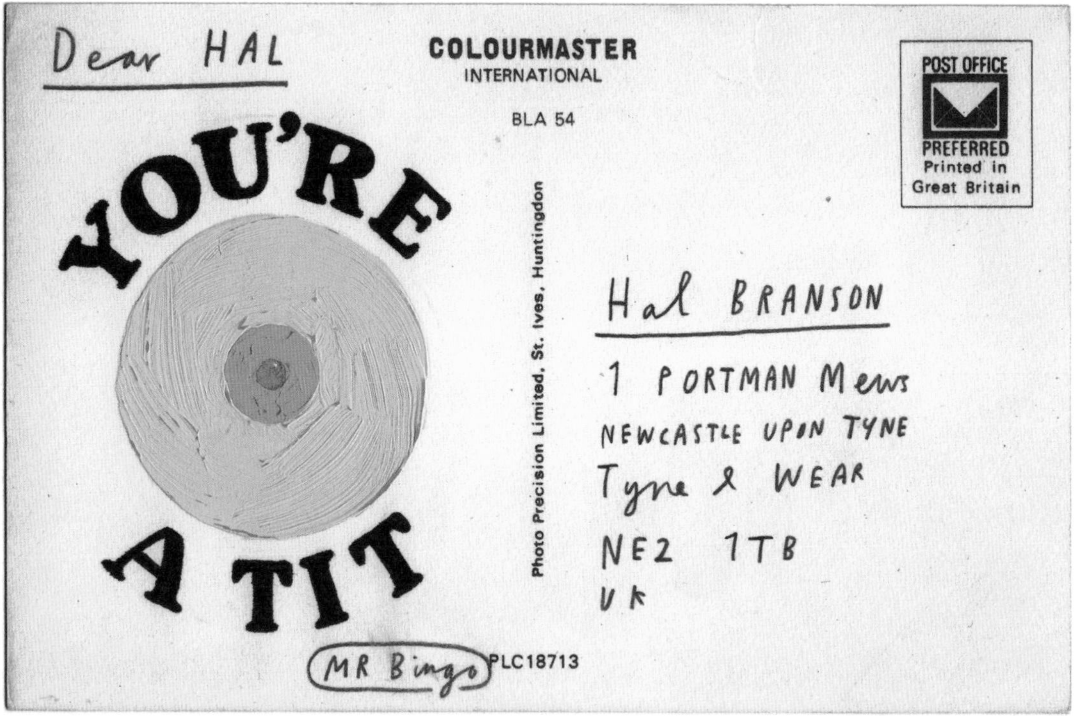
Dear HAL
COLOURMASTER
INTERNATIONAL
BLA 54
POST OFFICE
PREFERRED
Printed in
Great Britain
YOU'RE
A TIT
Photo Precision Limited, St. Ives, Huntingdon
Hal BRANSON
1 PORTMAN Mews
NEWCASTLE UPON TYNE
Tyne & WEAR
NE2 1TB
UK
MR Bingo
PLC18713

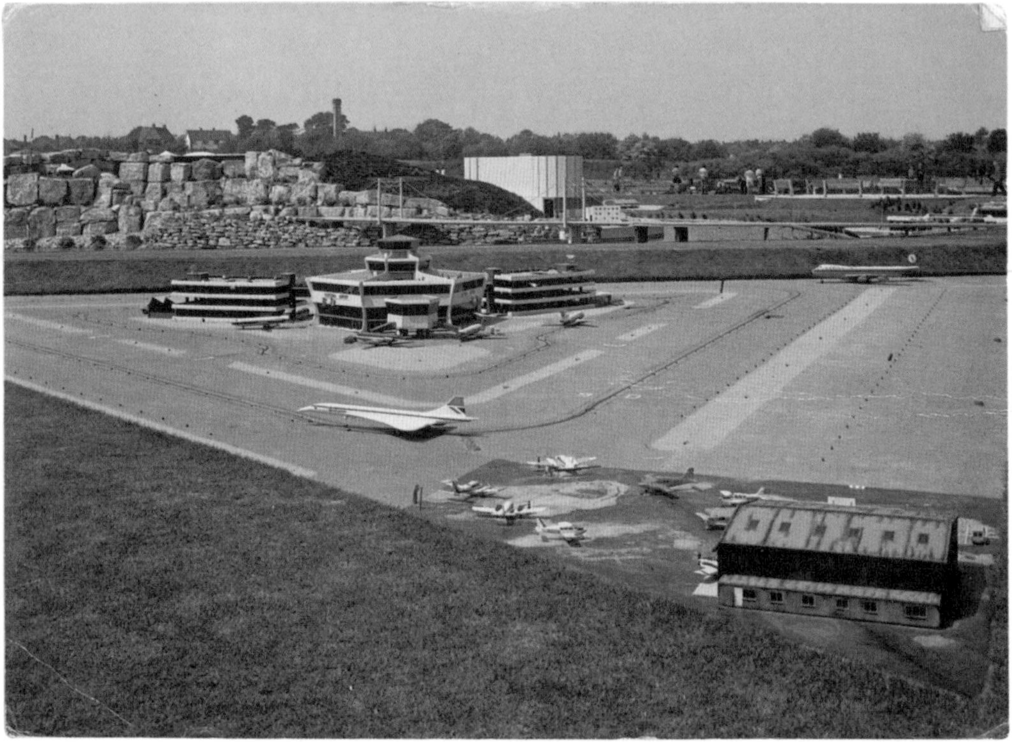

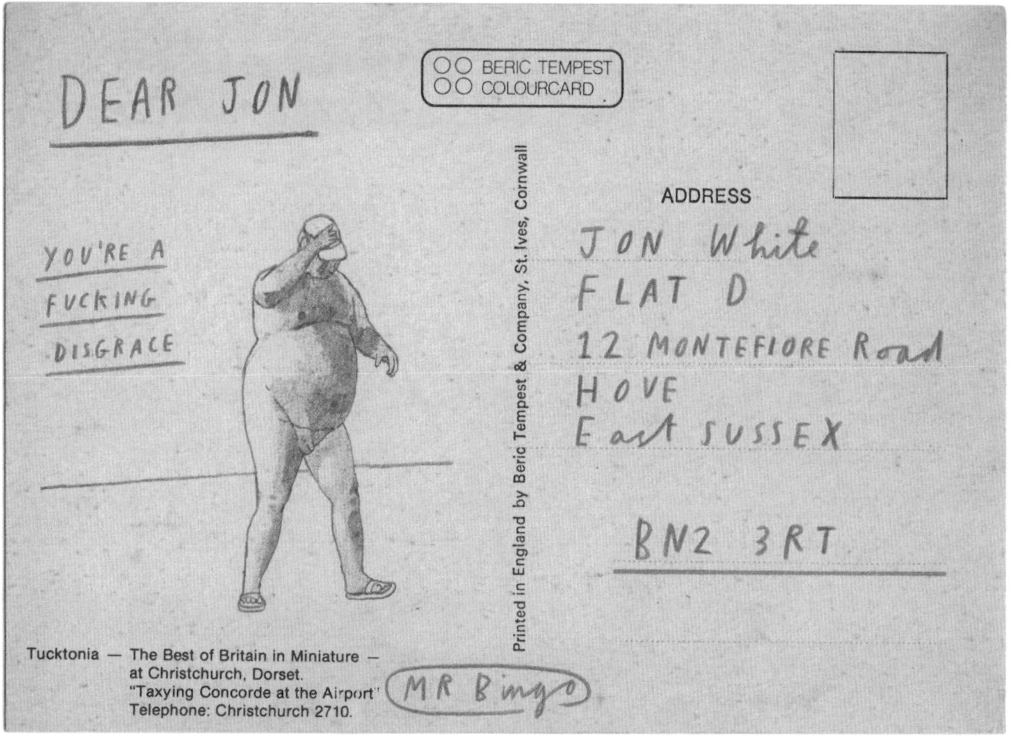
DEAR JON
YOU'RE A
FUCKING
DISGRACE
BERIC TEMPEST
COLOURCARD
Printed in England by Beric Tempest & Company, St. Ives, Cornwall
ADDRESS
JON White
FLAT D
12 MONTEFIORE Road
HOVE
East SUSSEX
BN2 3RT
Tucktonia — The Best of Britain in Miniature —
at Christchurch, Dorset.
"Taxying Concorde at the Airport"
Telephone: Christchurch 2710.
MR Bingo

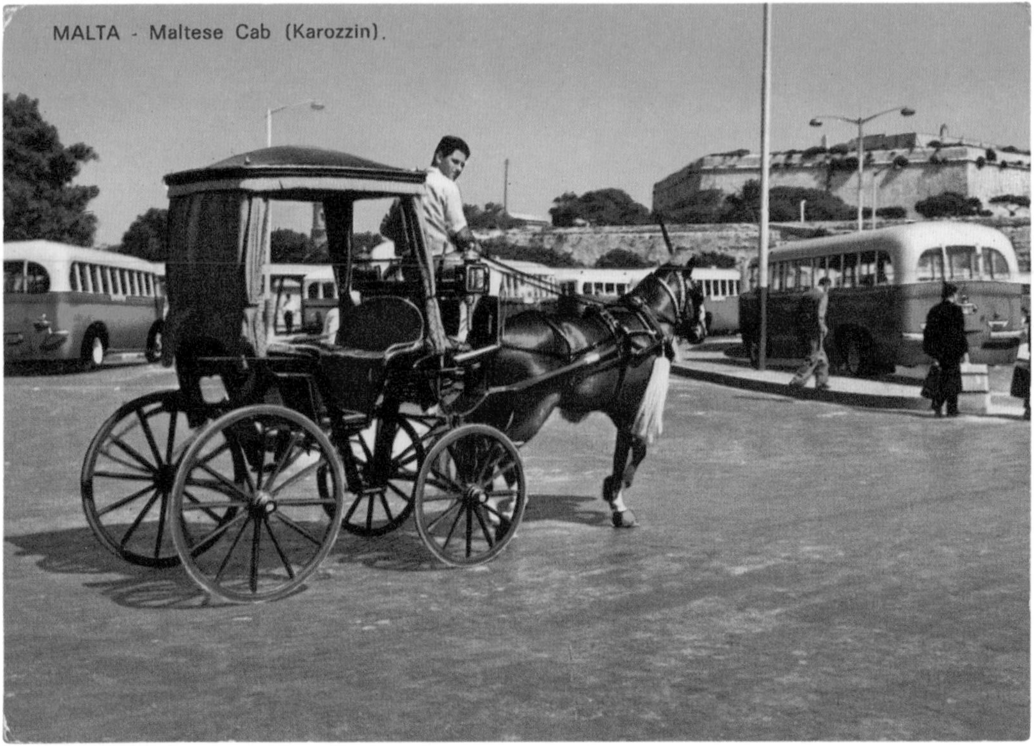
MALTA - Maltese Cab (Karozzin).

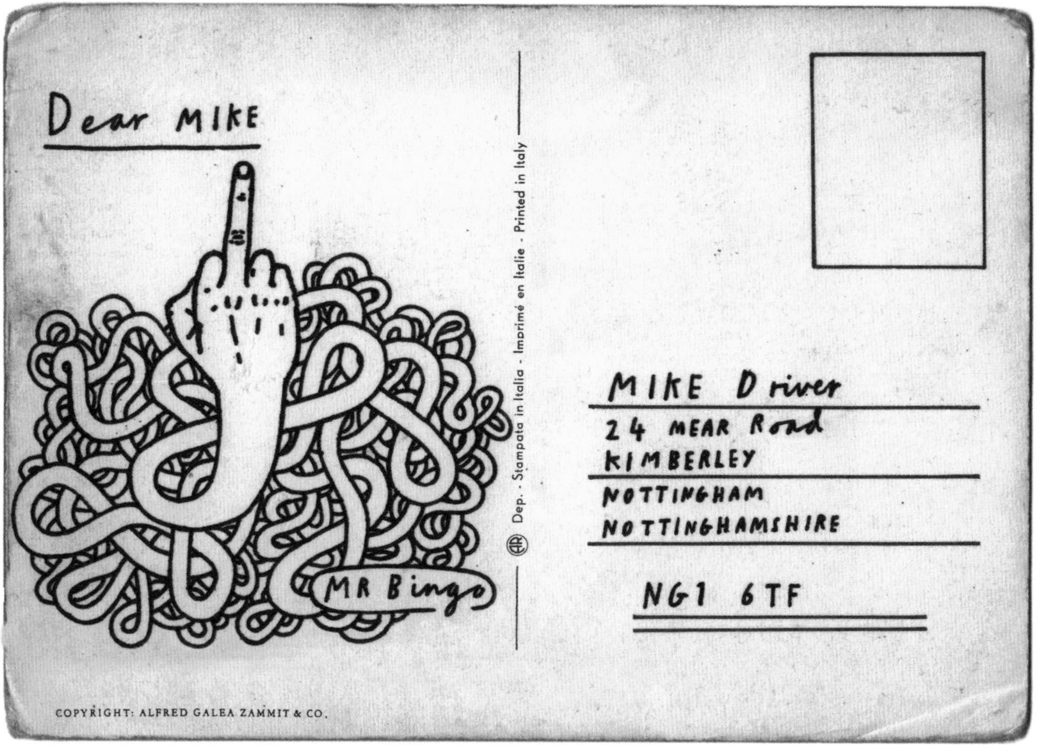
Dear MIKE
MR Bingo
Dep. - Stampata in Italia - Imprimé en Italie - Printed in Italy
MIKE Driver
24 MEAR Road
KIMBERLEY
NOTTINGHAM
NOTTINGHAMSHIRE
NG1 6TF
COPYRIGHT: ALFRED GALEA ZAMMIT & CO.

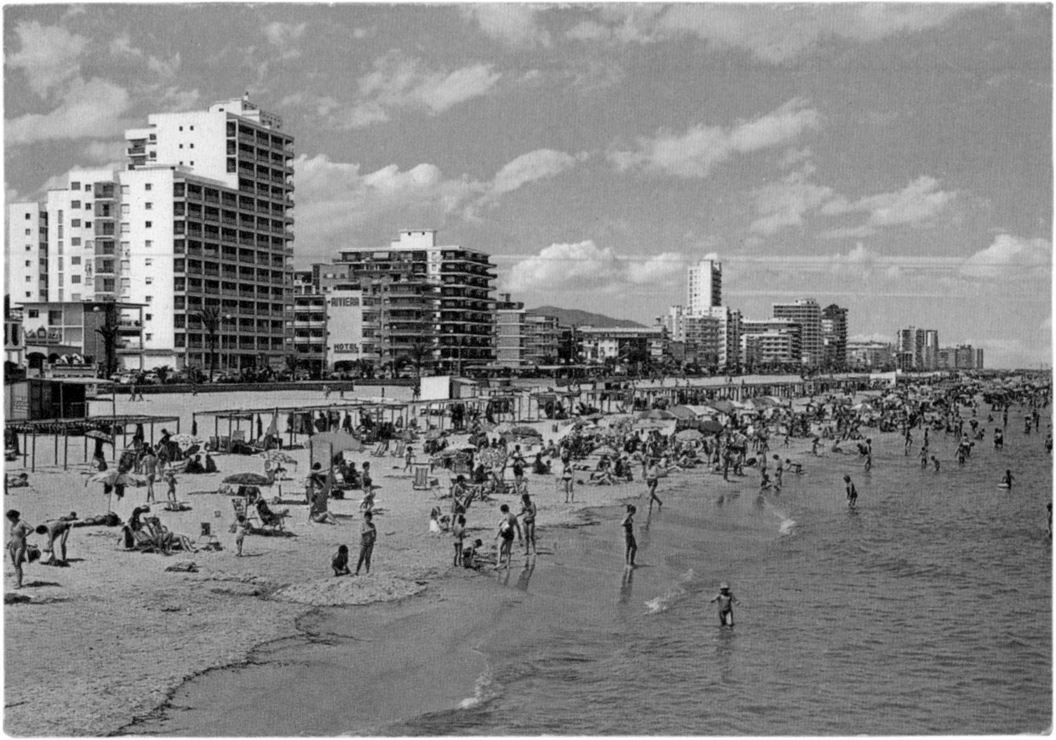
RIVIERA
HOTEL

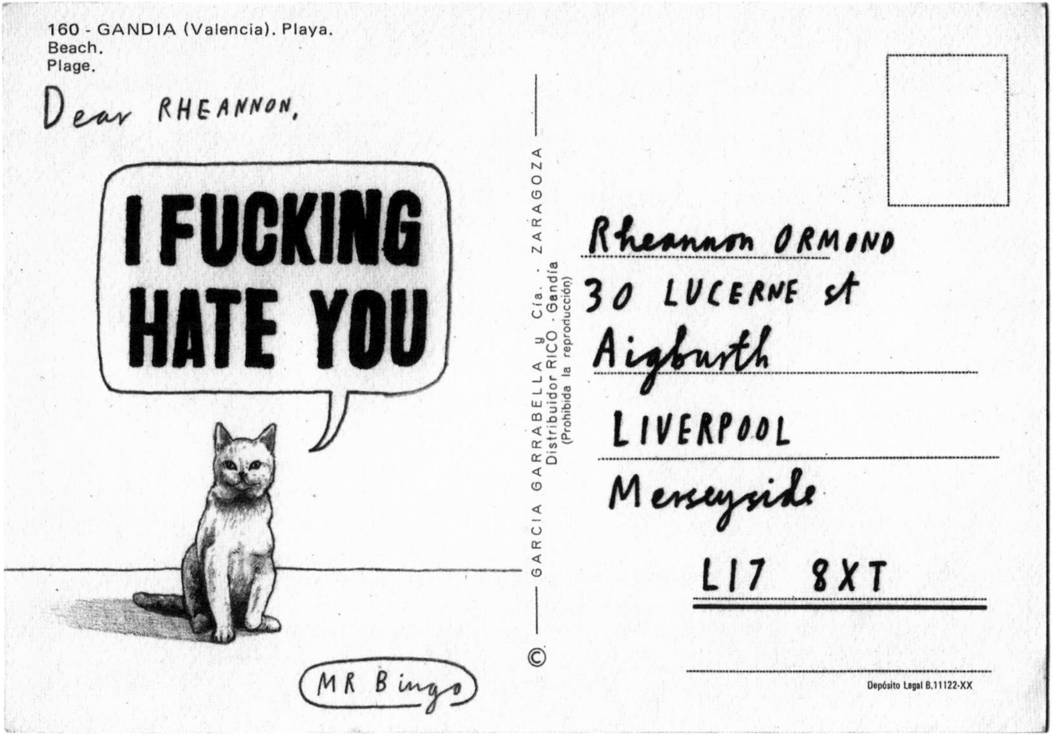
160 - GANDIA (Valencia). Playa.
Beach.
Plage.
Dear RHEANNON,
I FUCKING HATE YOU
MR Bingo
© GARCIA GARRABELLA y Cía. . ZARAGOZA
Distribuidor RICO . Gandía
(Prohibida la reproducción)
Rheannon ORMOND
30 LUCERNE st
Aigburth
LIVERPOOL
Merseyside
L17 8XT
Depósito Legal B.11122-XX

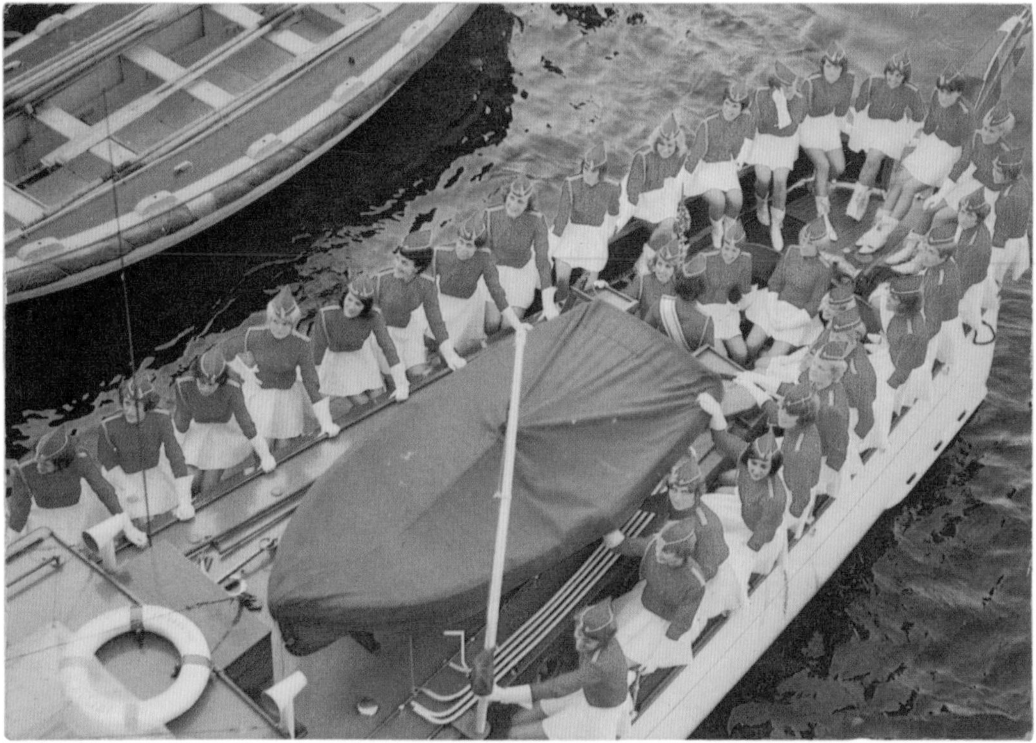

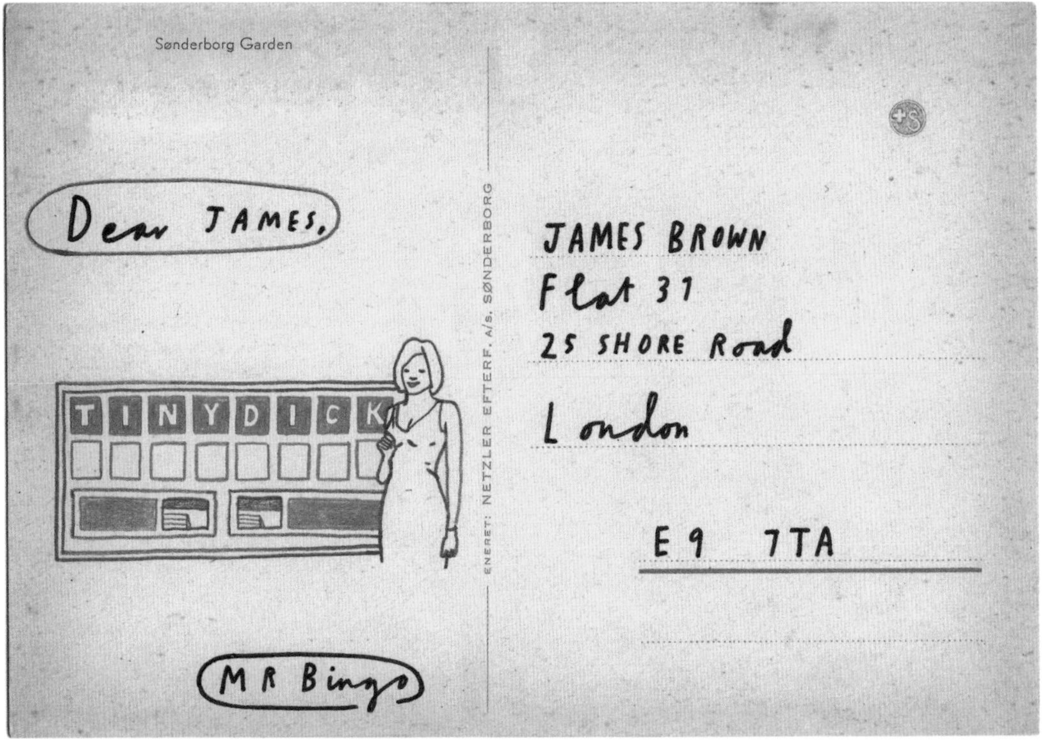

Sønderborg Garden

Dear JAMES,

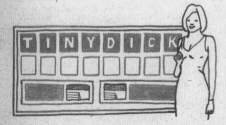

MR Bingo

ENERET: NETZLER EFTERF. A/s. SØNDERBORG

JAMES BROWN
Flat 37
25 SHORE Road

London

E9   7TA

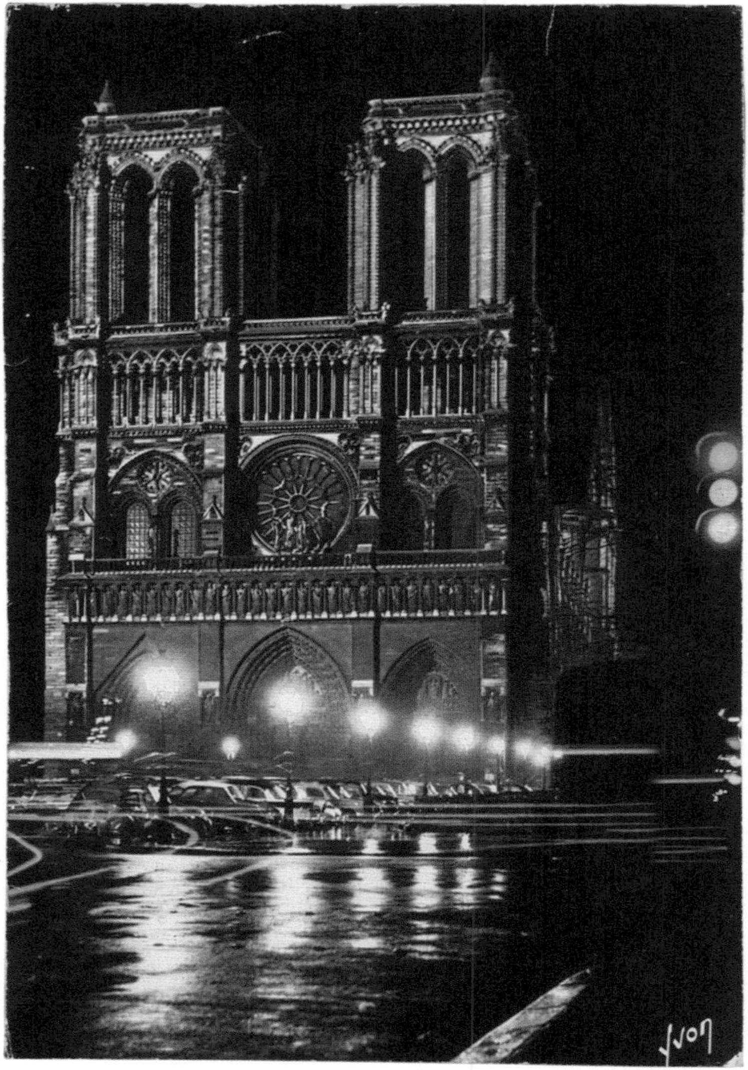
Yvon

Image de France
Imprimée en France

COULEURS ET LUMIERE DE FRANCE

Imprimé en France

Dear MARG

PEOPLE DON'T STARE AT YOU BECAUSE YOU'RE ATTRACTIVE.
PEOPLE STARE AT YOU BECAUSE YOU LOOK FUCKING ODD.

79

MR Bingo

MARG Laing
13 CONRCORD House
CLIFTON GROVE
London
E8 3DL

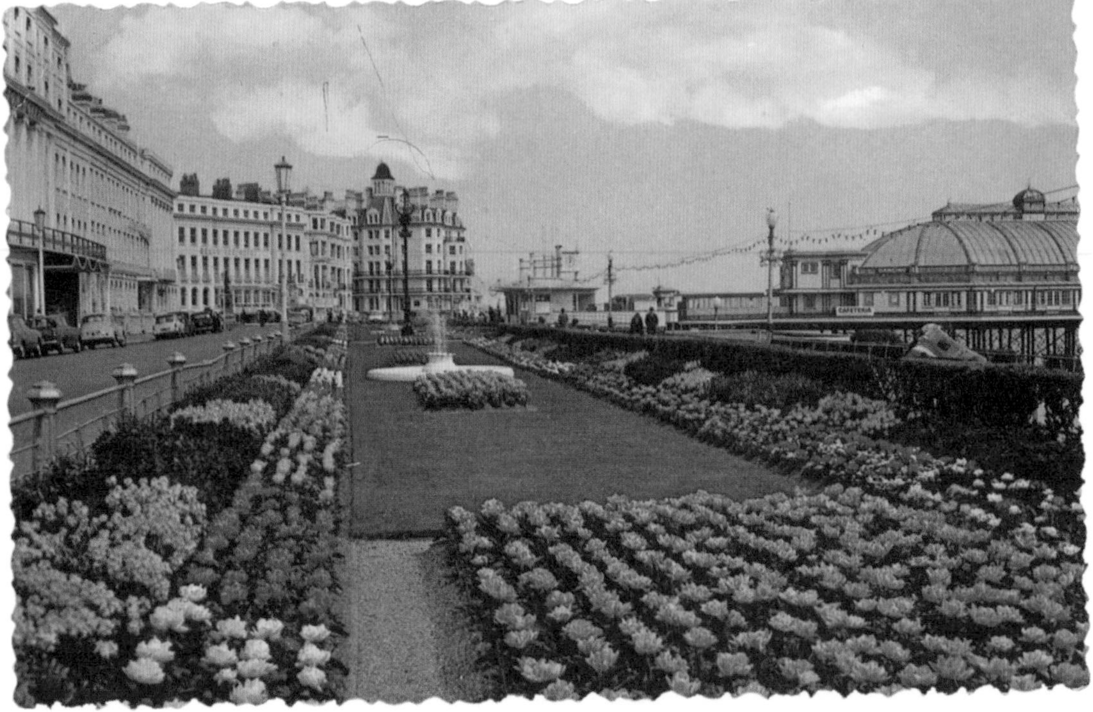
CAFETERIA

The Carpet Gardens, EASTBOURNE

SHOESMITH & ETHERIDGE LTD., HASTINGS

C9621

Dear DOUGAL

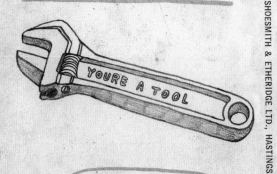

YOU'RE A TOOL

M R Bingo

Dougal Sadler

Hill TOP House
36B Valley ROAD
HENLEY on THAMES
OXFORDShire
RG9   1RR

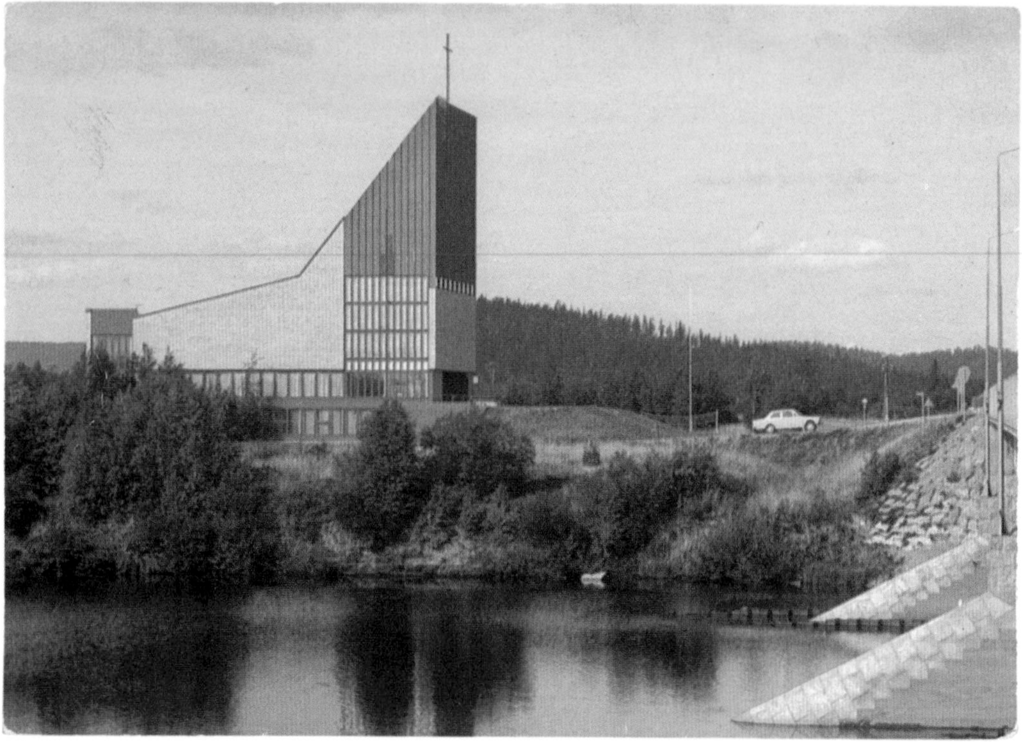

IVALO
Kirkko

SUOMI – FINLAND

Dear SAM

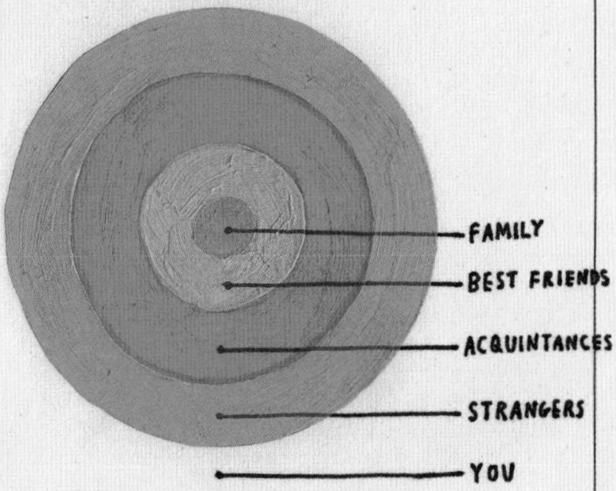
FAMILY
BEST FRIENDS
ACQUINTANCES
STRANGERS
YOU

SAM Baker

75B TAMWORTH Road

London

E3 ORH

MR Bingo

125

RM

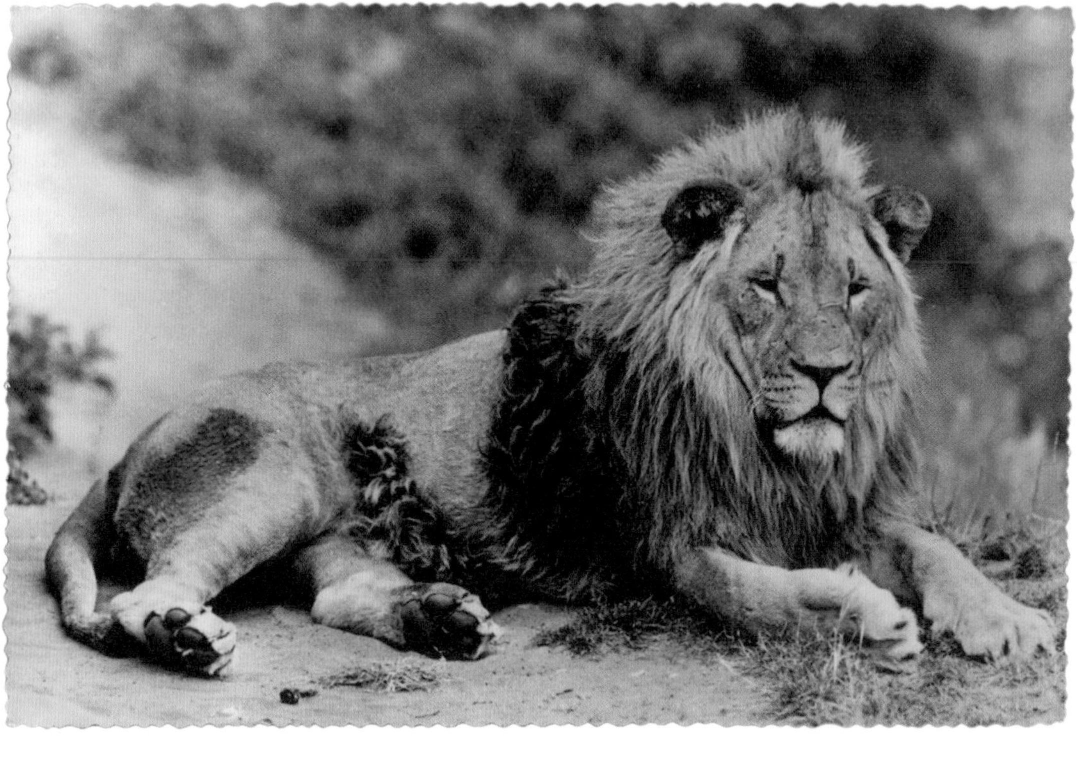

Dear LUKE & VANESSA

The Photographic Greeting Card Co. Ltd.

GO PHOTO SERIES GREETINGS

GREAT TO MEET YOU LAST WEEK
AT THE STOKE NEWINGTON DOGGING CLUB

Lion, London Zoo.   MR Bingo

GREETINGS AND BEST WISHES
Photo W. G. Vanderson, Fox Photos

LUKE & VANESSA

Flat 27, QUEBEC WHARF

315 Kingsland ROAD

London E8 4DJ

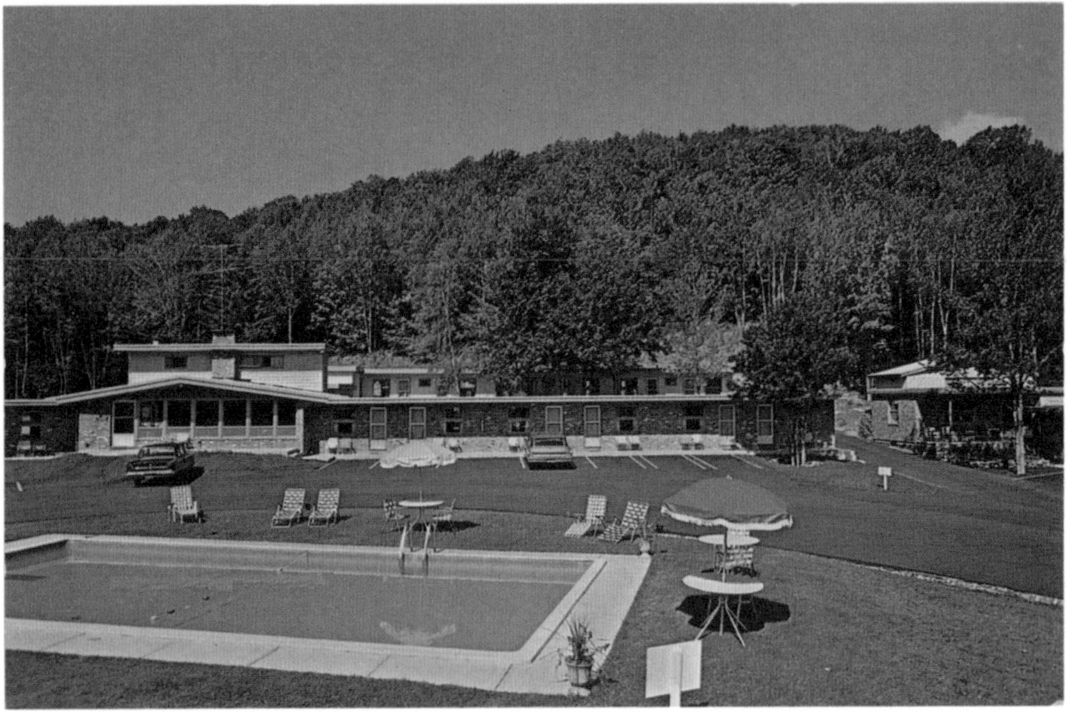

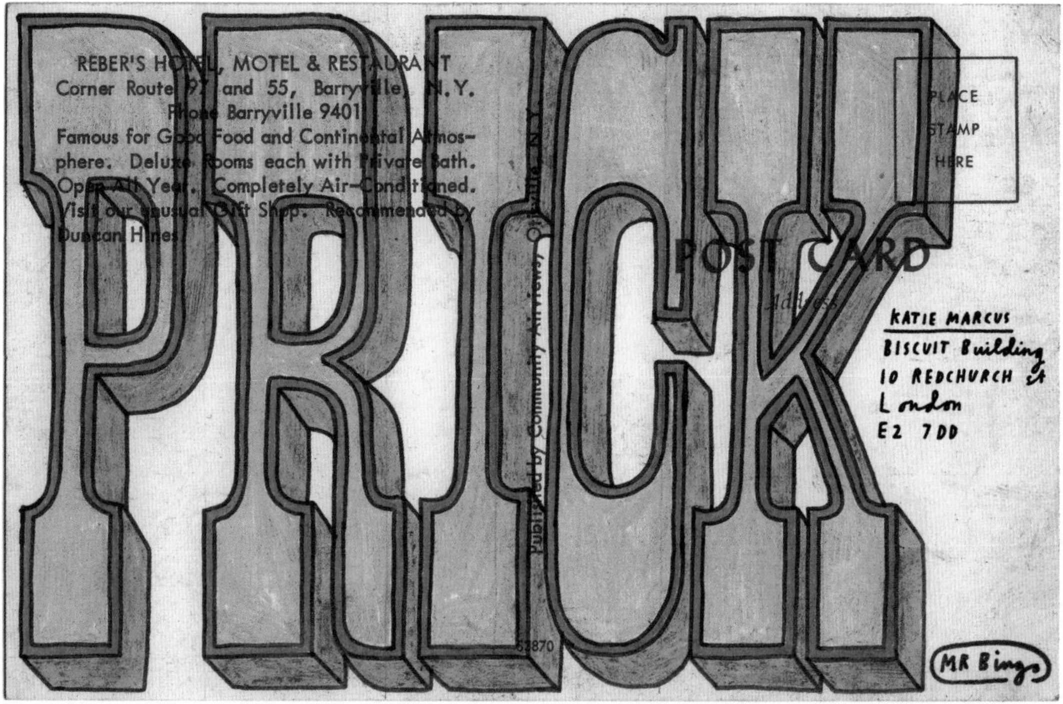
PRICK
REBER'S HOTEL, MOTEL & RESTAURANT
Corner Route 97 and 55, Barryville, N.Y.
Phone Barryville 9401
Famous for Good Food and Continental Atmosphere. Deluxe Rooms each with Private Bath. Open All Year. Completely Air-Conditioned. Visit our unusual Gift Shop. Recommended by Duncan Hines.
Published by Community Airviews
53870
POST CARD
PLACE
STAMP
HERE
Address
KATIE MARCUS
BISCUIT Building
10 REDCHURCH St
London
E2 7DD
MR Bingo

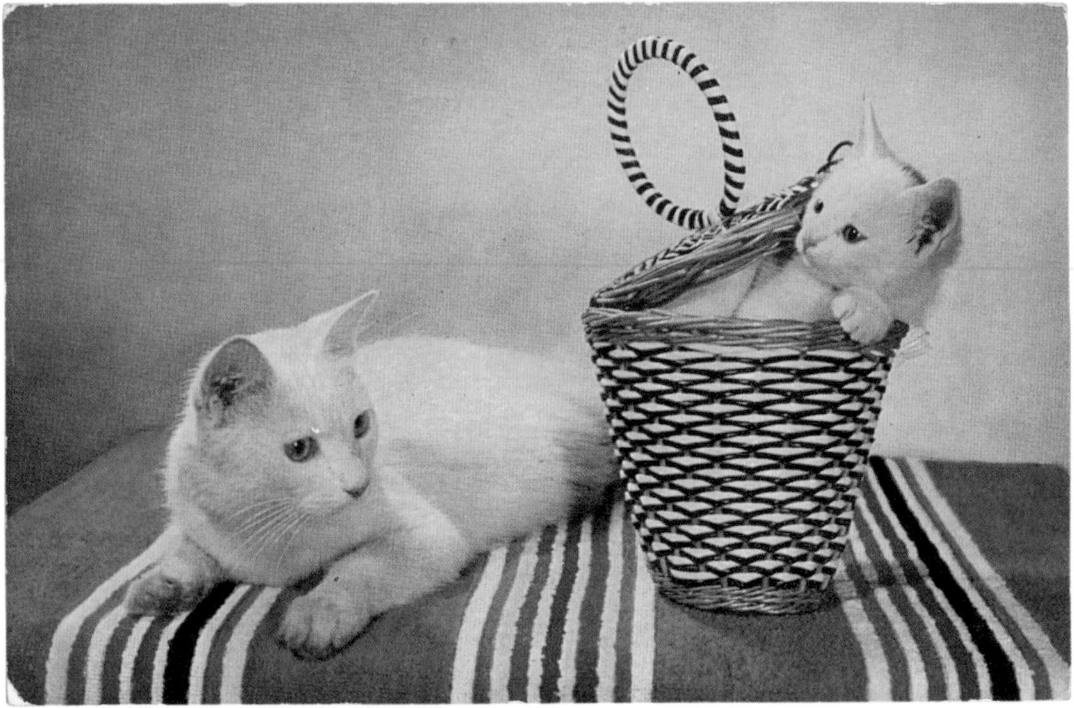

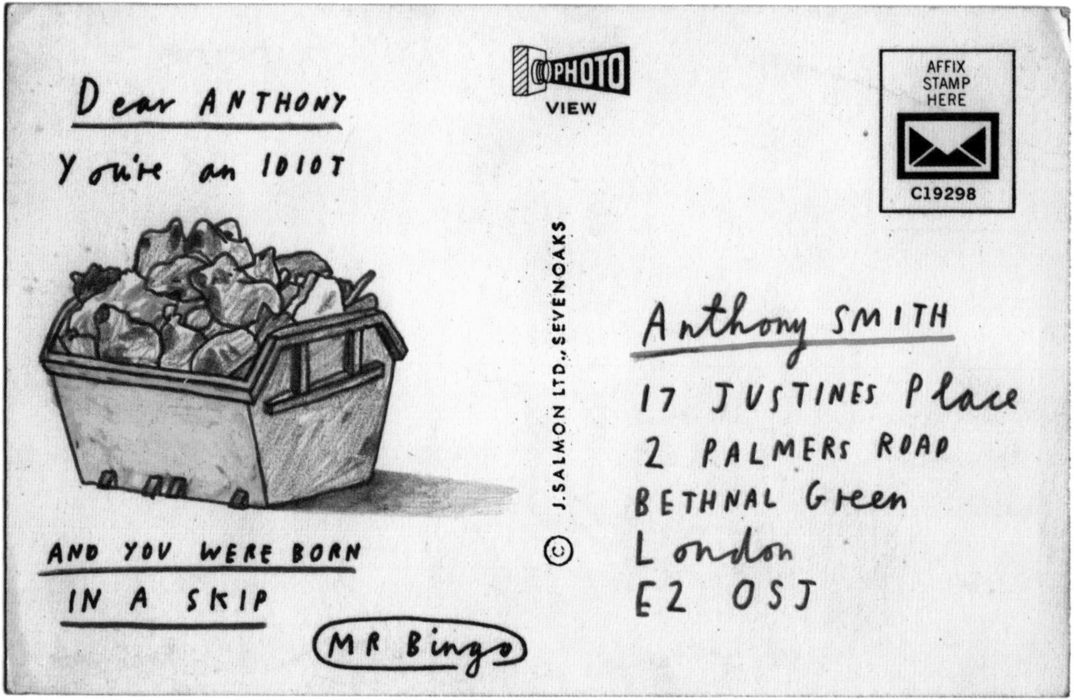

Dear ANTHONY

You're an IDIOT

AND YOU WERE BORN
IN A SKIP

MR Bingo

PHOTO VIEW

© J. SALMON LTD., SEVENOAKS

AFFIX STAMP HERE

C19298

Anthony SMITH
17 JUSTINES Place
2 PALMERS ROAD
BETHNAL Green
London
E2 0SJ

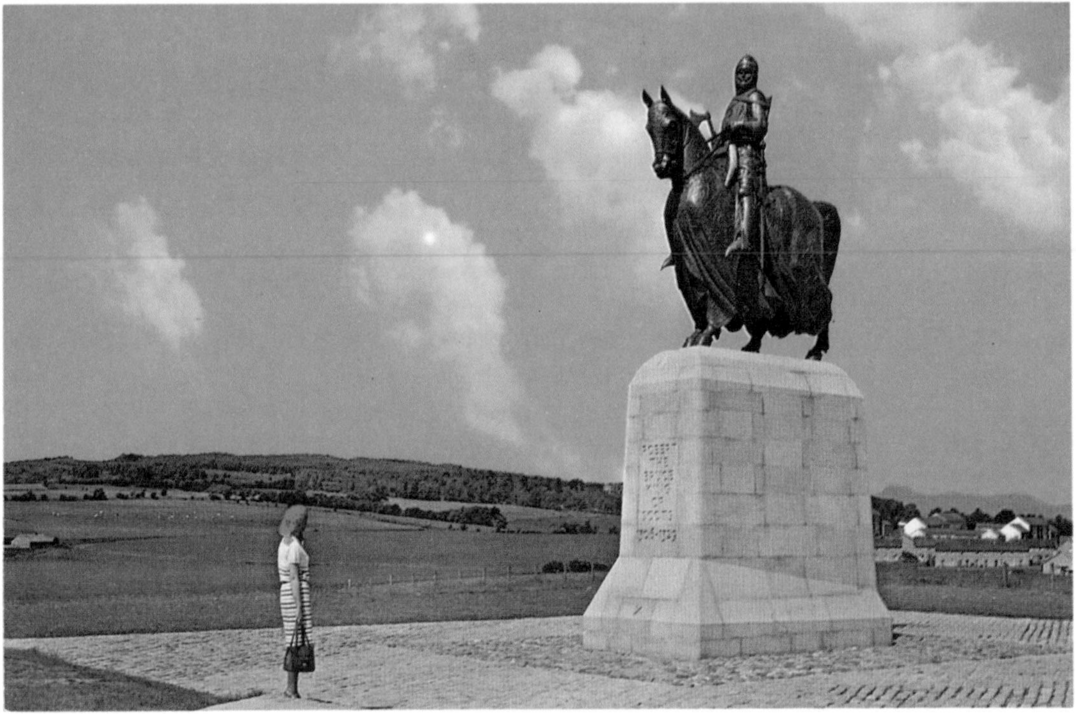

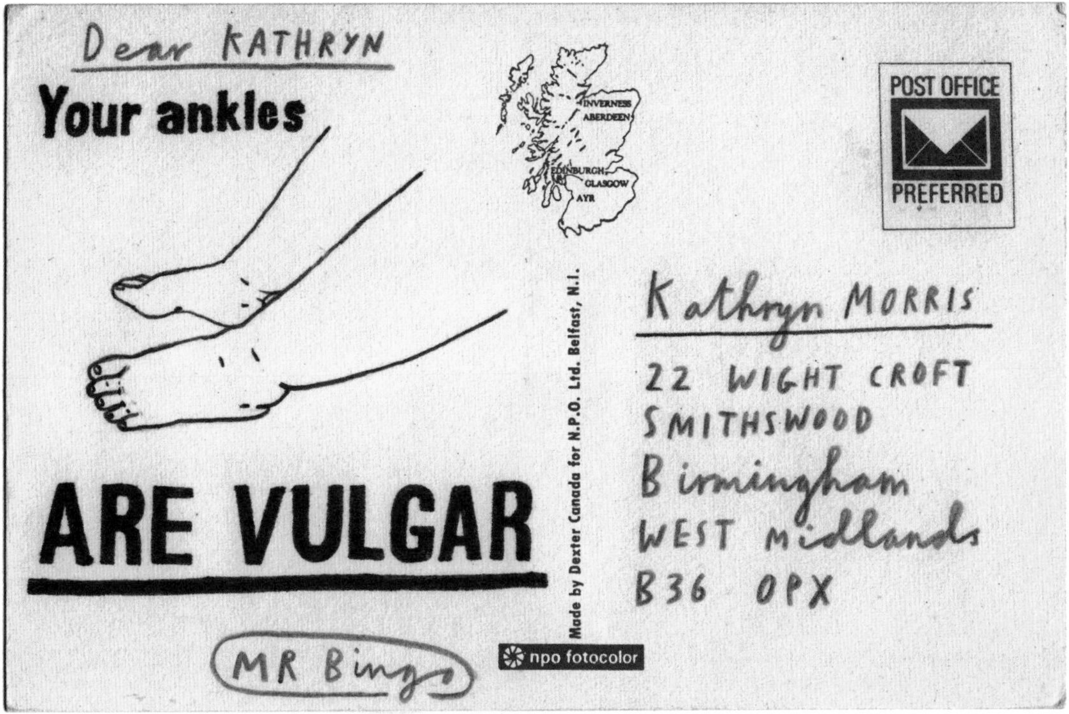
Dear KATHRYN
Your ankles
ARE VULGAR
MR Bingo
INVERNESS
ABERDEEN
EDINBURGH
GLASGOW
AYR
POST OFFICE
PREFERRED
Made by Dexter Canada for N.P.O. Ltd. Belfast, N.I.
npo fotocolor
Kathryn MORRIS
22 WIGHT CROFT
SMITHSWOOD
Birmingham
WEST midlands
B36 OPX

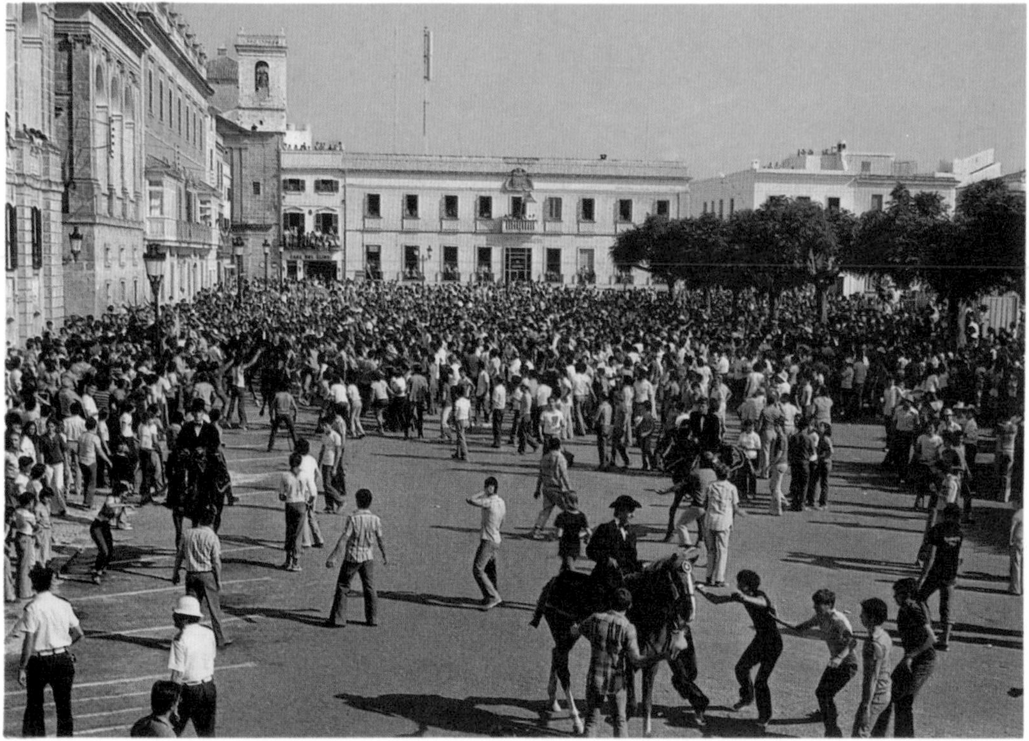

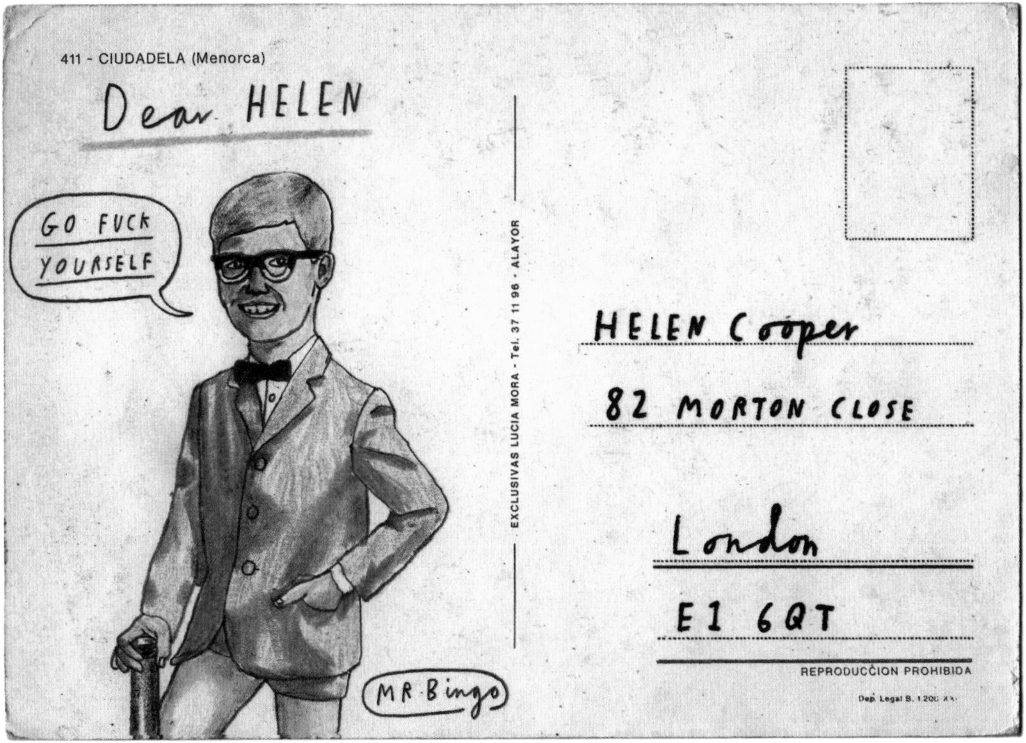
411 - CIUDADELA (Menorca)
Dear HELEN
GO FUCK YOURSELF
MR Bingo
EXCLUSIVAS LUCIA MORA - Tel. 37 11 96 - ALAYOR
HELEN Cooper
82 MORTON CLOSE
London
E1 6QT
REPRODUCCION PROHIBIDA

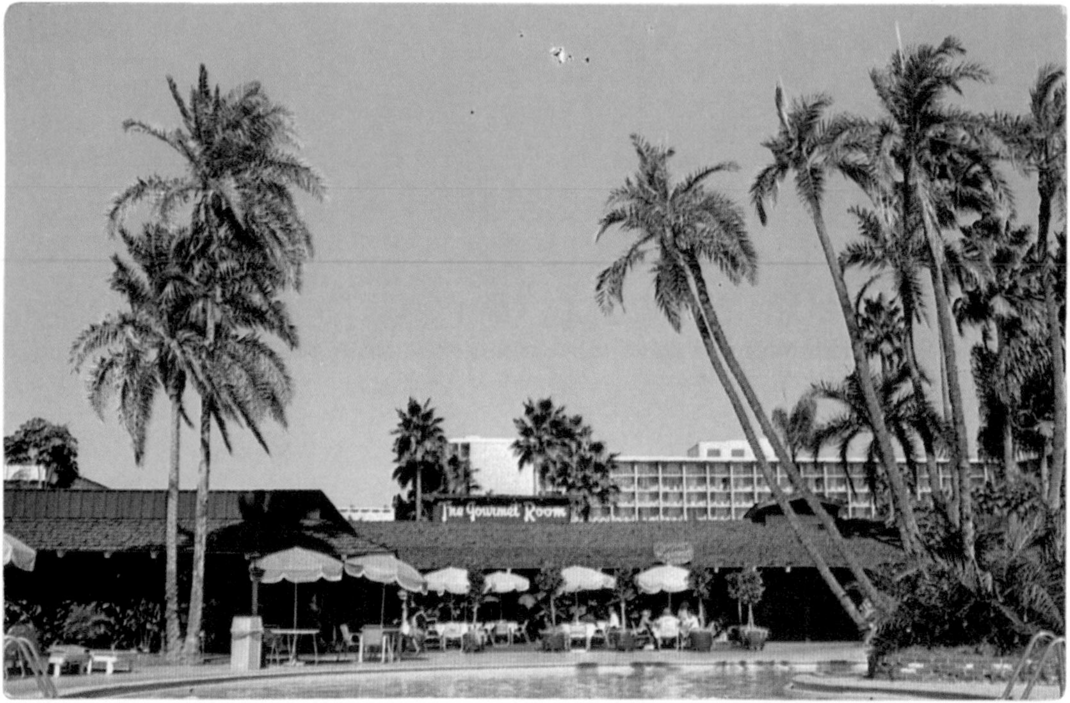
The Gourmet Room

Town and Country HOTEL

The Town and Country Hotel is located in the heart of San Diego in relaxing, peaceful surroundings, just 10 minutes from the San Diego International Airport, close to the San Diego Zoo, Sea World and San Diego's many other attractions . . . fine dining and entertainment just footsteps away.

Dear ALEX

YOU ARE JUST ANOTHER GENERIC DRONE, WANDERING AROUND, WAITING FOR THE WEEKEND

MR Bingo

ATLAS ah HOTELS

McGREW COLOR GRAPHICS mcg KANSAS CITY MO 64102
541060

PLACE 5c STAMP HERE

POST CARD

Address

ALEX Morris

8 LAUGHARNE Court
OFF CALDY CLOSE
Barry
The VALE of GLAMORGAN
CF62 9DW

Litho in U.S.A.

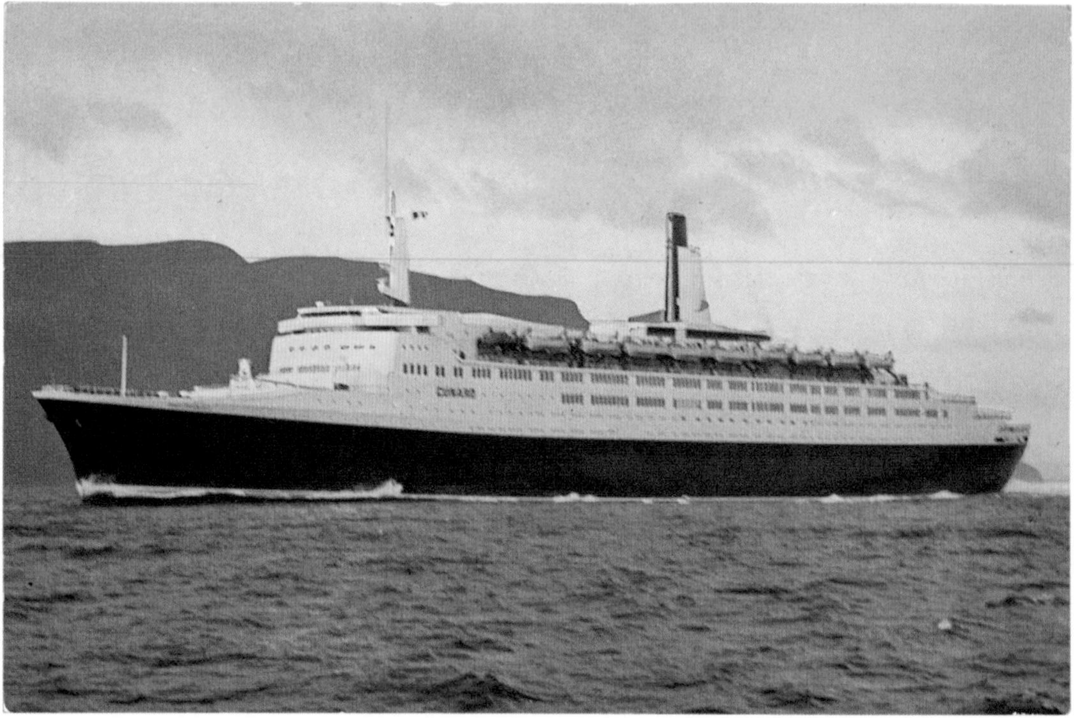
CUNARD

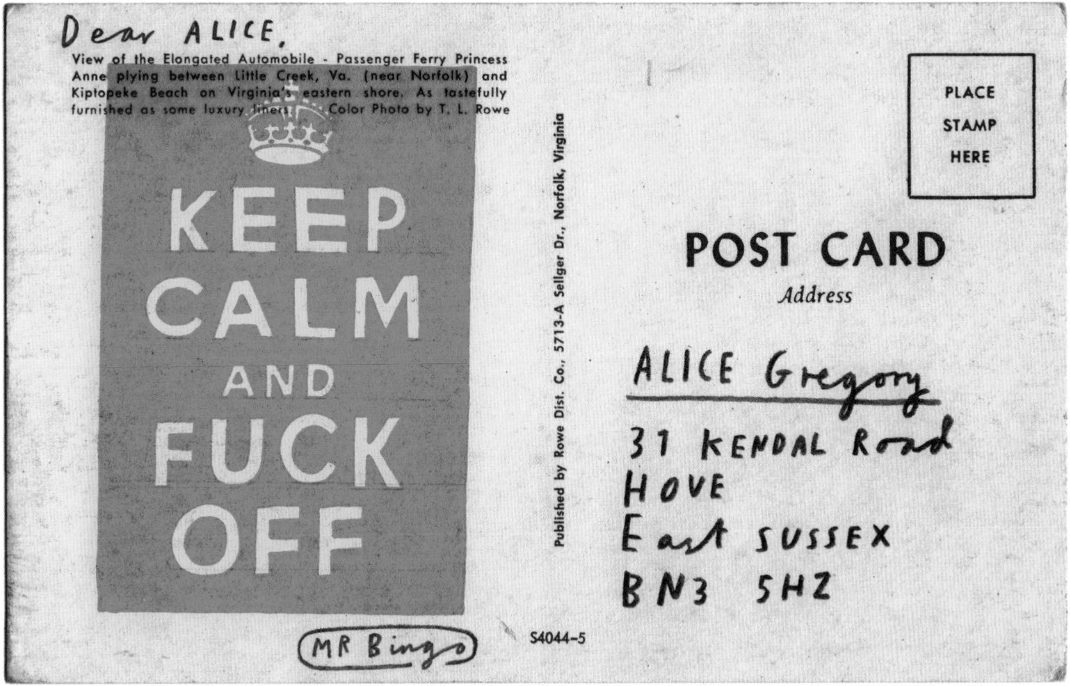
Dear ALICE,

View of the Elongated Automobile - Passenger Ferry Princess Anne plying between Little Creek, Va. (near Norfolk) and Kiptopeke Beach on Virginia's eastern shore. As tastefully furnished as some luxury liners. Color Photo by T. L. Rowe

KEEP
CALM
AND
FUCK
OFF

MR Bingo

S4044-5

Published by Rowe Dist. Co., 5713-A Sellger Dr., Norfolk, Virginia

PLACE
STAMP
HERE

POST CARD

Address

ALICE Gregory
31 KENDAL Road
HOVE
East SUSSEX
BN3 5HZ

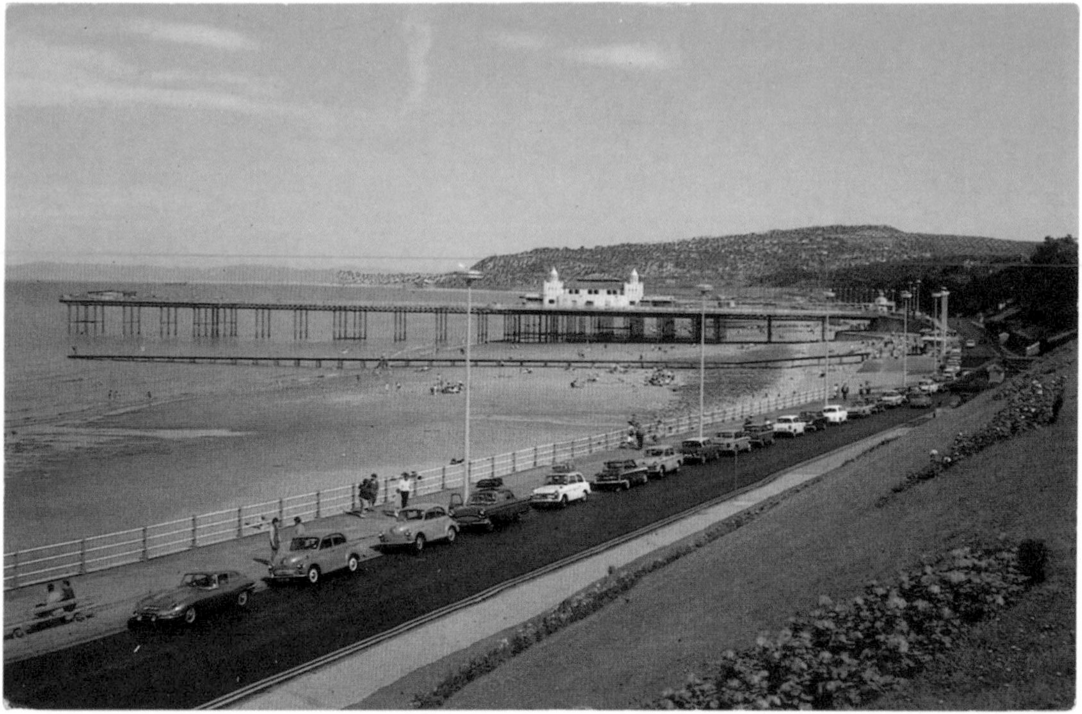

Dear PAUL

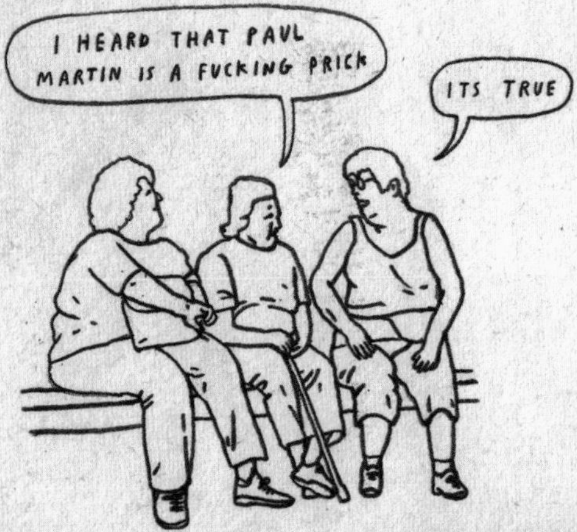
I HEARD THAT PAUL MARTIN IS A FUCKING PRICK
ITS TRUE

PRINTED IN GREAT BRITAIN

POST OFFICE PREFERRED

Paul MARTIN

28 RAYNOR Road
WEYBRIDGE
Surrey
KT13 5JU

MR Bingo

PIER AND PROMENADE. COLWYN BAY

PT23687

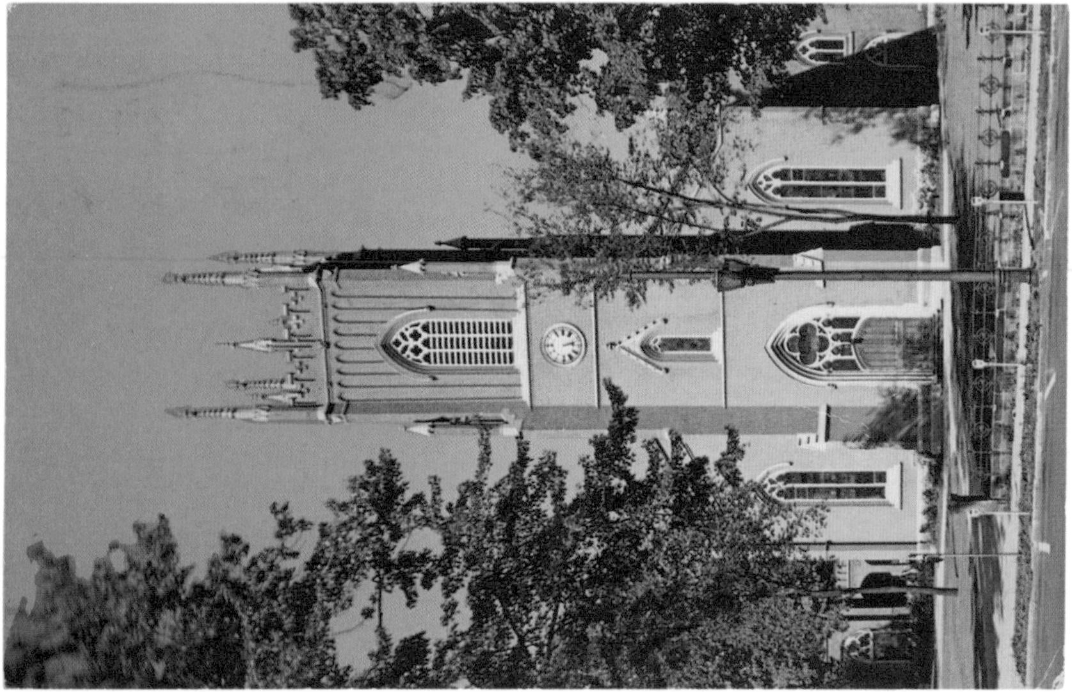

ST. PAUL'S CATHEDRAL
London, Ontario, Canada

Dear EMMA

LOOKS - WISE,
I'D RATE YOU

3 OUT OF 10

MR Bingo

Photographed & Distributed by Victor Aziz Photography Ltd., London, Ontario, Canada.

Plastichrome
by COLOURPICTURE
Boston 30, Mass.

POST CARD

Emma COOKE

120 STERLING Gardens
NEW CROSS
London
SE14 6DZ

PUT
STAMP
HERE

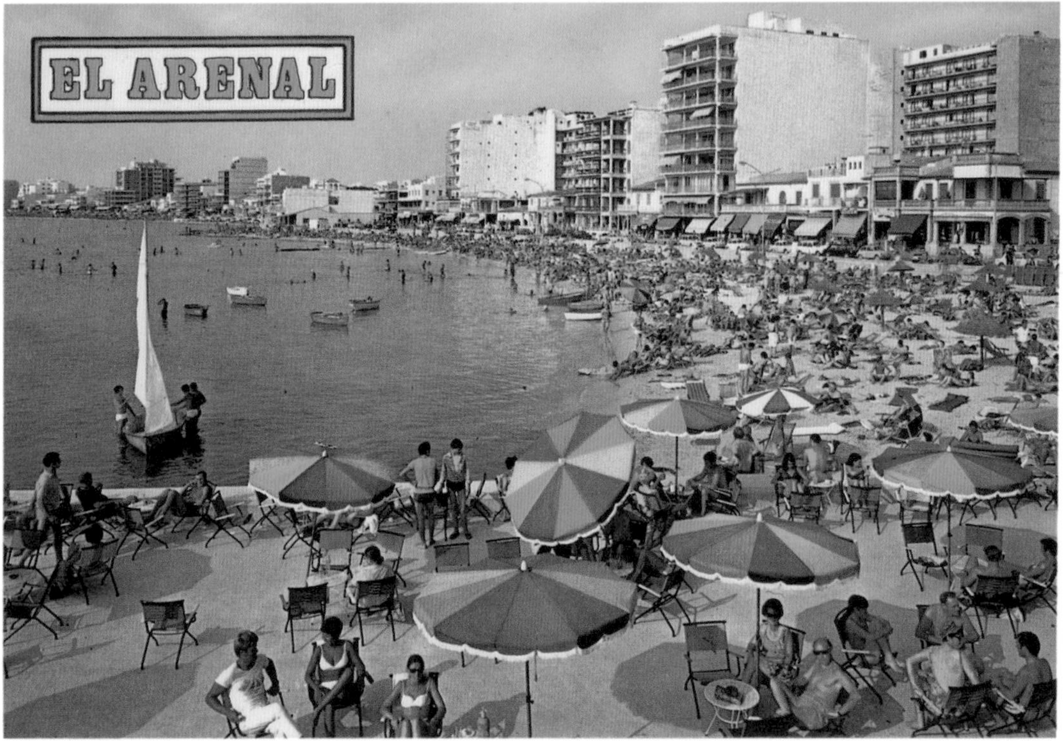
EL ARENAL

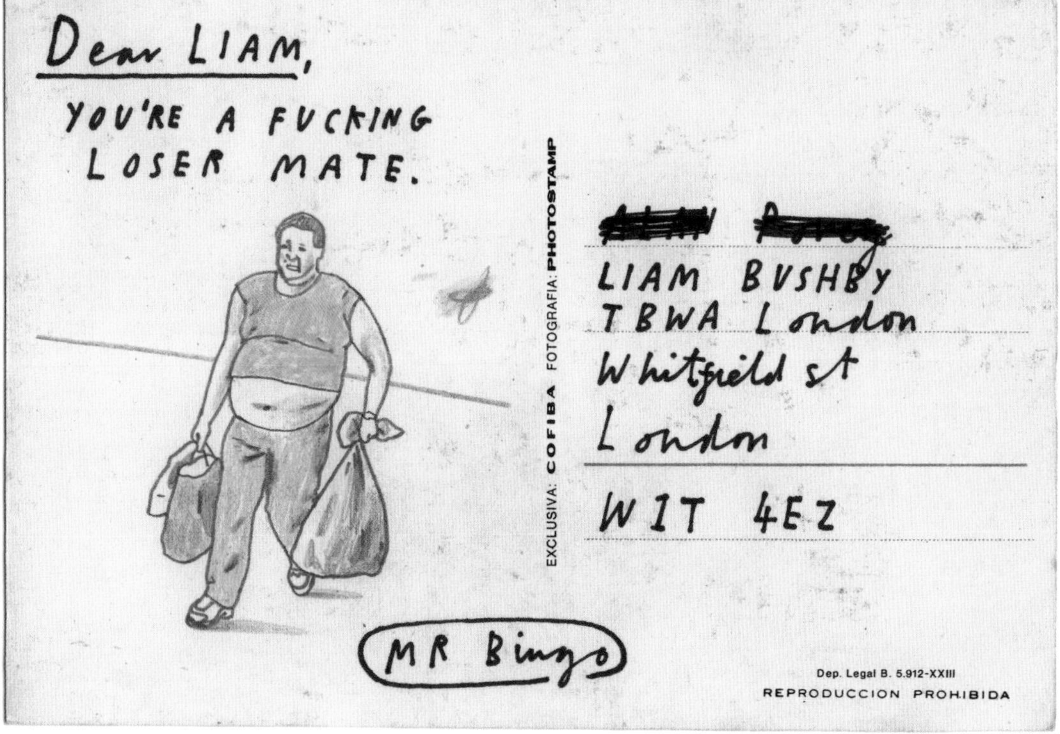

Dear LIAM,

YOU'RE A FUCKING LOSER MATE.

MR Bingo

EXCLUSIVA: COFIBA FOTOGRAFIA: PHOTOSTAMP

[redacted]

LIAM BUSHBY

TBWA London

Whitfield st

London

WIT 4EZ

Dep. Legal B. 5.912-XXIII

REPRODUCCION PROHIBIDA

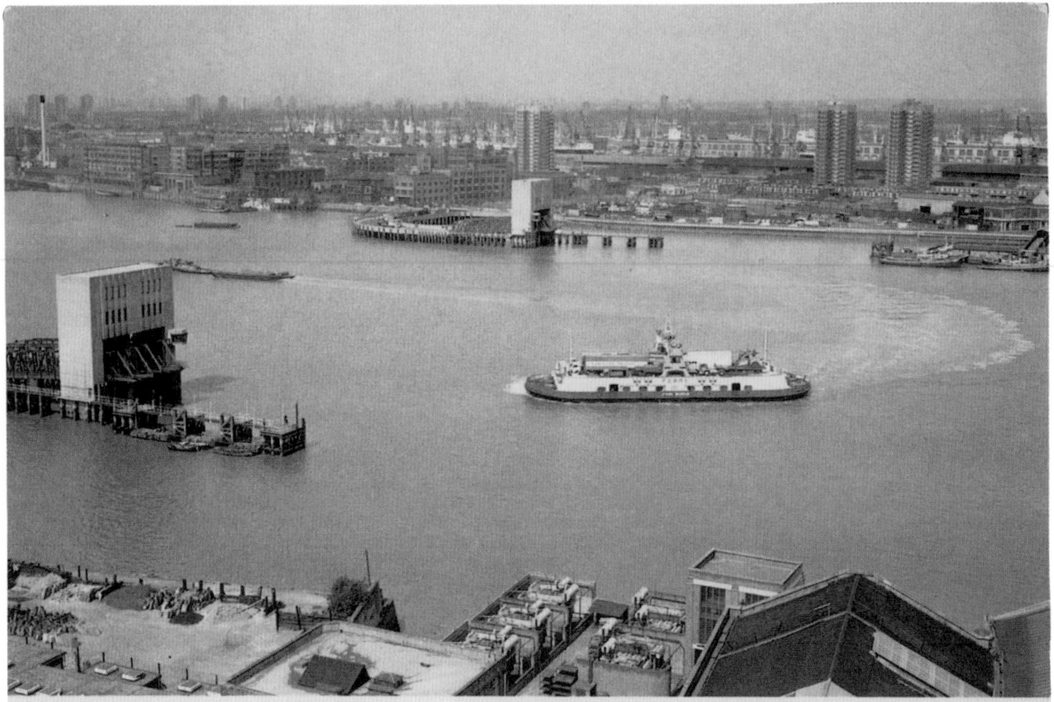

THE WOOLWICH FERRY, LONDON

Dear ROGER

IT REALLY
IS ALL YOUR
FAULT

COLOURMASTER
INTERNATIONAL

Photo Precision Limited, St. Ives, Huntingdon

PT15643

POST OFFICE
PREFERRED
Printed in
Great Britain

ROGER Kelly
74 Old FORD MEWS
PRINTERS Road
London
E5 3NZ

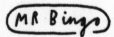

MR Bingo

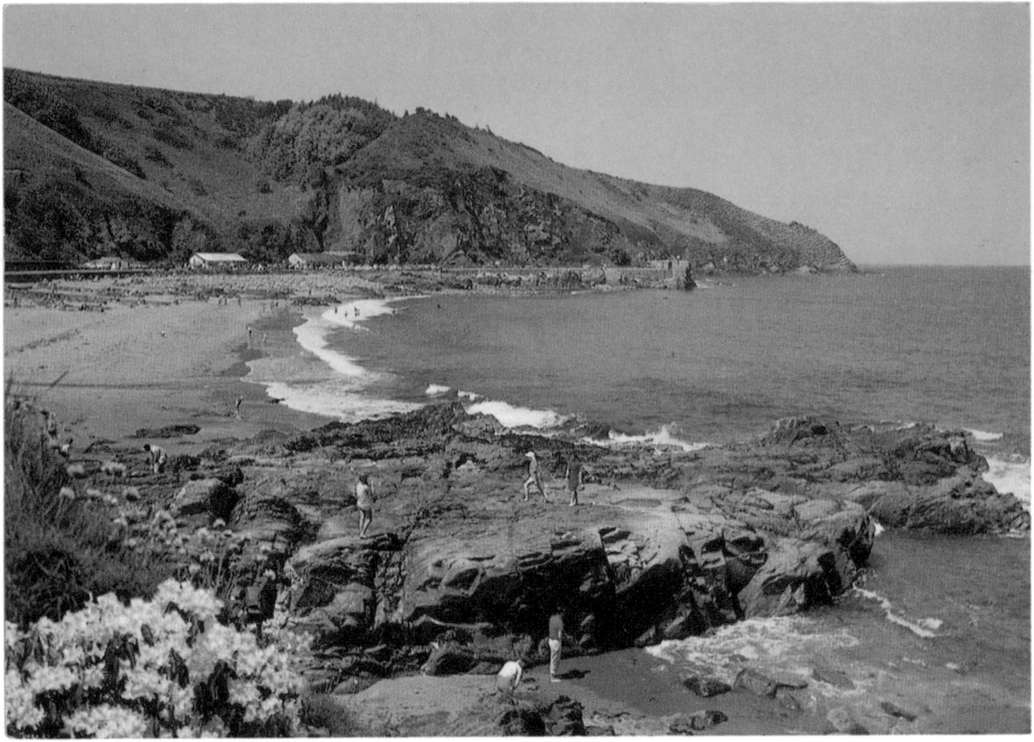

Dear IAN

I DID A 'GOOGLE IMAGE SEARCH'
FOR 'IAN ALLARDYCE' AND THIS CAME UP.

COLOURMASTER
INTERNATIONAL

POST OFFICE
PREFERRED
Printed in
Great Britain

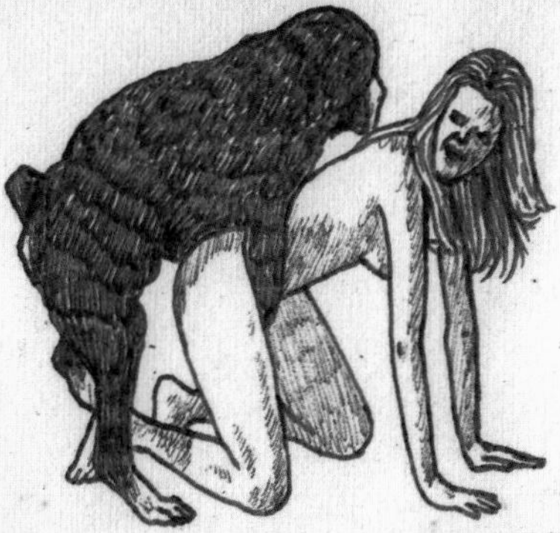

Photo Precision Limited, St. Ives, Huntingdon

IAN Allardyce
90 WARWICK Building
366 QUEENSTOWN ROAD
London
SW8 4NL

MR Bingo

GREVE DE LECQ, JERSEY

PT28778

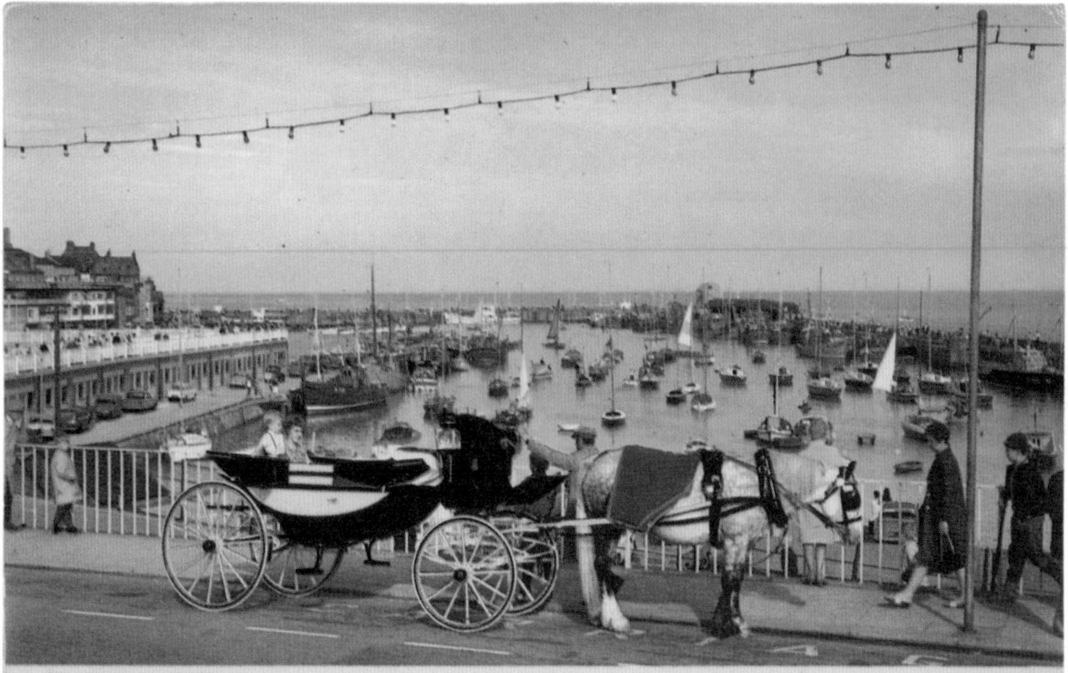

The Harbour, Bridlington B.2269

90

POST DENNIS Productions CARD

Dear OWEN

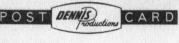

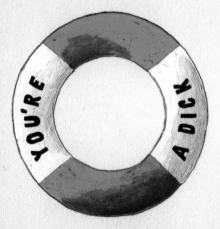

YOU'RE
A DICK

Printed & Published by E. T. W. DENNIS & SONS LTD., SCARBOROUGH

POST OFFICE PREFERRED

AFFIX STAMP HERE

ALL BRITISH PRODUCTION

MR OWEN JOHNSON

See What You Mean

126 BUTE st

Cardiff BAY

CARDIFF

CF10 5LE

MR Bings

Photocolour
C.1226

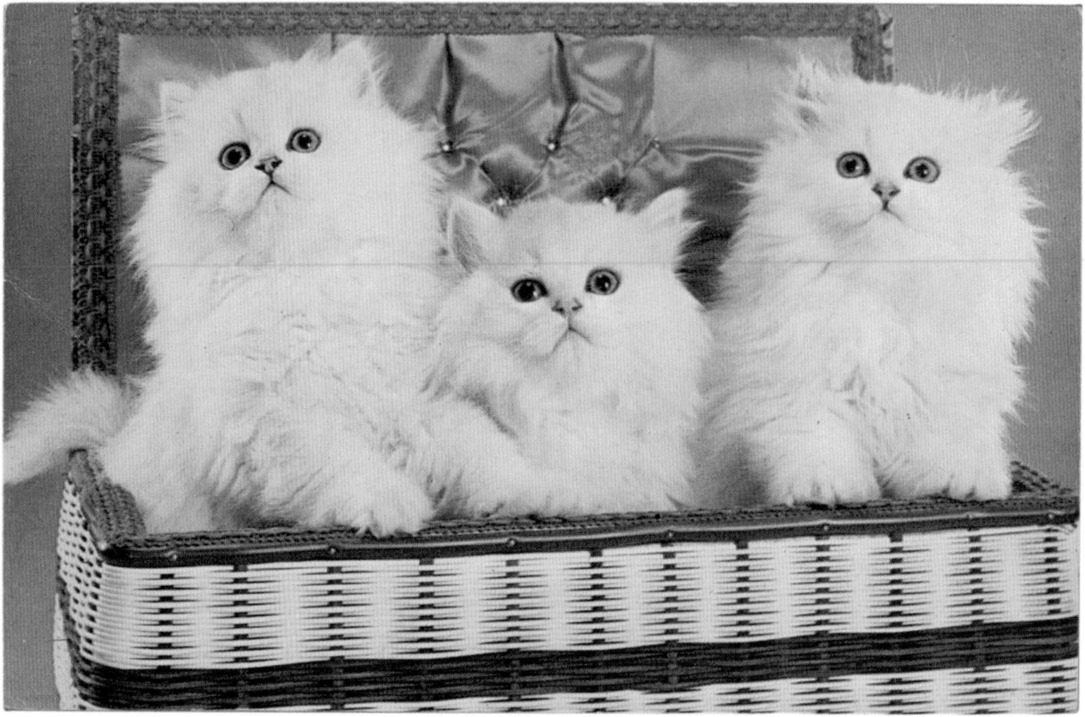

POST CARD

Dear CHARLIE

I HAVE BEEN INFORMED THAT YOU ARE A WANKER

MR Binge

PRINTED IN ENGLAND

CHARLIE Burton
WIRED Magazine
5th FLOOR
6-8 Old BOND st
London
W1S 4PH
United Kingdom

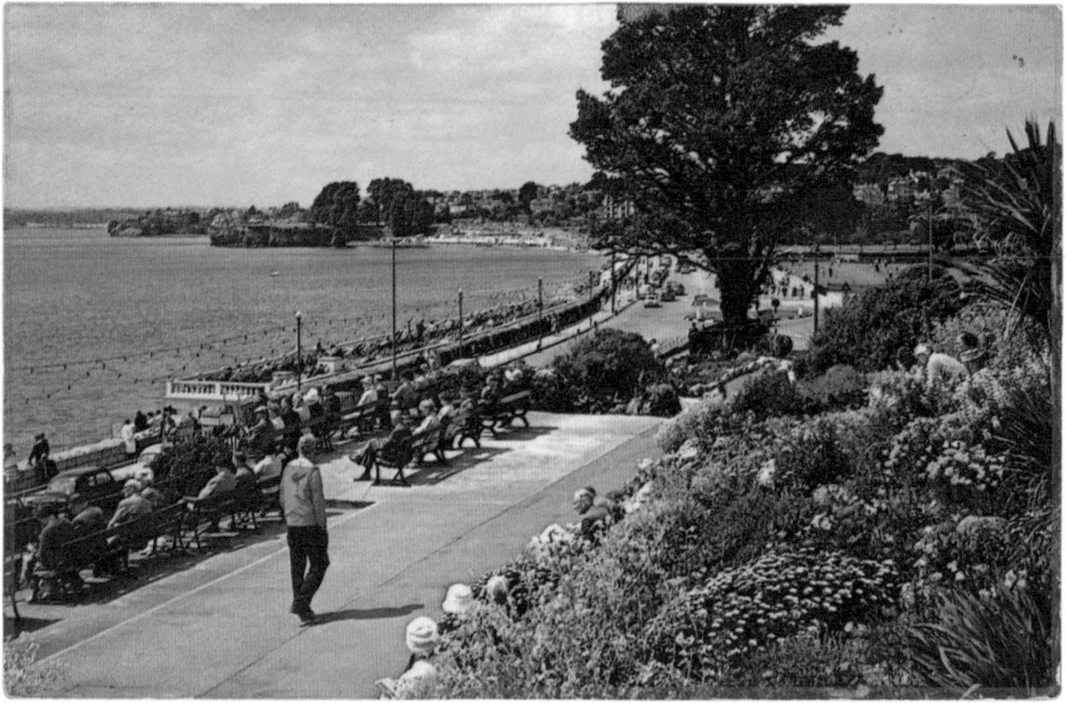

POST CARD

GREETINGS AND BEST WISHES

ADDRESS ONLY

British Manufacture
H B

Dear HEFIN

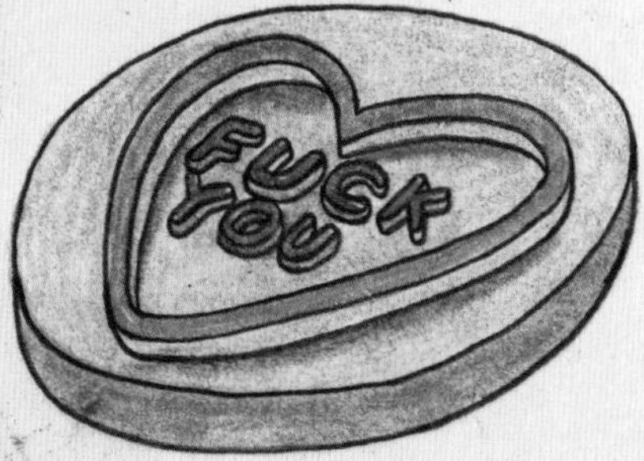
FUCK YOU

MR Bingo

HEFIN Jones

SURREY House
80 LEWISHAM WAY
NEW Cross
London
SE14 6PB

GT 4207 SUB TROPICAL GARDENS, TORQUAY.

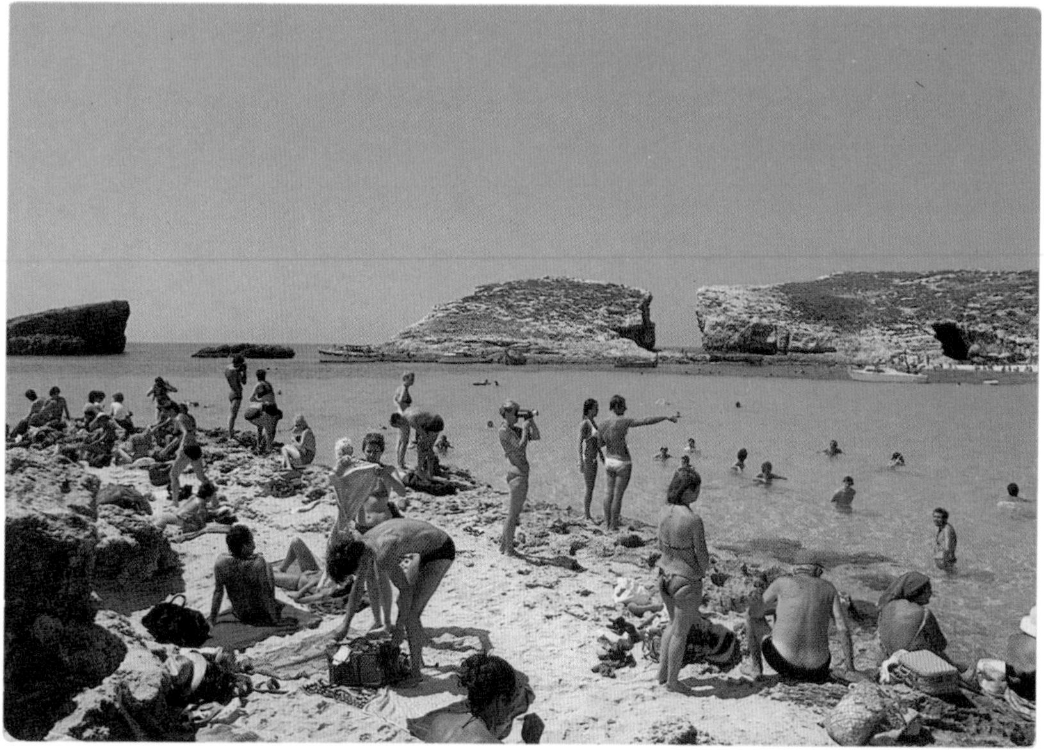

Blue Lagoon
COMINO

303

Copyright: Perfecta Advertising Ltd – Malta Tel: 29068

Dear CHRIS

CHRIS George

FLAT 1

The OLD GERMAN Hospital

66 RITSON ROAD

London E8 1FP

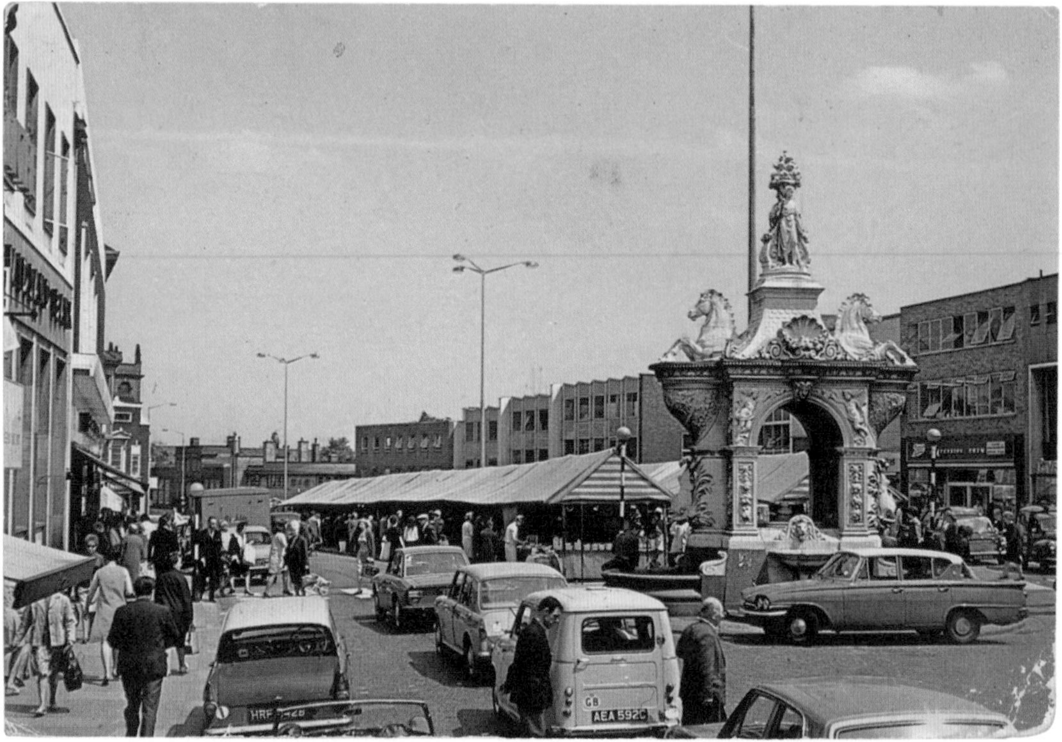
GB
AEA 592C

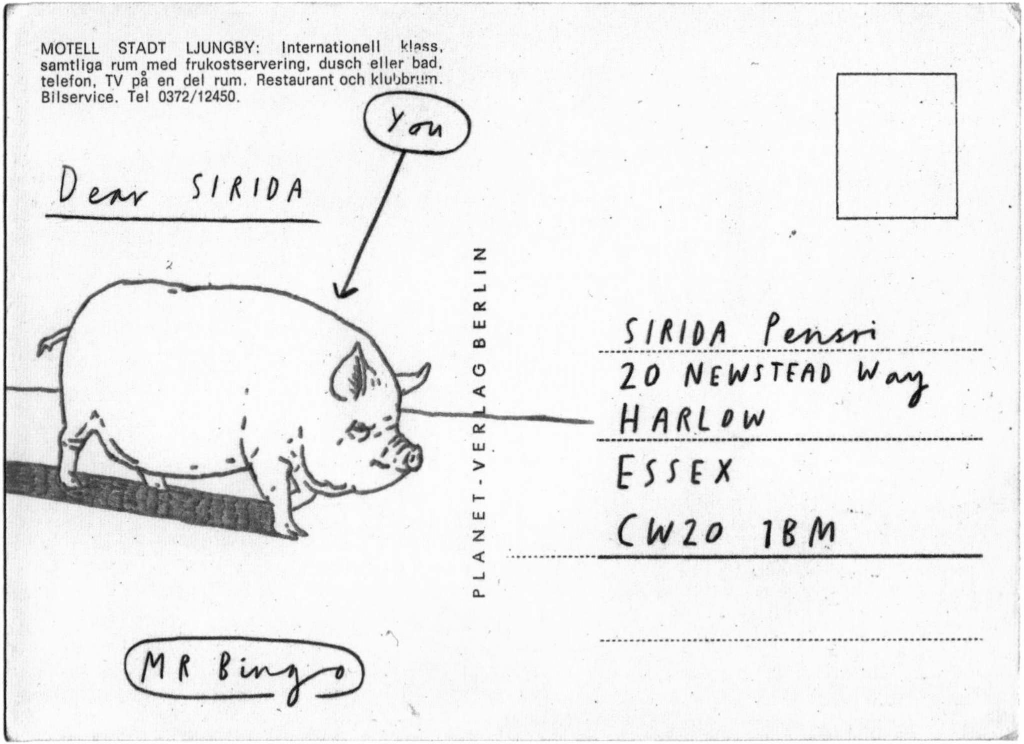
MOTELL STADT LJUNGBY: Internationell klass, samtliga rum med frukostservering, dusch eller bad, telefon, TV på en del rum. Restaurant och klubbrum. Bilservice. Tel 0372/12450.
You
Dear SIRIDA
PLANET-VERLAG BERLIN
SIRIDA Pensri
20 NEWSTEAD Way
HARLOW
ESSEX
CW20 1BM
MR Bingo

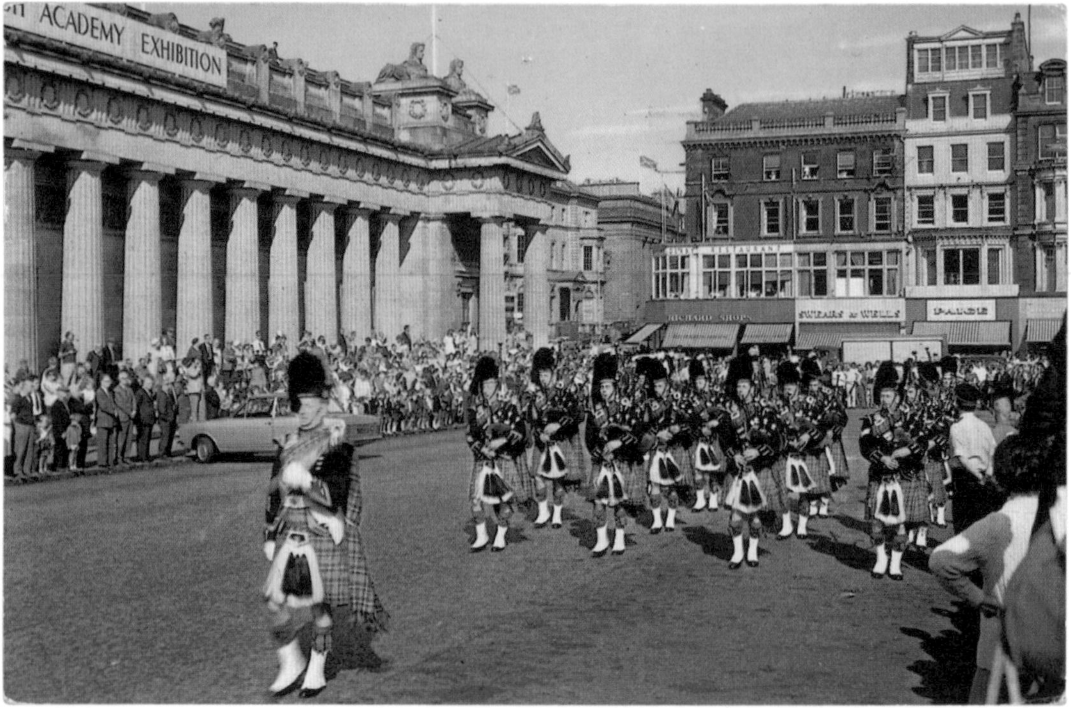
ACADEMY EXHIBITION

Dear MATTHEW

1. I HAVE REMOVED YOU AS A FRIEND
   ON FACEBOOK
2. I HAVE UNFOLLOWED YOU ON TWITTER
3. WE ARE NO LONGER 'LINKED-IN'

BECAUSE I REALISED THAT
   YOU ARE A CUNT.

COLOURMASTER
INTERNATIONAL

Photo Precision Limited, St. Ives.

PIPES AND DRUMS IN EDINBURGH   PT37030

MR Bingo

AFFIX STAMP
HERE
POST OFFICE
PREFERRED

MATTHEW Booth
16 MAYTREE ROAD
ADLINGTON
Chorley
LANCASHIRE
PR9 6SL

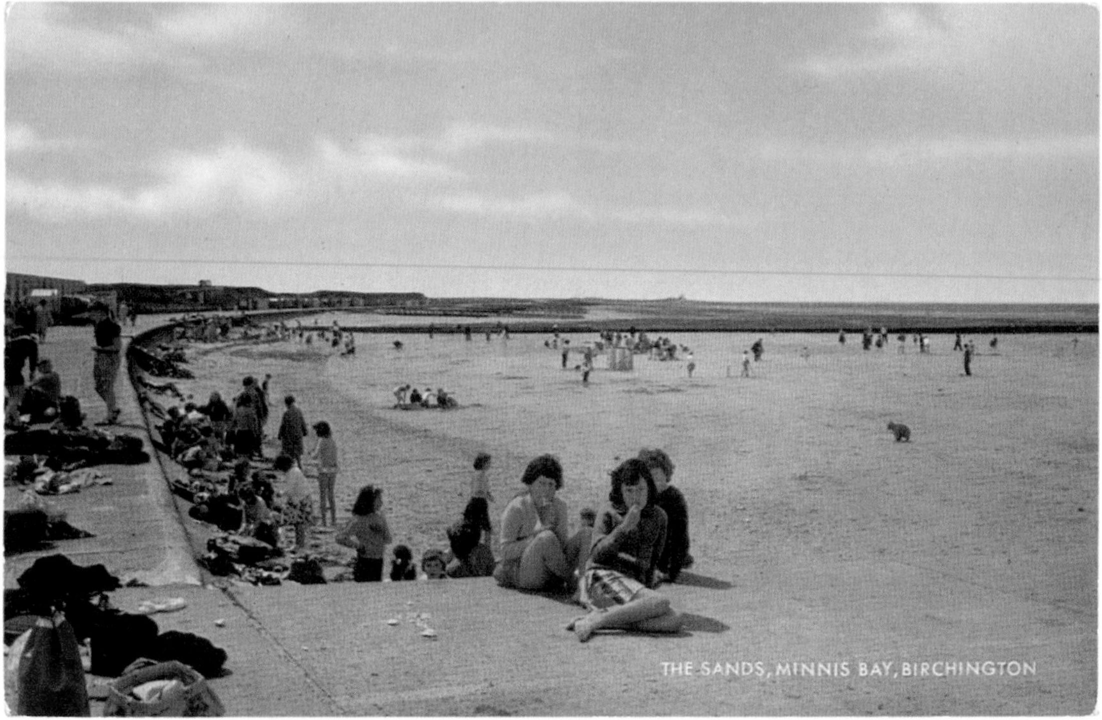
THE SANDS, MINNIS BAY, BIRCHINGTON

POST **Salmon** SERIES "CAMERACOLOUR" © CARD

Dear ALEXA

TW AT

MR Bingo

Printed & Published by J. Salmon Ltd., Sevenoaks, Eng. ©

3280c

ALEXA Chung

8 SMOKEHOUSE Yard
44-46 PEAR St
London
EC1Y 4FD

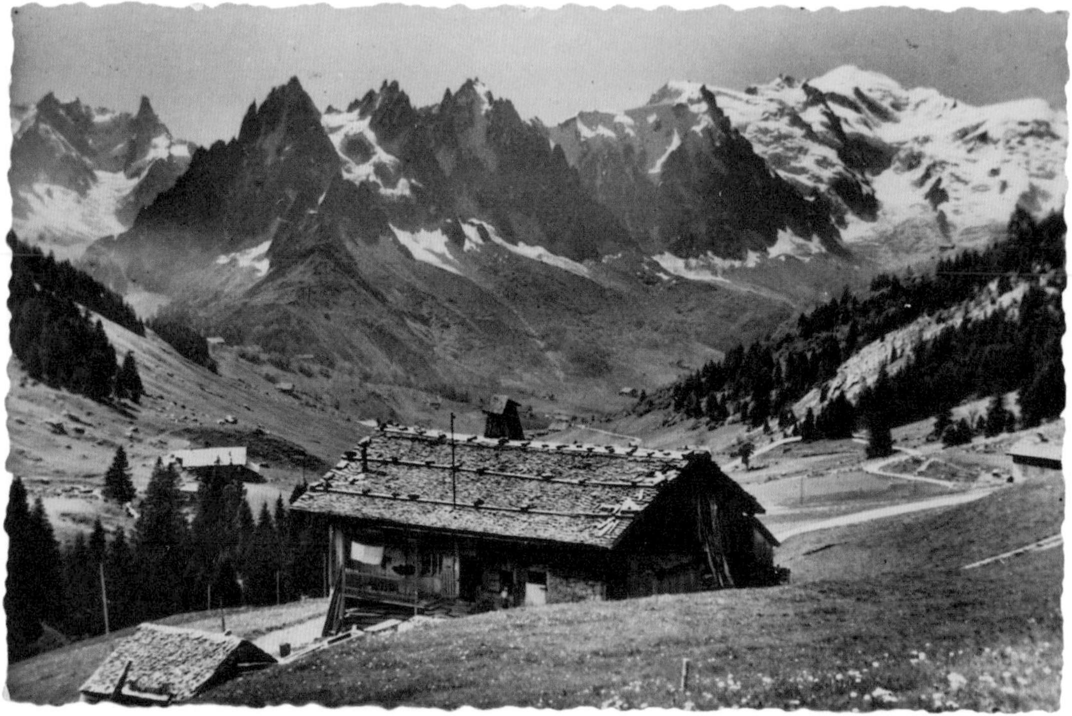

2515. Paysage Savoyard au
PAYS du MONT-BLANC.

Dear JEZ BURROWS

FUCK JEZ

C'est un cliché du célèbre chasseur d'images

JEZ Burrows

2F2, 10 STEEL's Place

EDINBURGH

MIDLOTHIAN

EH10 4QS

MR Bingo

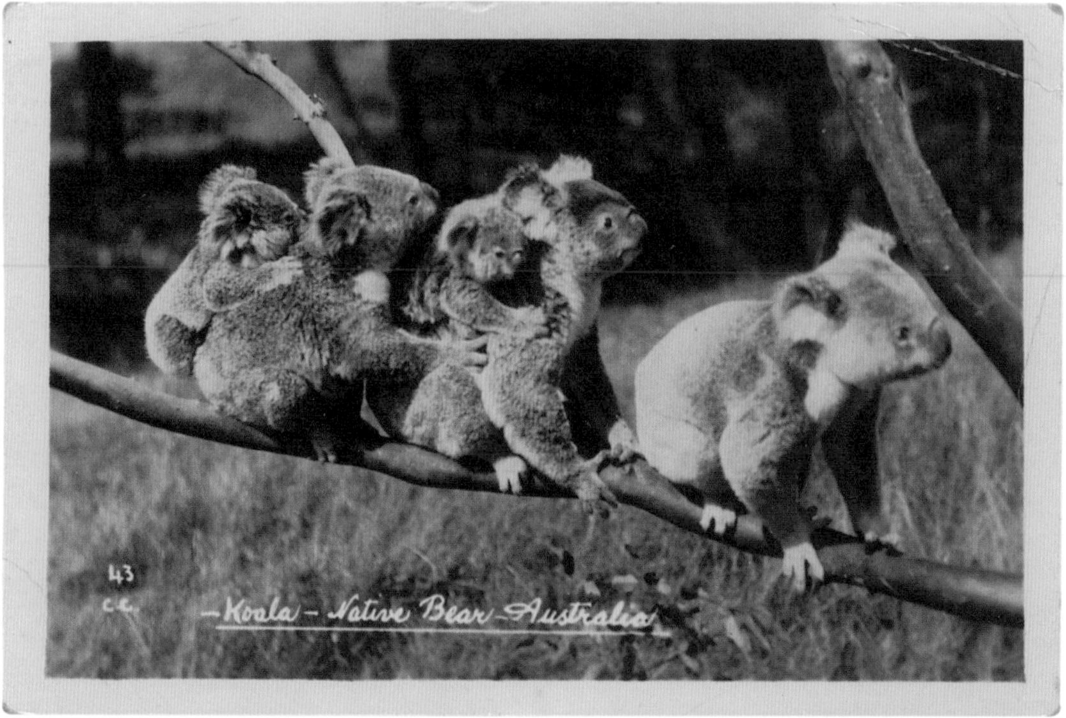
43
C.C.
-Koala - Native Bear - Australia

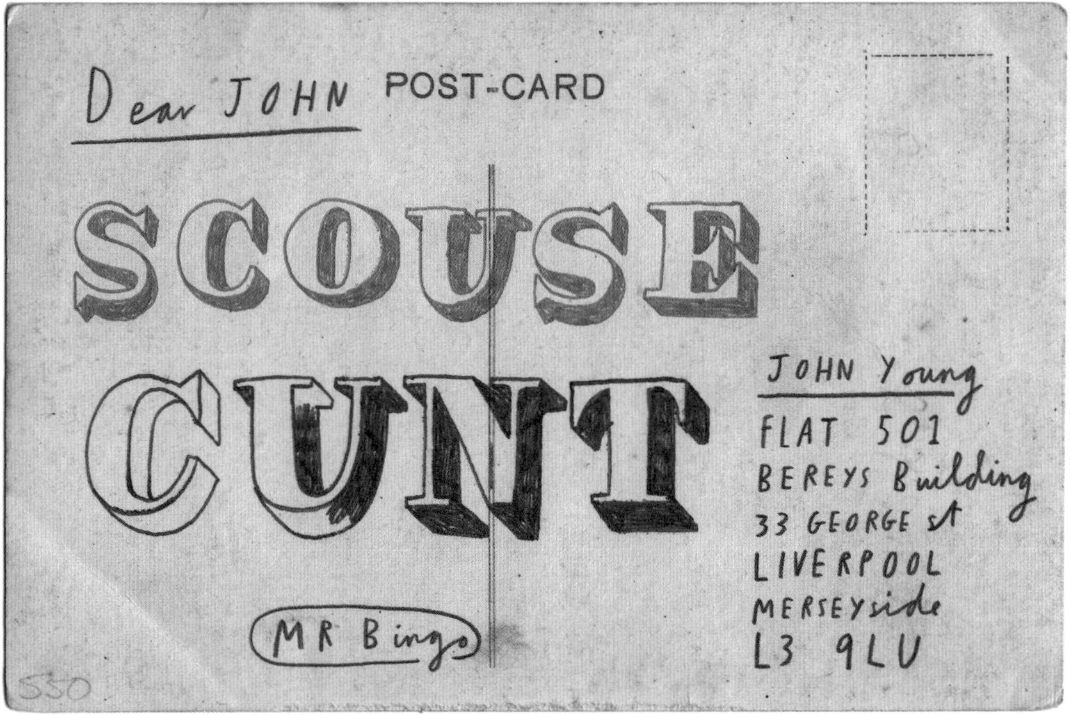
Dear JOHN
POST-CARD
SCOUSE
CUNT
MR Bingo
JOHN Young
FLAT 501
BEREYS Building
33 GEORGE st
LIVERPOOL
MERSEYside
L3 9LU
550

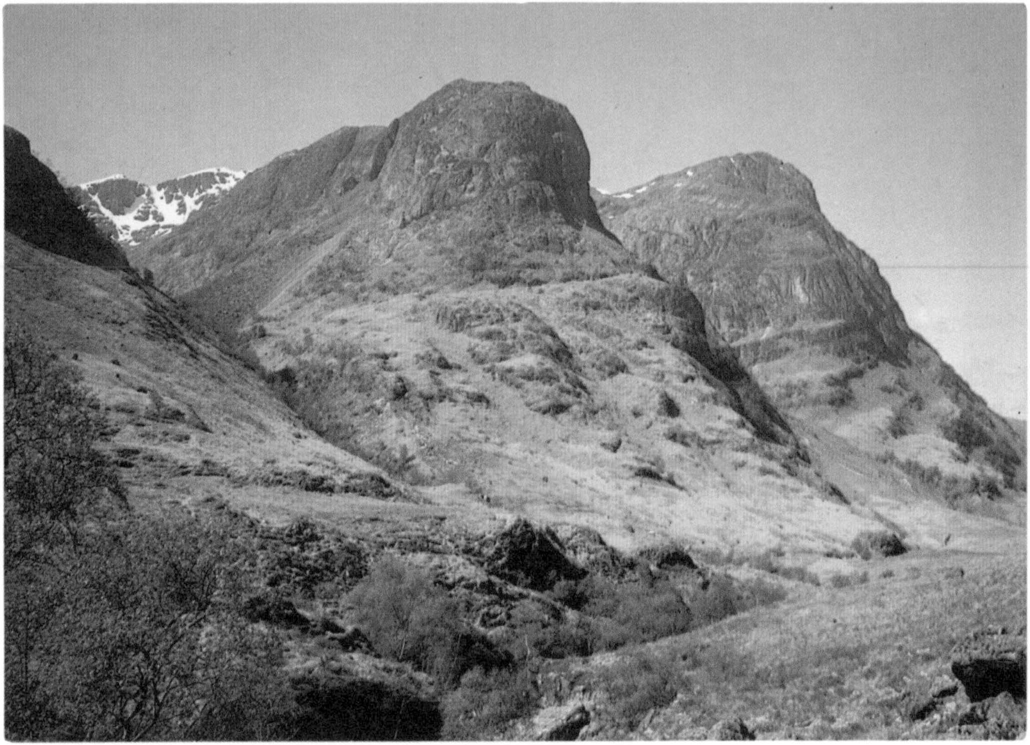

Dear THOMAS. A Dickinson Robinson Group Product

I SAW YOU GETTING YOUR LUNCH
OUT THE BIN AGAIN

J. ARTHUR DIXON LTD

Printed in Scotland by J. ARTHUR DIXON LTD.

Glencoe, Argyllshire
Two of the Three Sisters, Beinn Fhadja
and Biden nam Bian

PAR/22492   MR Bingo   DRG

Thomas LEACH

FLAT 17
King EDWARD MANSIONS
MARE st
London
E8 4As

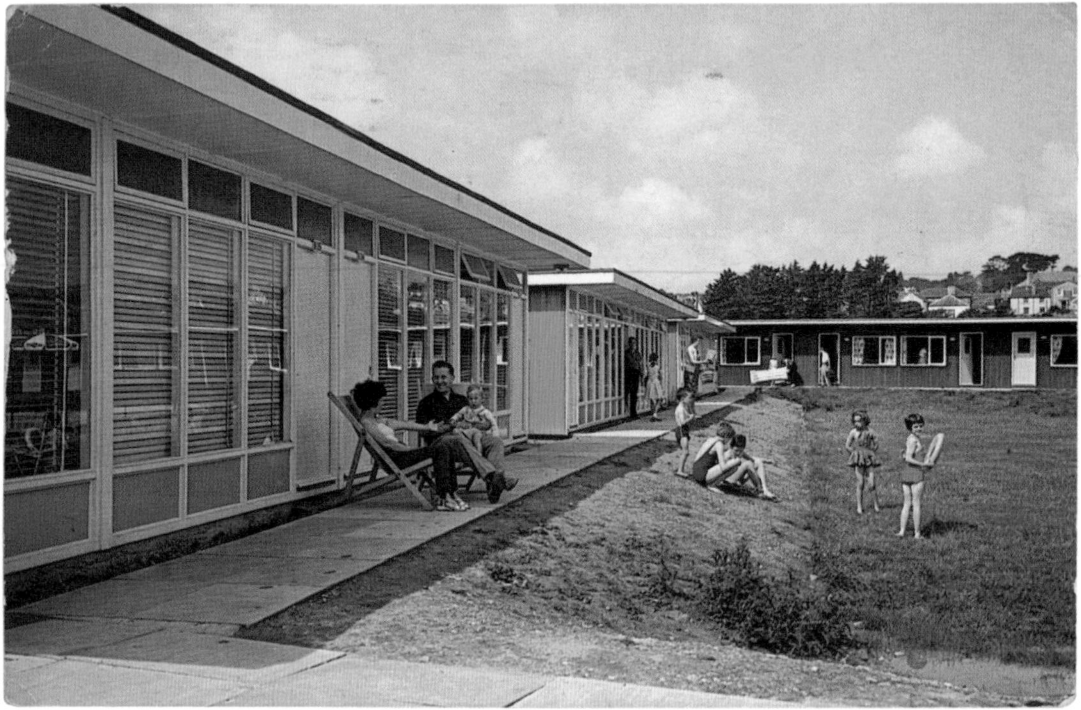

GREETINGS FROM BLUE WATERS PARK, SEATON
A CORNER OF THE PARK SHOWING
DE LUXE CHALETS

P56452

PLACE
STAMP
HERE

Dear JAMES,

YOUR NEW HAIRCUT

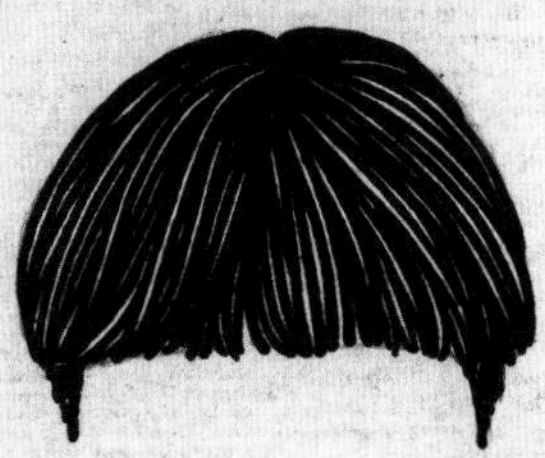

MAKES YOU LOOK LIKE A CUNT

MR Bingo

Pub. by Two Counties Match Co., Honiton

Plastichrome ® by COLOURPICTURE PUBLISHERS

Post Card

JAMES Withers

VENTURETHREE
5d SHEPHERD st
London
W1J 7HP

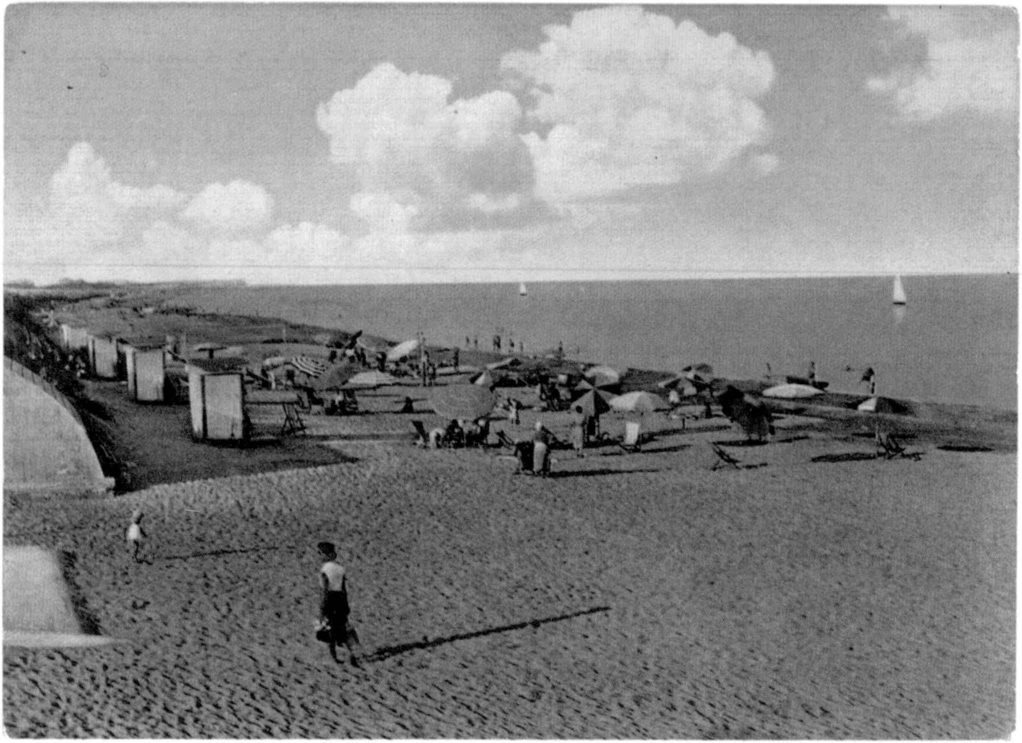

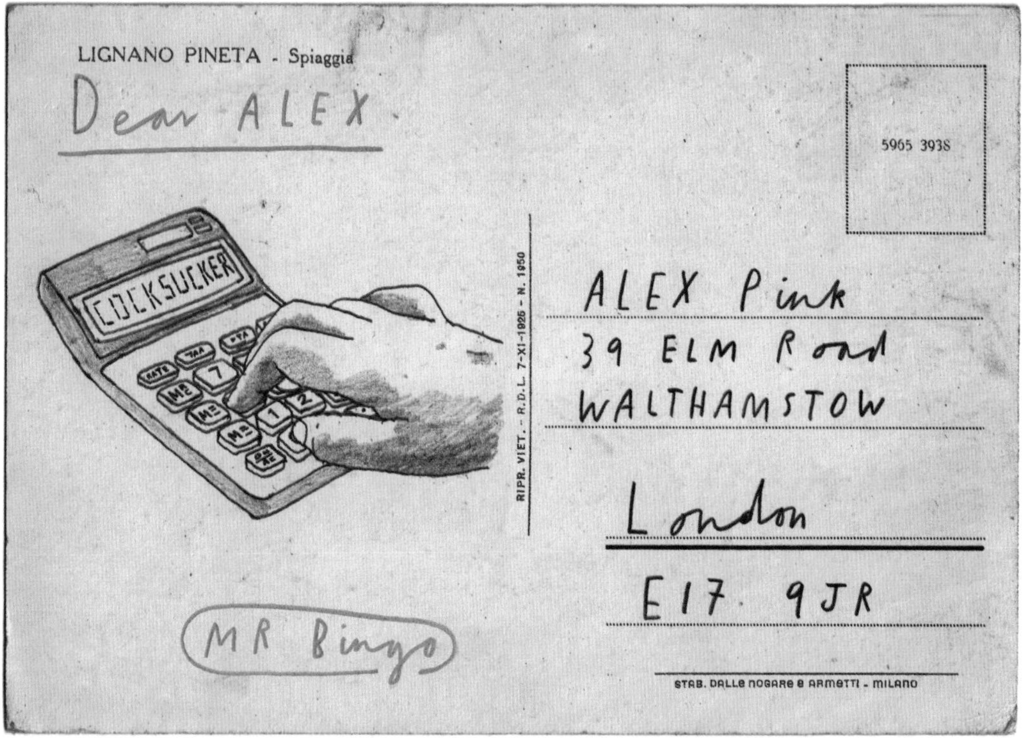
LIGNANO PINETA - Spiaggia
Dear ALEX
COCKSUCKER
MR Bingo
RIPR. VIET. - R.D.L. 7-XI-1925 - N. 1950
5965 3938
ALEX Pink
39 ELM Road
WALTHAMSTOW
London
E17 9JR
STAB. DALLE NOGARE E ARMETTI - MILANO

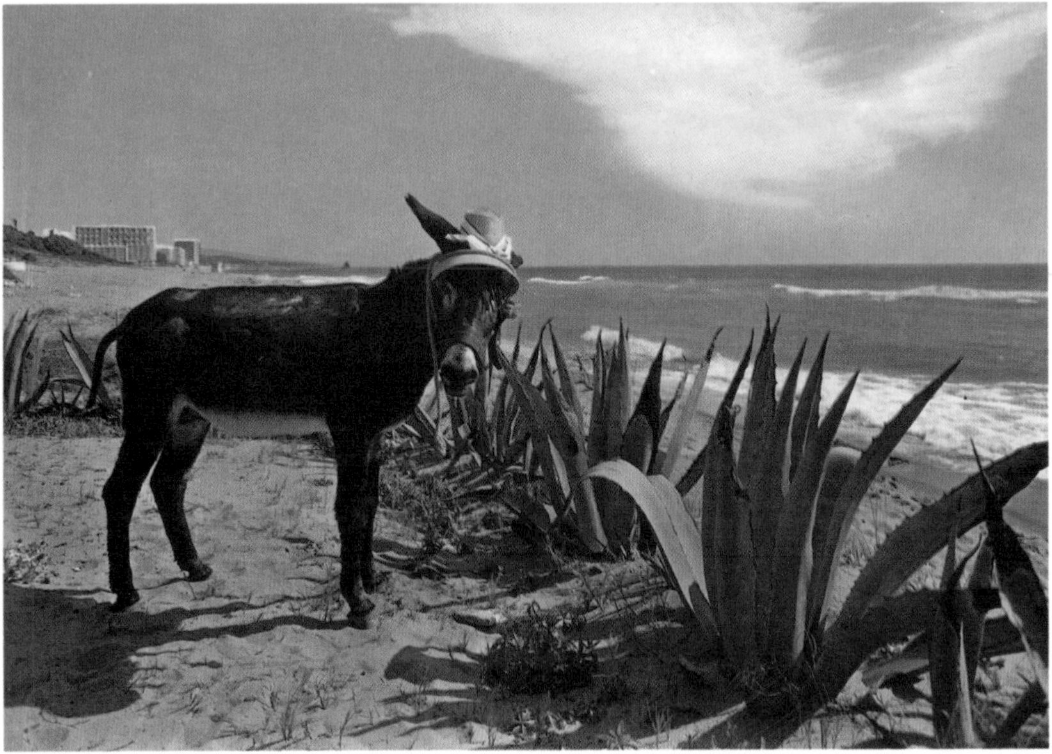

Dear LEAH,

YOUR WALK

IRRITATES THE FUCK OUT OF ME

MR Bingo

TONI RIBAS - POSTALES FIGUERETAS
TEL. 34·00 53 - SAN ANTONIO (IBIZA)

LEAH de SILVA

30 STIRLING Road

WOOD GREEN

London

N22 5BT

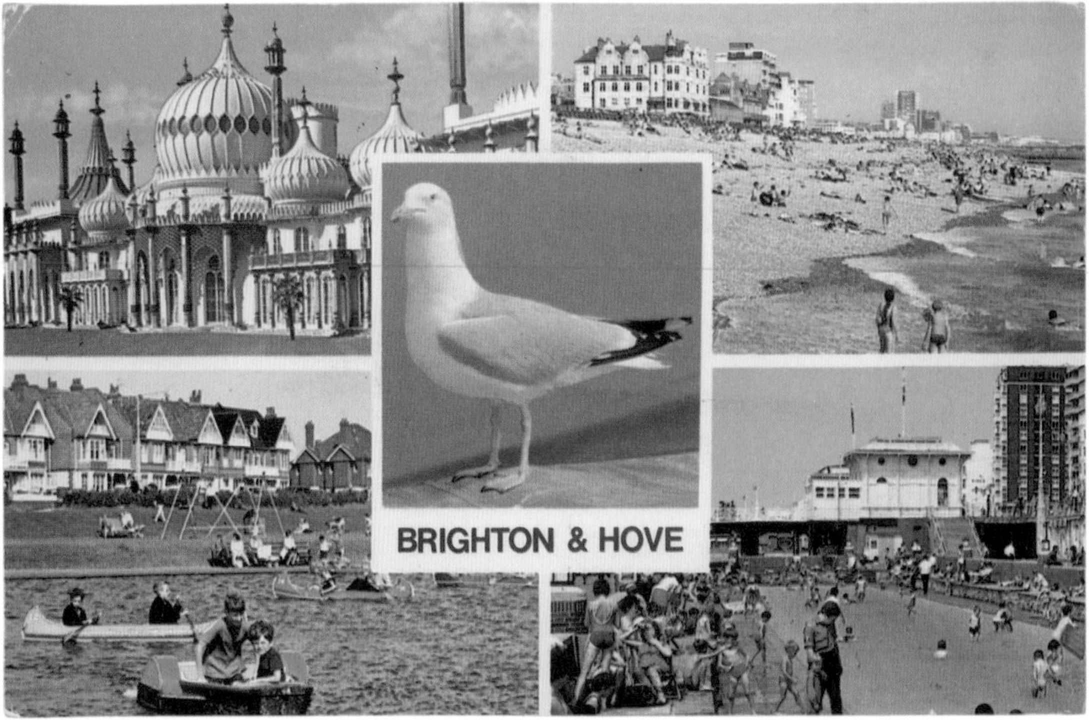
BRIGHTON & HOVE

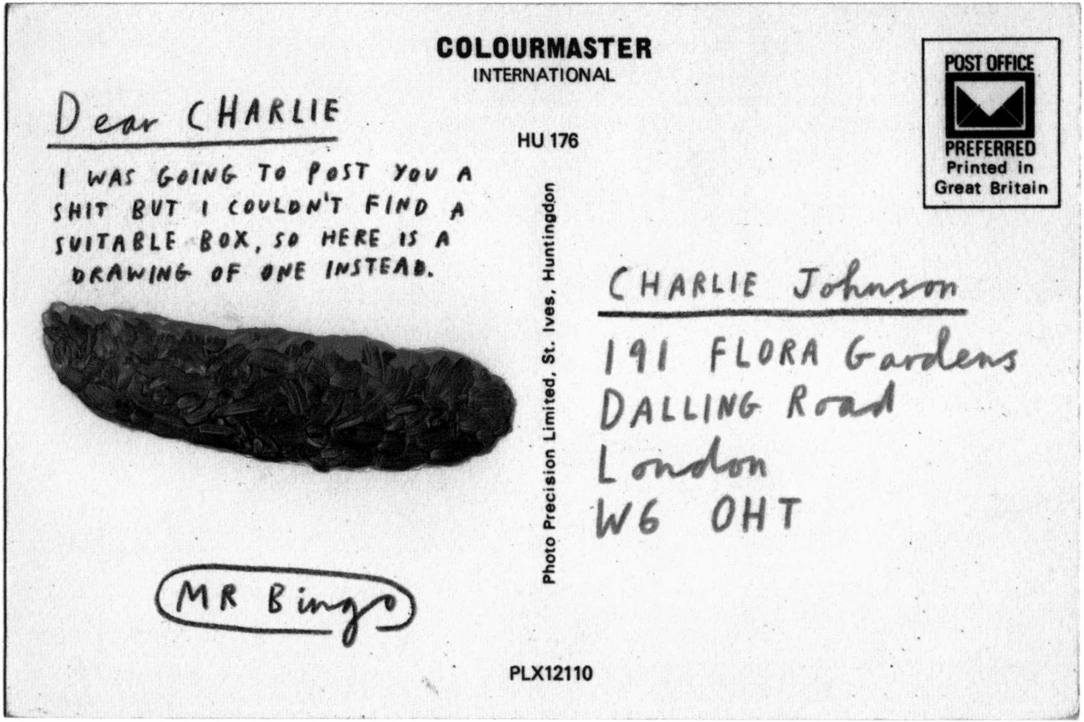

COLOURMASTER
INTERNATIONAL

HU 176

Dear CHARLIE

I WAS GOING TO POST YOU A SHIT BUT I COULDN'T FIND A SUITABLE BOX, SO HERE IS A DRAWING OF ONE INSTEAD.

MR Bingo

Photo Precision Limited, St. Ives, Huntingdon

POST OFFICE PREFERRED
Printed in Great Britain

CHARLIE Johnson
191 FLORA Gardens
DALLING Road
London
W6 OHT

PLX12110

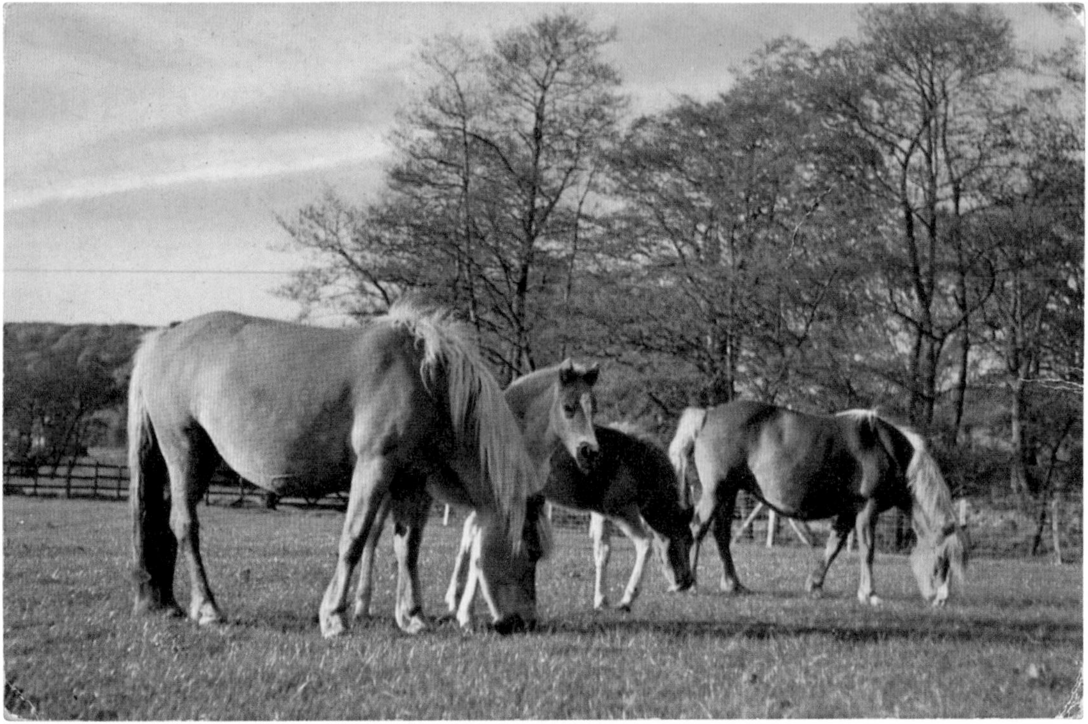

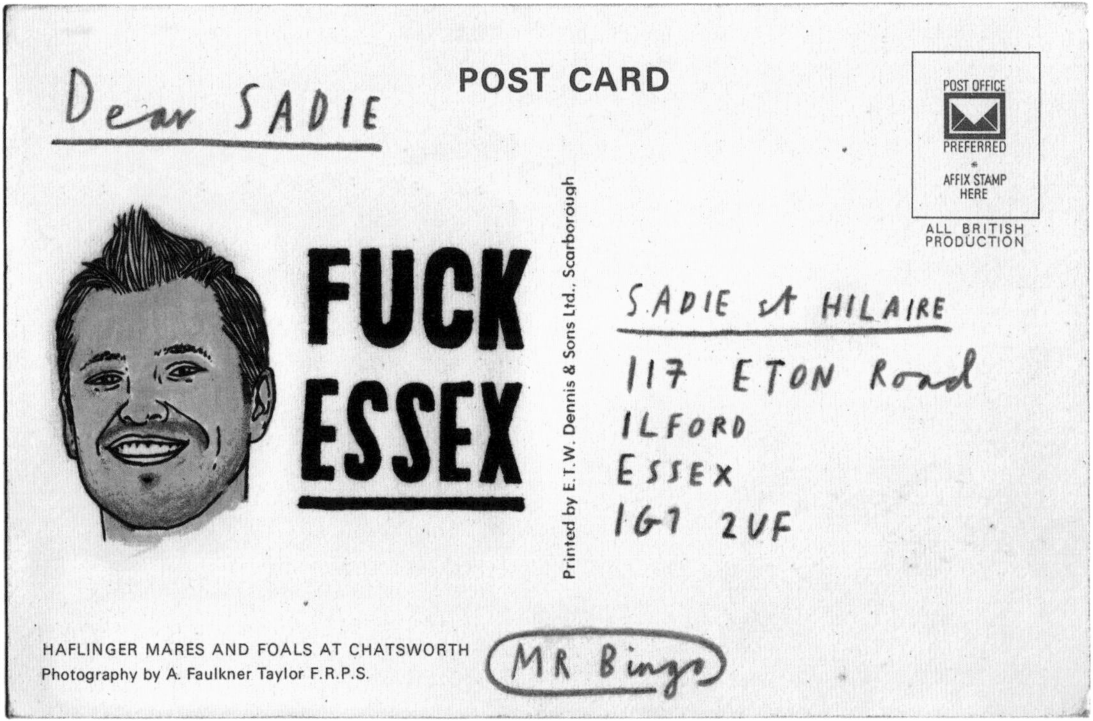
Dear SADIE

POST CARD

POST OFFICE PREFERRED

AFFIX STAMP HERE

ALL BRITISH PRODUCTION

FUCK ESSEX

Printed by E.T.W. Dennis & Sons Ltd., Scarborough

SADIE St HILAIRE
117 ETON Road
ILFORD
ESSEX
IG7 2UF

HAFLINGER MARES AND FOALS AT CHATSWORTH
Photography by A. Faulkner Taylor F.R.P.S.

MR Bingo

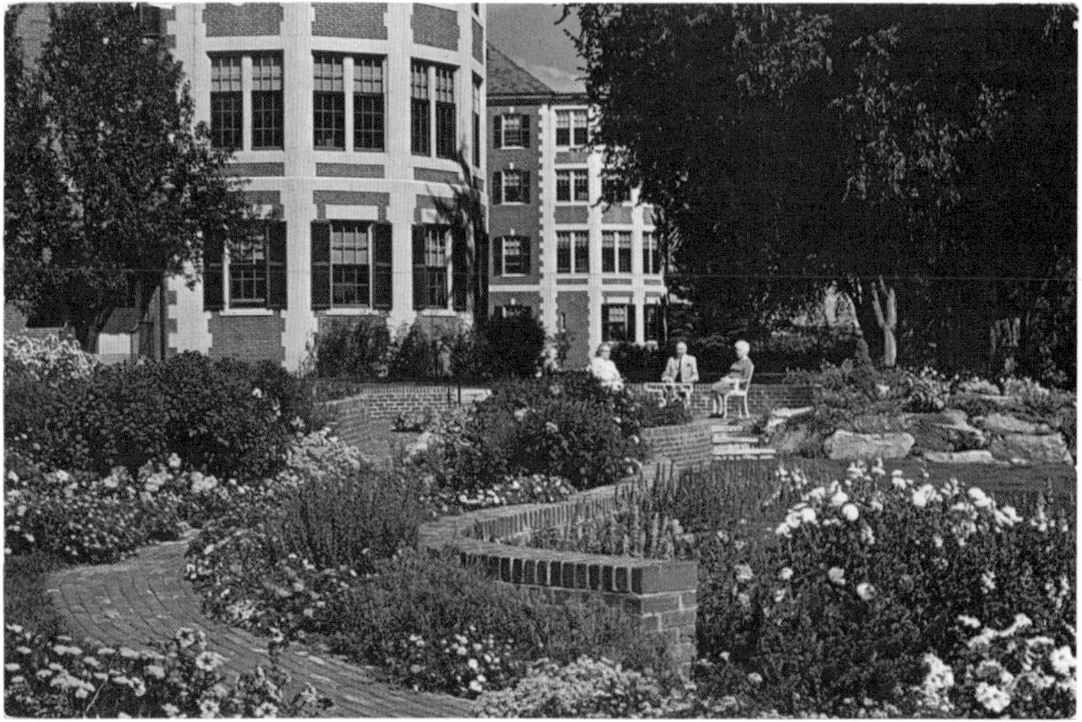

Dear SOMA Gallery,

KISS MY

MR Bingo

Photography by Stephen T. Whitney

Eastern Illustrating & Publishing Co., Inc.,

SOMA Gallery

4 BOYCES Avenue

CLIFTON, BRISTOL

BS8 4AA

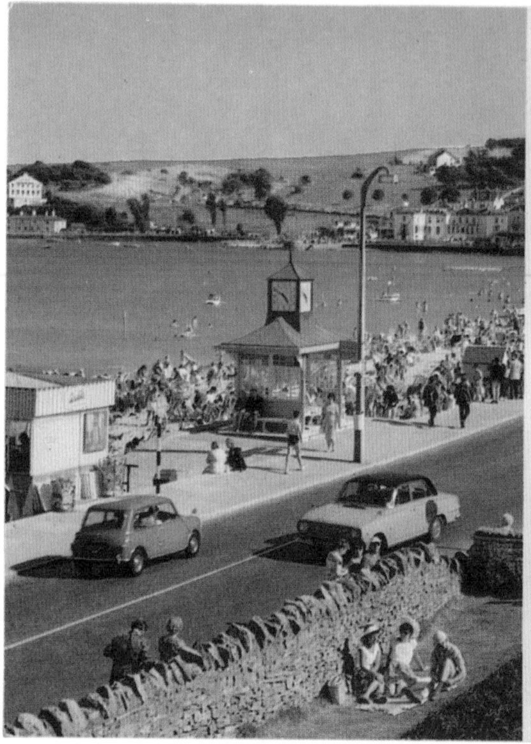

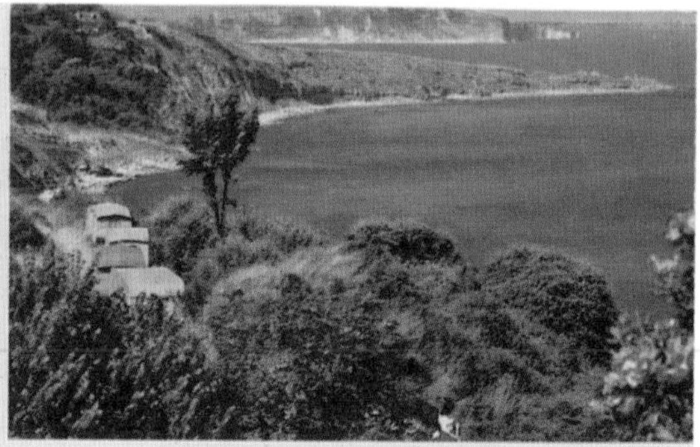

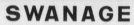

SWANAGE

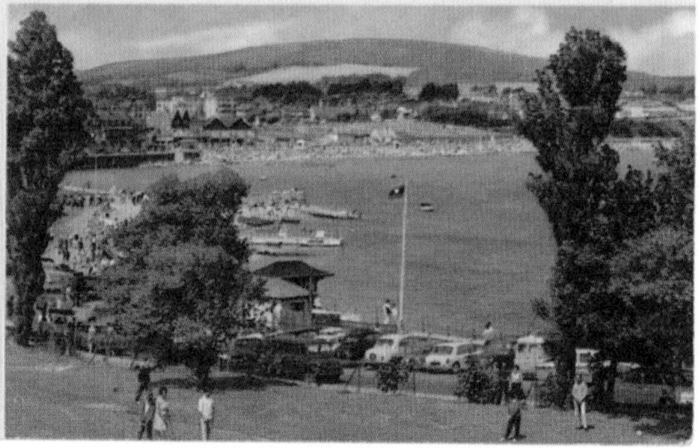

3BM53   Photos : John Hinde F.R.P.S.

<u>Dear PHILIP</u>

YOU'RE A DICK

Distributed by Thunder & Clayden, Bearden & Wade Ltd., Bournemouth.

JOHN HINDE ORIGINAL

Philip CHRISTER

91 Nether St

Middle HEYFORD

Northampton

NORTHAMPTONSHIRE NN3 7LR

MR Bingo

THE ESPLANADE AND BAYS, SWANAGE, DORSET.
Published by John Hinde (Distributors) Ltd., 3/5, Dunn Street, London. E.O. Printed in the Republic of Ireland.

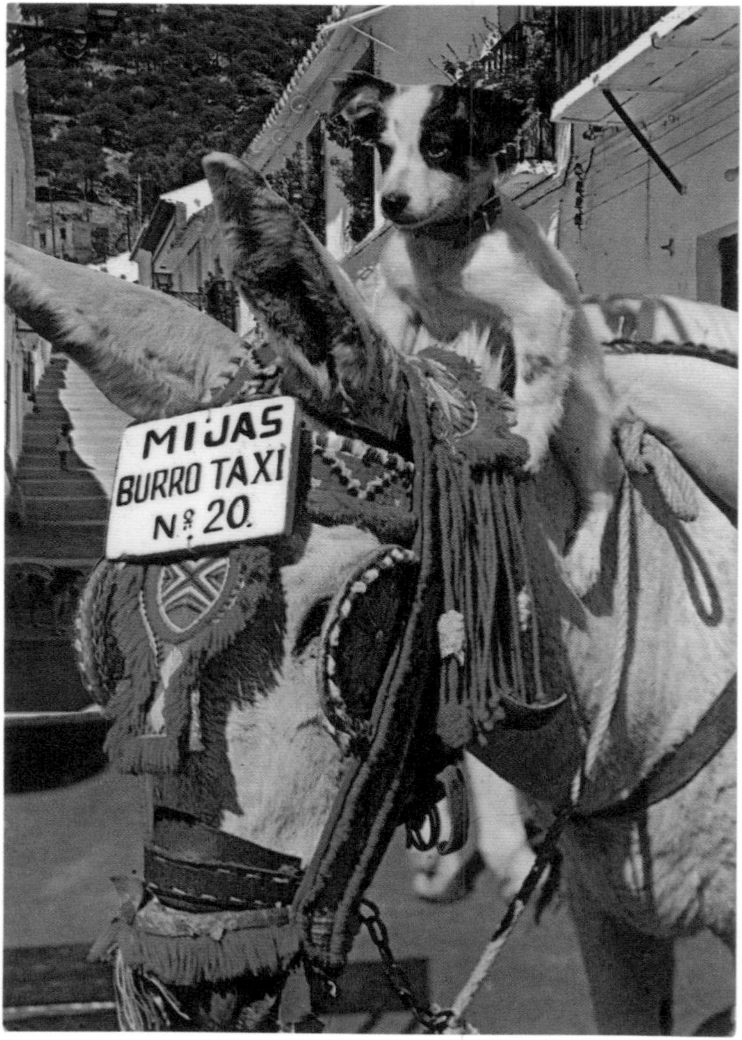
MIJAS
BURRO TAXI
Nº 20.

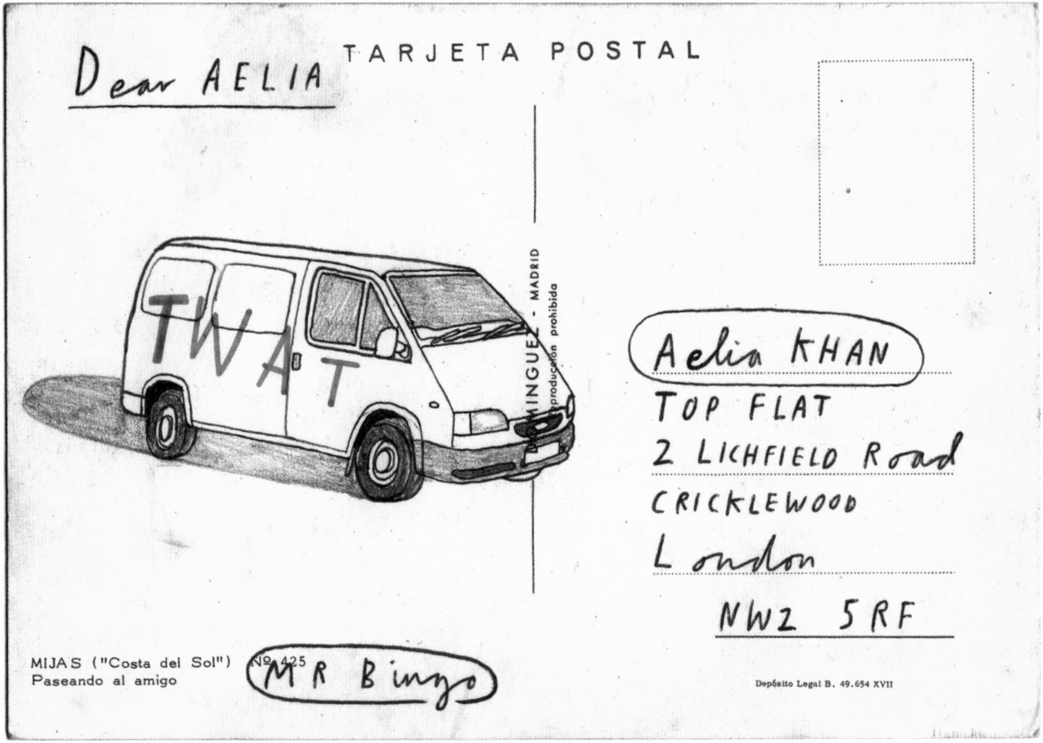
TARJETA POSTAL
Dear AELIA
TWAT
DOMINGUEZ - MADRID
Reproducción prohibida
Aelia KHAN
TOP FLAT
2 LICHFIELD Road
CRICKLEWOOD
London
NW2 5RF
MIJAS ("Costa del Sol") Nº 425
Paseando al amigo
MR Bingo
Depósito Legal B. 49.654 XVII

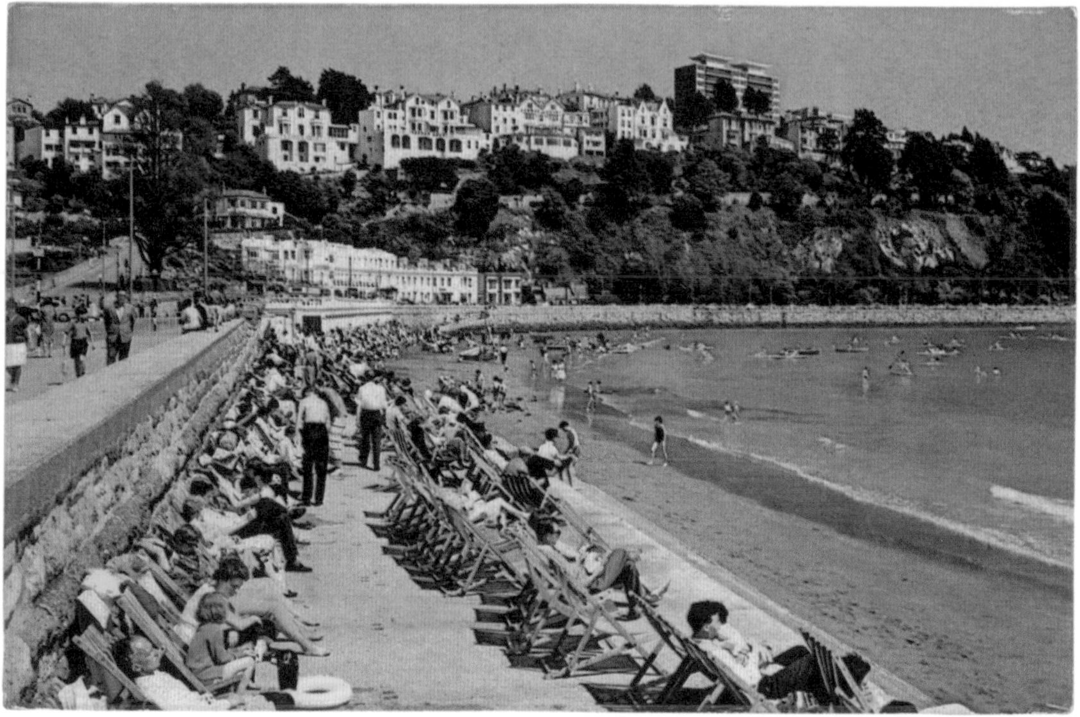

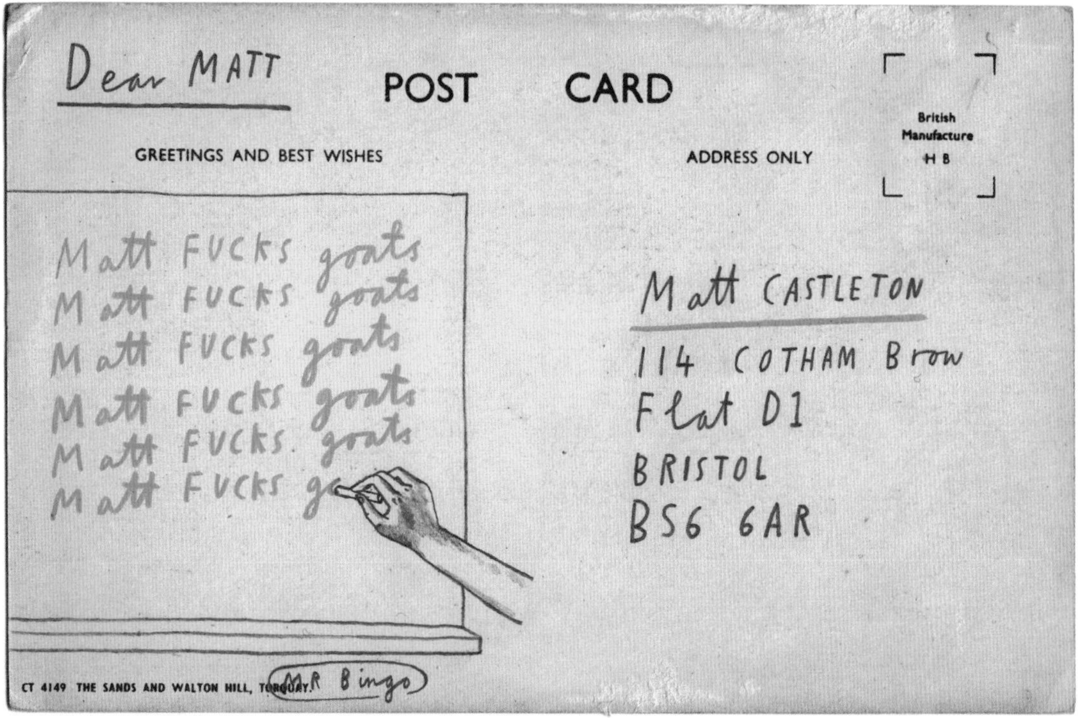
Dear MATT
POST CARD
British Manufacture H B
GREETINGS AND BEST WISHES
ADDRESS ONLY
Matt FUCKS goats
Matt FUCKS goats
Matt FUCKS goats
Matt FUCKS goats
Matt FUCKS goats
Matt FUCKS g
Matt CASTLETON
114 COTHAM Brow
Flat D1
BRISTOL
BS6 6AR
CT 4149 THE SANDS AND WALTON HILL, TORQUAY.
MR Bingo

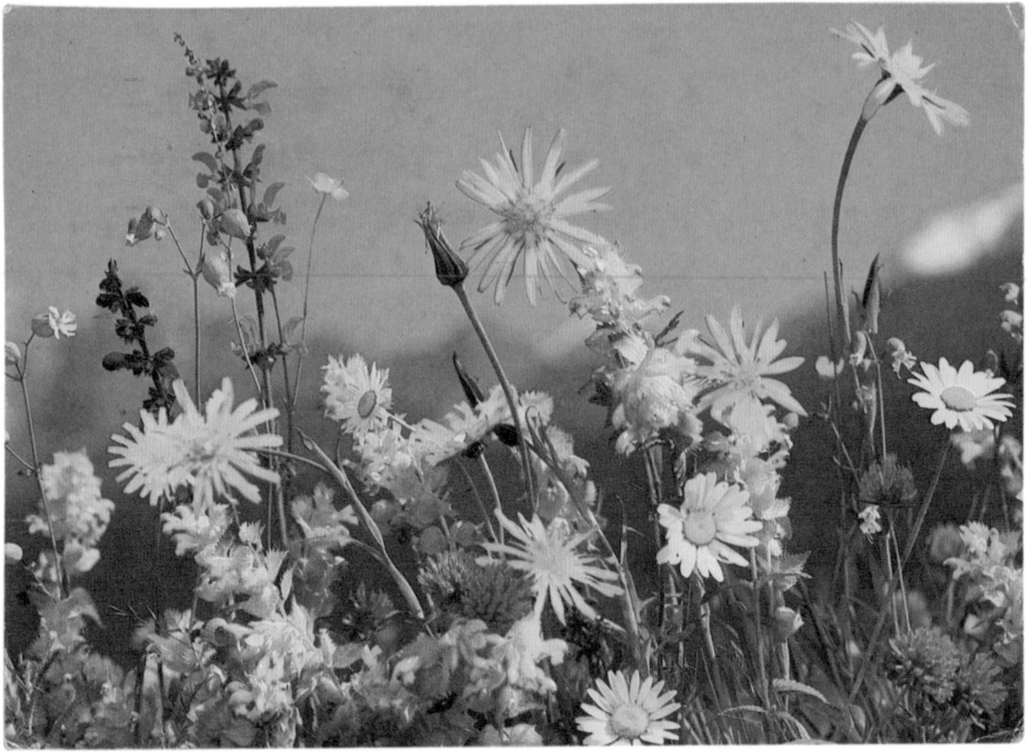

Dear NICHOLAS,

YOU HAVE NOTHING
GOING FOR YOU

MR Bingo

Imprimé en Suisse – Edition Stehli – Printed in Switzerland

NICOLAS WAVISH
Flat 7
1 SEAL St

London

E8 2EE

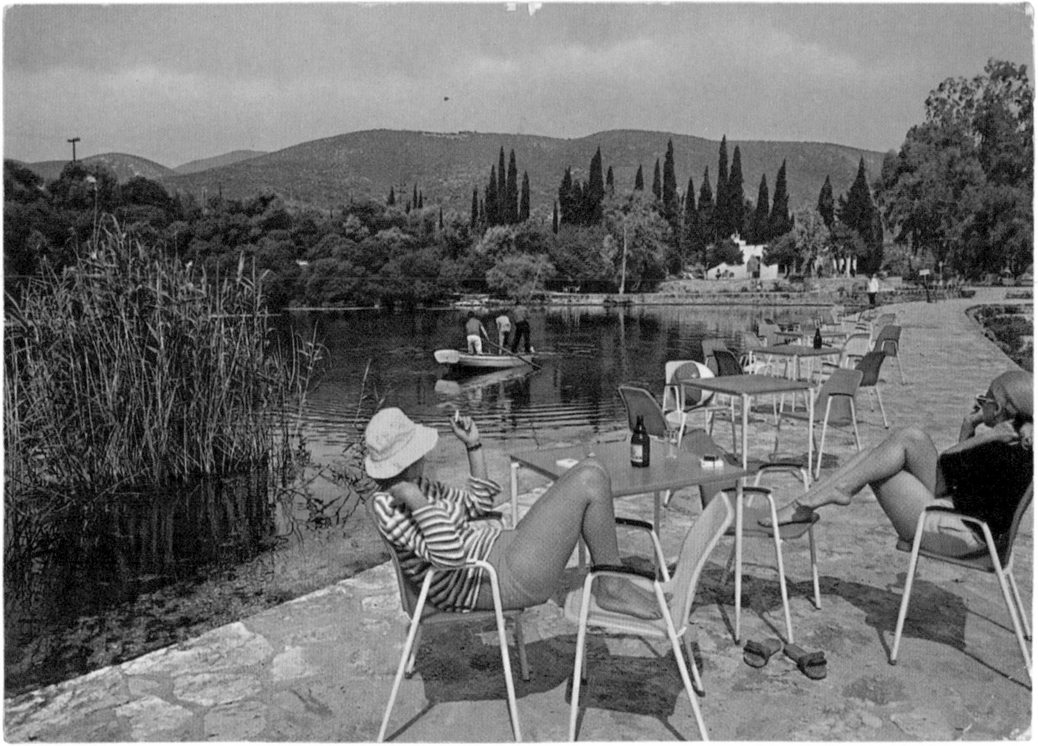

Dear BEN.

YOU'RE SHITTER
THAN JEDWARD

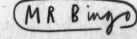

MR Bingo

Ben BATESON

61 STANE A

Bingley

WEST YORKSHIRE

BD11 4HN

Distributors: N.G. TRIARCHOS & Co. Ltd P.O.B. 1296. Tel.: 49886, Nicosia, Cyprus

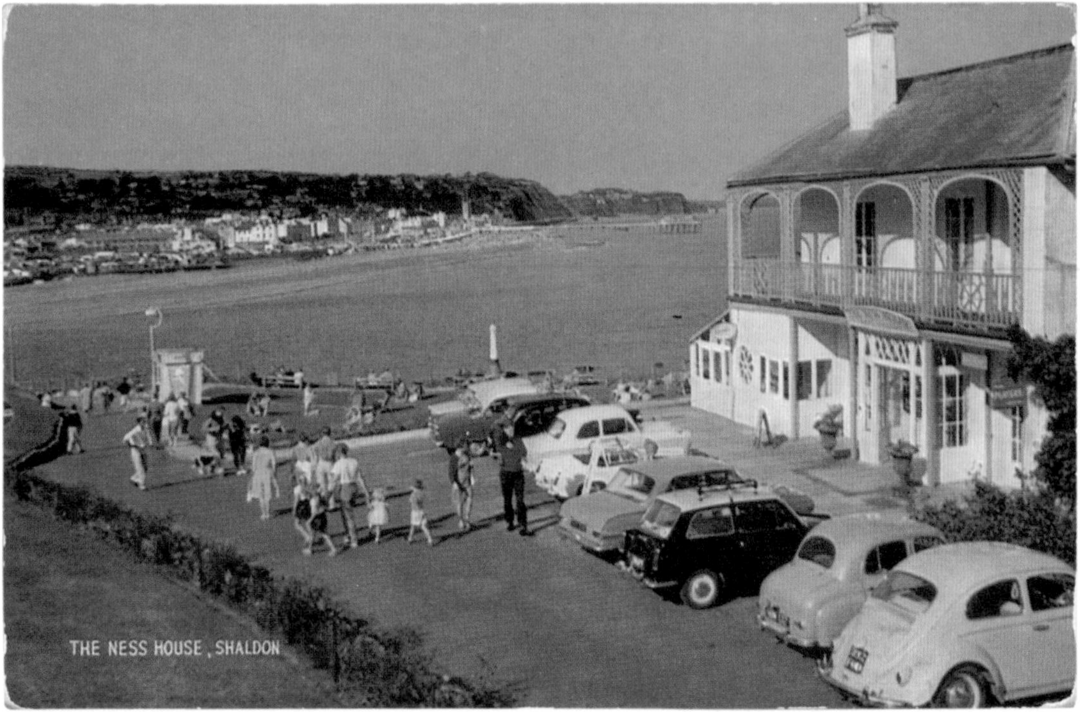
THE NESS HOUSE, SHALDON

Dear NEIL

A SALMON
CAMERACOLOUR
POST CARD
PRINTED IN ENGLAND

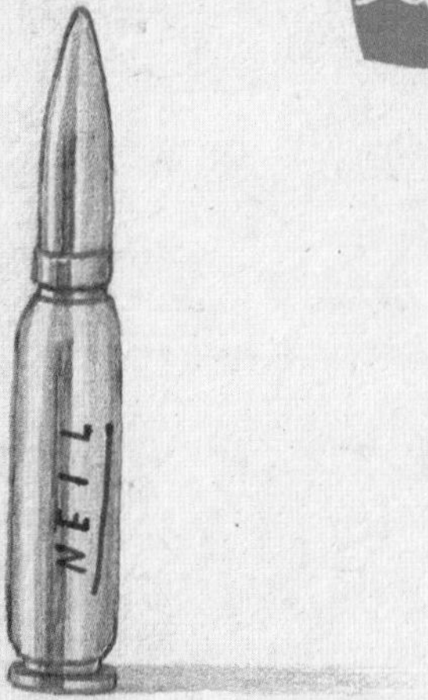
NEIL

© J.SALMON LTD., SEVENOAKS

NEIL Haas

106 TRENT House
Fann St
GOLDEN Lane ESTATE
London
EC1 0SJ

1 – 50 – 02 – 02 / 2836c

MR Bingo

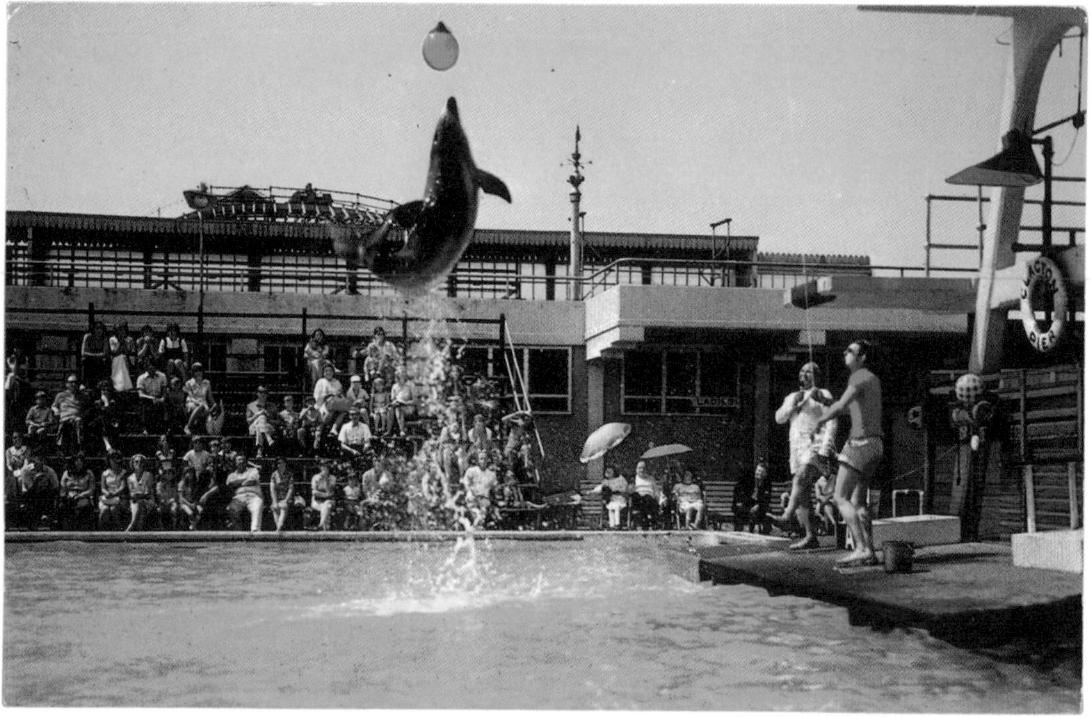
CLACTON
PIER
LADIES

Dear EMMA

COLOURMASTER
INTERNATIONAL

POST OFFICE
PREFERRED
Printed in
Great Britain

YOUR FACE

CLT 402

IS NOT IDEAL

Photo Precision Limited, St. Ives, Huntingdon

EMMA Wood

92A LACON Road
EAST DULWICH
London
SE22 9TH

MR Bingo

PT8665

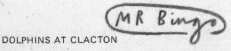

DOLPHINS AT CLACTON

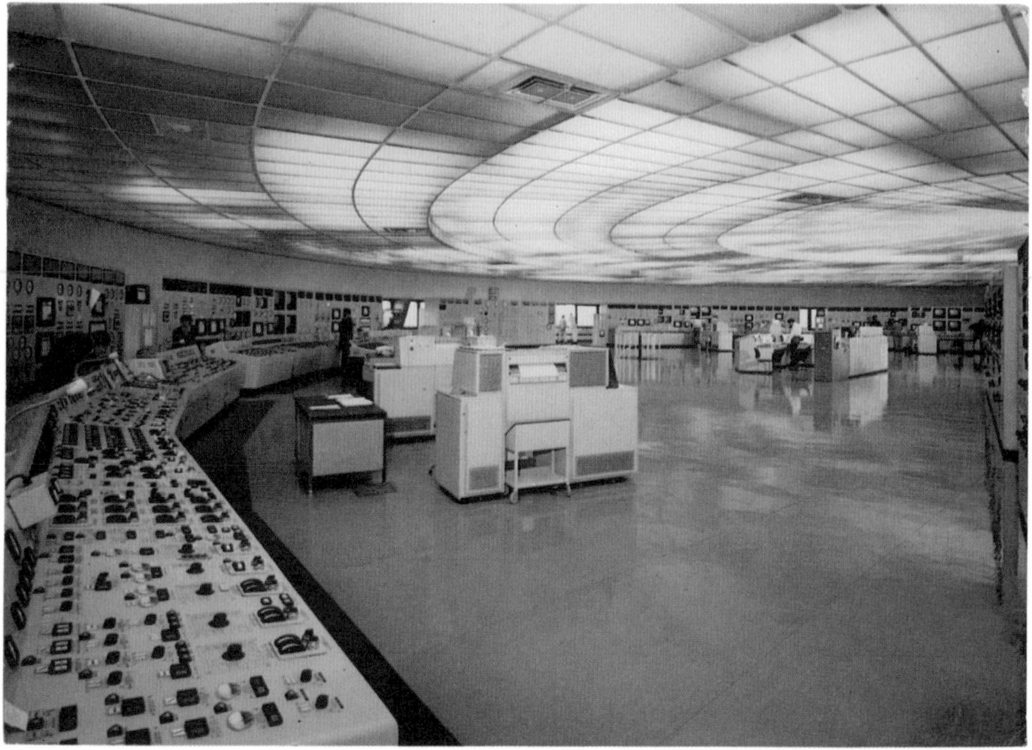

A Dickinson Robinson Group Product

J. ARTHUR DIXON

POST OFFICE PREFERRED

AFFIX STAMP HERE

ALL BRITISH PRODUCTION

Dear JAMES

9 OUT OF 10 CATS

Printed in Great Britain by J. ARTHUR DIXON

THINK YOU'RE A CUNT

James PEEL

9 BRITANNIA Mills
HULME Road
Manchester
M5 5TB

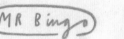

MR Bingo

DRG

Fawley Power Station

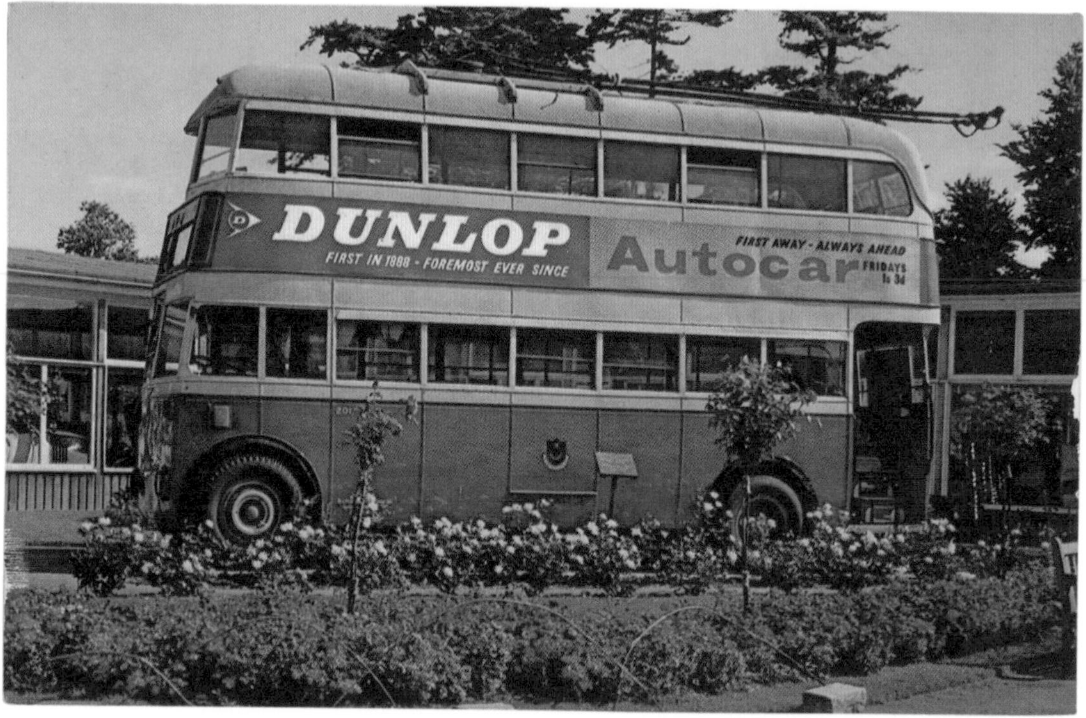
DUNLOP
FIRST IN 1888 - FOREMOST EVER SINCE
FIRST AWAY - ALWAYS AHEAD
Autocar
FRIDAYS
1s 3d

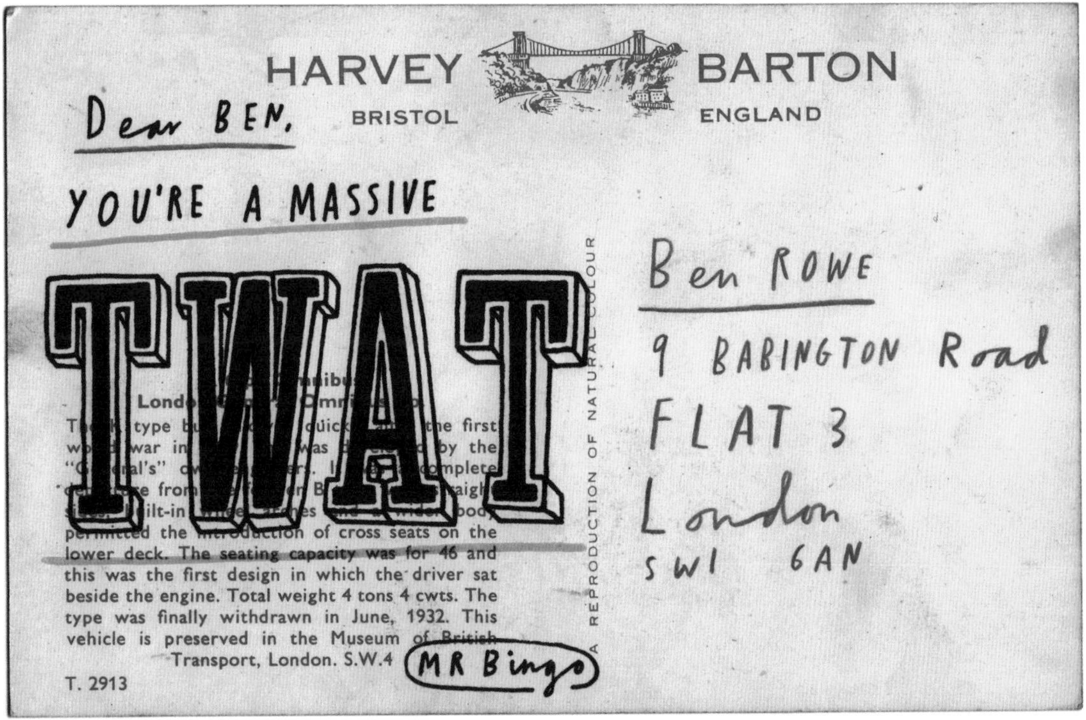
HARVEY BARTON
BRISTOL ENGLAND

Dear BEN,

YOU'RE A MASSIVE

TWAT

...Omnibus
London ... Omnibus Co.
The K type bu... quick... the first
wo... war in ... was ... by the
"G...al's" ow... I... complete
de...re from ... B ... straigh...
s... ...ilt-in ... ...es ... body
permitted the introduction of cross seats on the
lower deck. The seating capacity was for 46 and
this was the first design in which the driver sat
beside the engine. Total weight 4 tons 4 cwts. The
type was finally withdrawn in June, 1932. This
vehicle is preserved in the Museum of British
Transport, London. S.W.4

T. 2913

MR Bingo

A REPRODUCTION OF NATURAL COLOUR

Ben ROWE
9 BABINGTON Road
FLAT 3
London
SW1 6AN

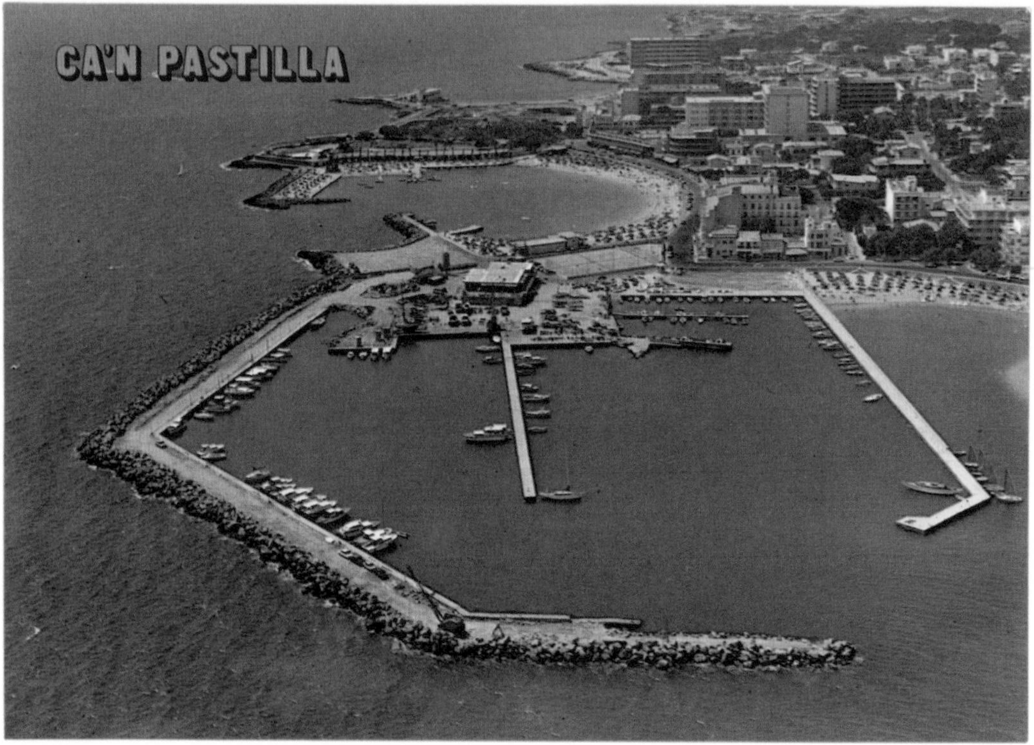
CA'N PASTILLA

N° 228
CA'N PASTILLA (Mallorca)

Dear MATT

The reason I'm 'FRIENDS' with you
on Facebook is so I can look at
your photos and monitor how
FAT you're getting.

MR Bingo

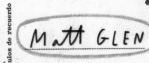

Matt GLEN

FLAT 7
303-309 LAVENDER Hill
CLAPHAM Junction

London

SW11 7LN

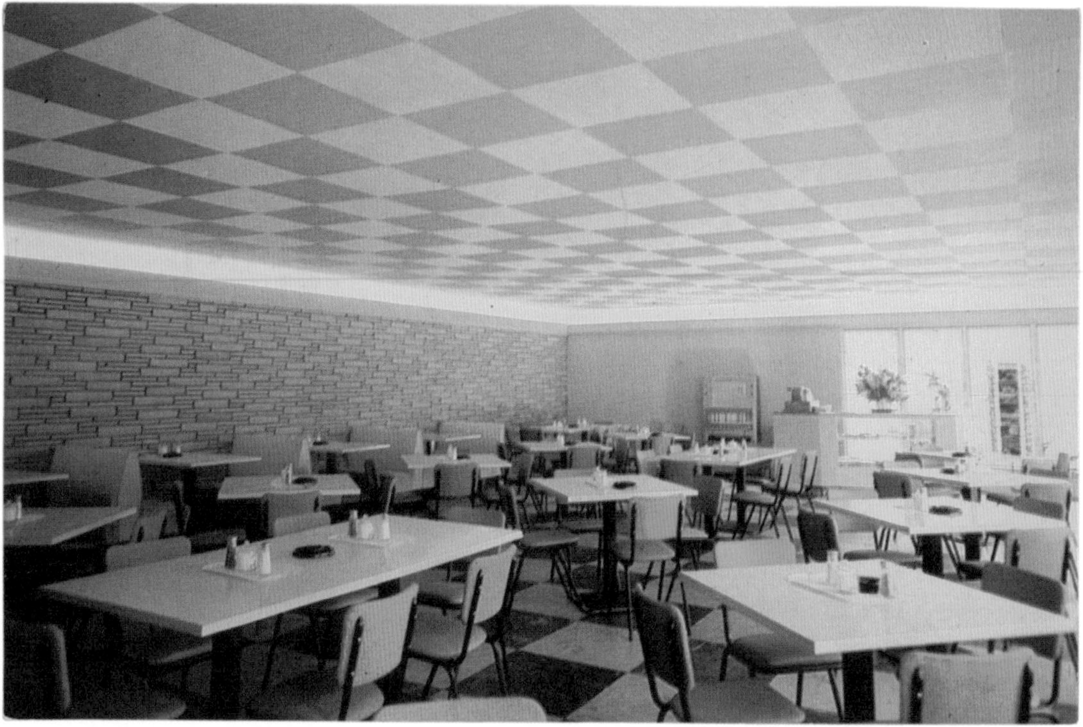

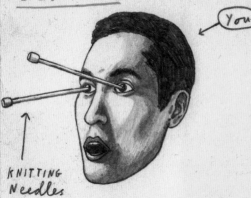

COLVILLE DINING ROOM
Ela, North Carolina

Published by Thomas B. Kehoe, P.O. Box 192, Asheville, N.C.

S3920

Dear NEIL

You

KNITTING
Needles

MR Bingo

PLACE
STAMP
HERE

POST CARD

Address

NEIL Sparshott

34 MEADOW Close
NORWICH
Norfolk
NR6 6XY

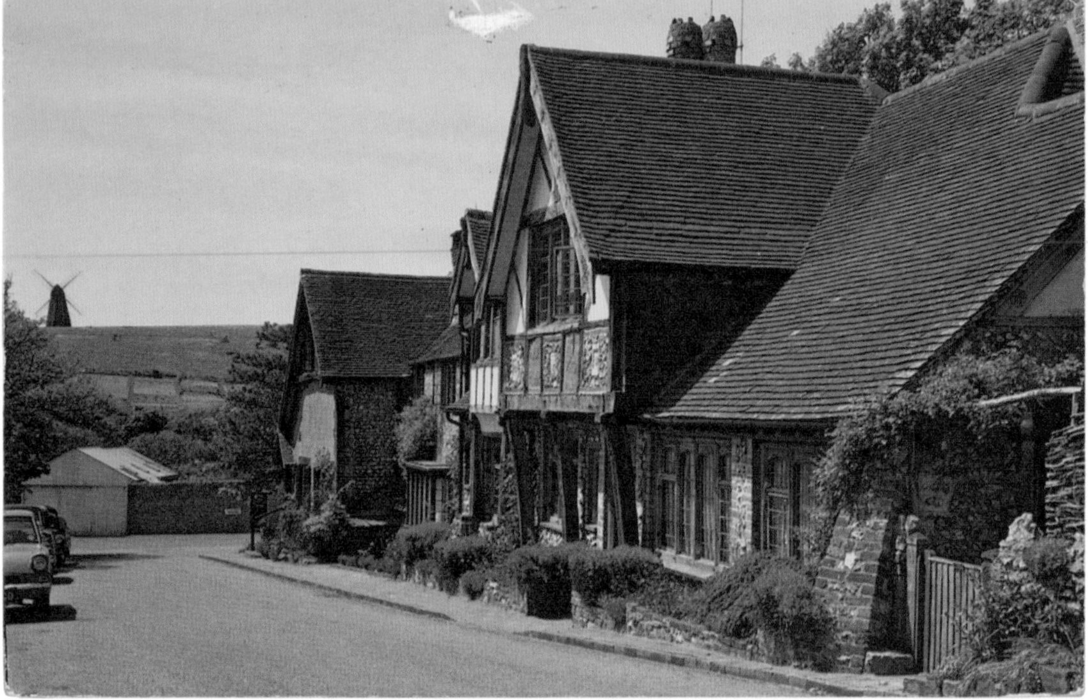

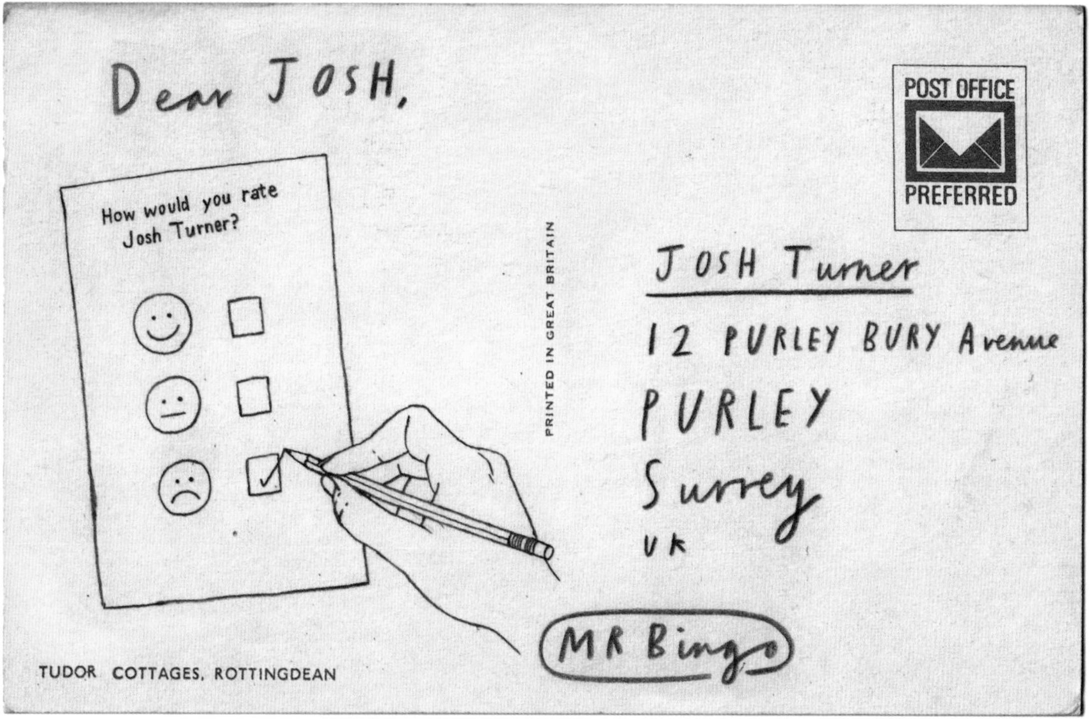
Dear JOSH,
How would you rate Josh Turner?
PRINTED IN GREAT BRITAIN
POST OFFICE PREFERRED
JOSH Turner
12 PURLEY BURY Avenue
PURLEY
Surrey
UK
MR Bingo
TUDOR COTTAGES, ROTTINGDEAN

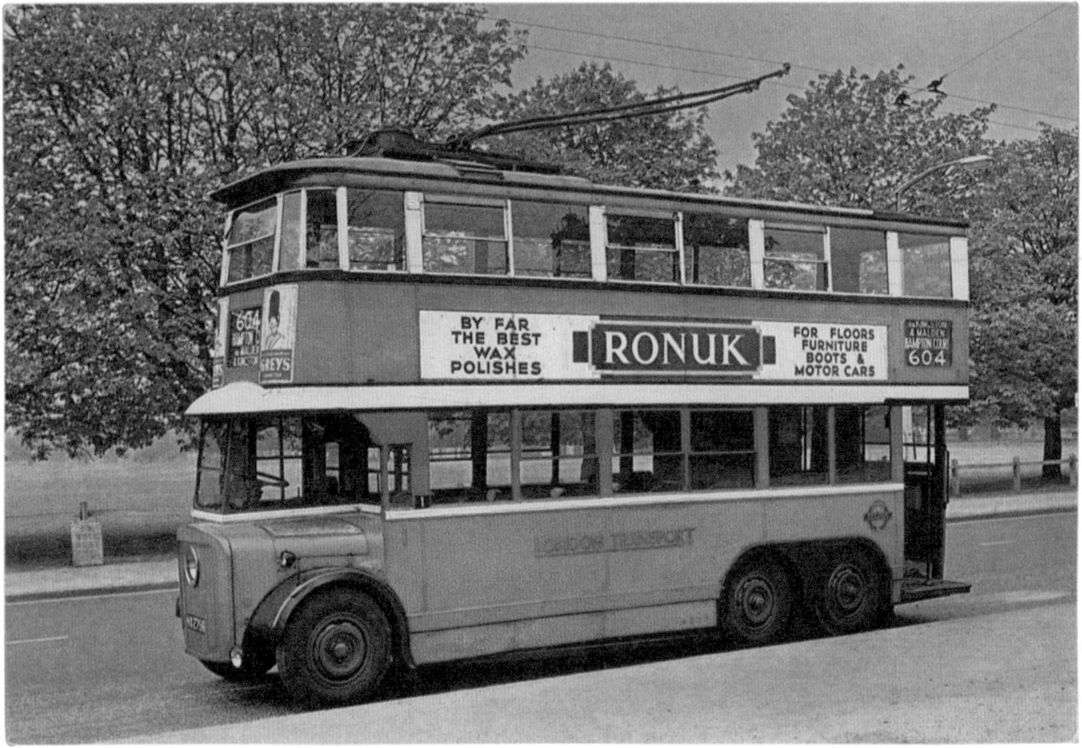
BY FAR
THE BEST
WAX
POLISHES
RONUK
FOR FLOORS
FURNITURE
BOOTS &
MOTOR CARS
604
604
GREYS
LONDON TRANSPORT

Dear ANYA

NATURAL COLOUR
J. Arthur Dixon
PHOTOGRAVURE
POST CARD

I DON'T LOVE YOU ANYMORE

Trolleybus 1
London United Tramways

Trolleybus 1 was the first of two batches of similar trolleybuses of type A1 (35 buses) and A2 (25 buses) which formed the initial fleet of 60 trolley buses owned by the London United Tramways, for operation in the Kingston area. On 15th May 1931 by the passenger public. The chassis is exemplified by Trolleybus 1 is not extreme, but was succeeded by three experimental vehicles with electrically operated motors. It had a single electric motor mounted in orthodox motor bus position at the front under a bonnet. The chassis was identical except for the power unit and transmission, with the LT double-deck bus. This trolleybus is preserved in the Museum of British Transport, London, S.W.4

T.2908

Printed and Published by J. Arthur Dixon Ltd., Newport, I.W., England

MR Bingo

ANYA SAGE COWLEY

19 EASTGATE
COWBRIDGE
VALE of GLAMORGAN
CF71 7EL
United Kingdom

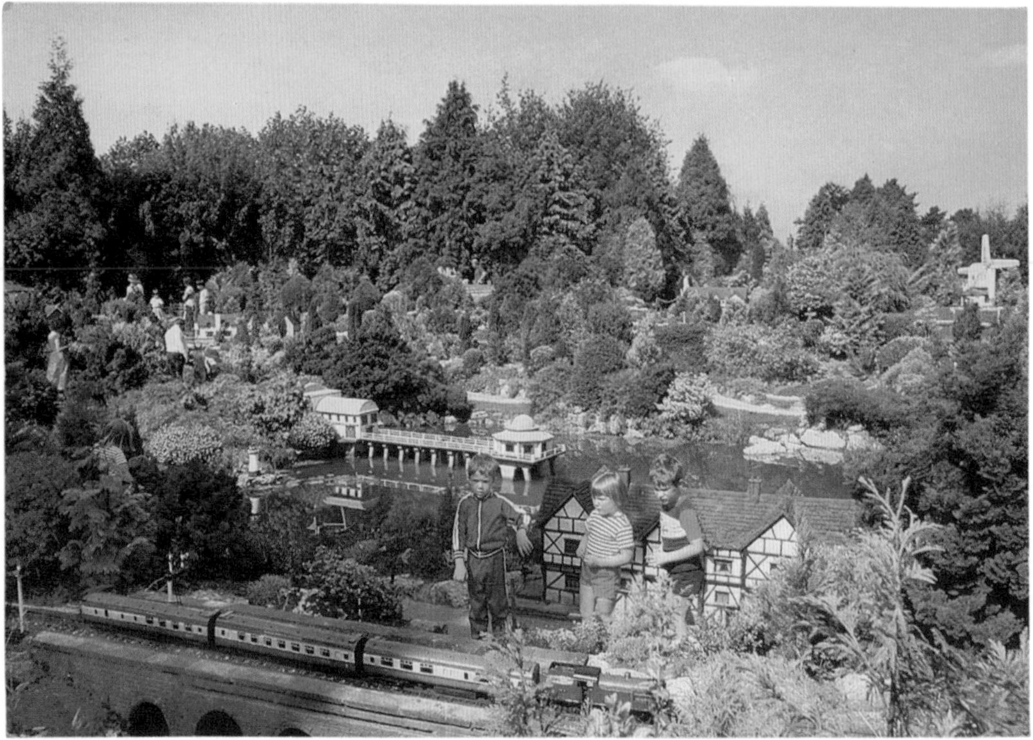

Dear JONATHAN

JARROLD

Printed and Published by Jarrold & Sons Ltd. Norwich

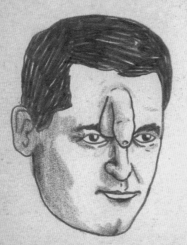

YOU'RE A DICK-HEAD MATE

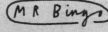

MR Bingo

Jonathan McNAMARA
65 PRINCESS House
144 Princess St
MANCHESTER
Lancashire

M1 7EP

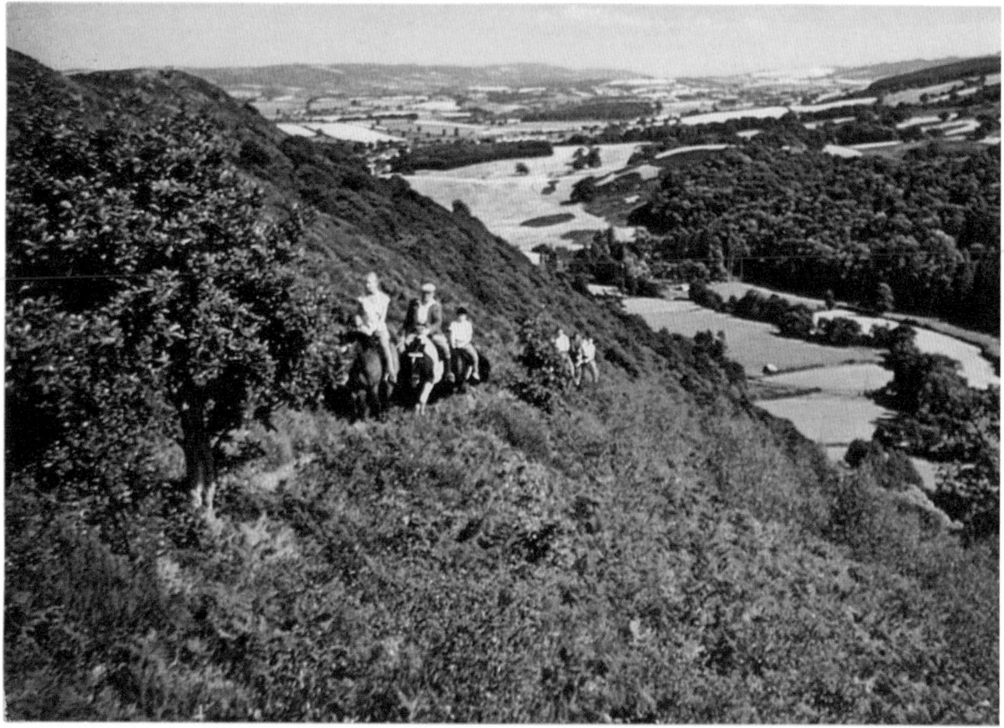

WHS 4693 **PONY TREKKING ON EXMOOR**

Dear HAYLEY

I'VE MET SOMEONE BETTER LOOKING SO I'D LIKE TO SPLIT UP WITH YOU.

IS IT OK IF I COME ROUND AT THE WEEKEND TO PICK UP MY MINIDISC COLLECTION?

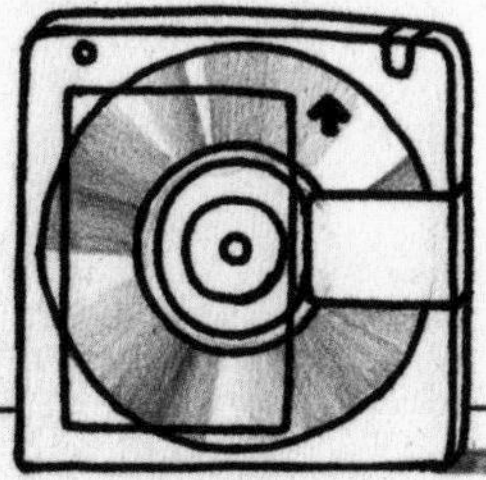

MR Bingo

84B
A POST OFFICE PREFERRED SIZE

POST CARD

Hayley MARTIN
81 PAGITT st
CHATHAM
Kent
ME4 6RE

Plastichrome®
by COLOURPICTURE
MADE IN U.S.A.

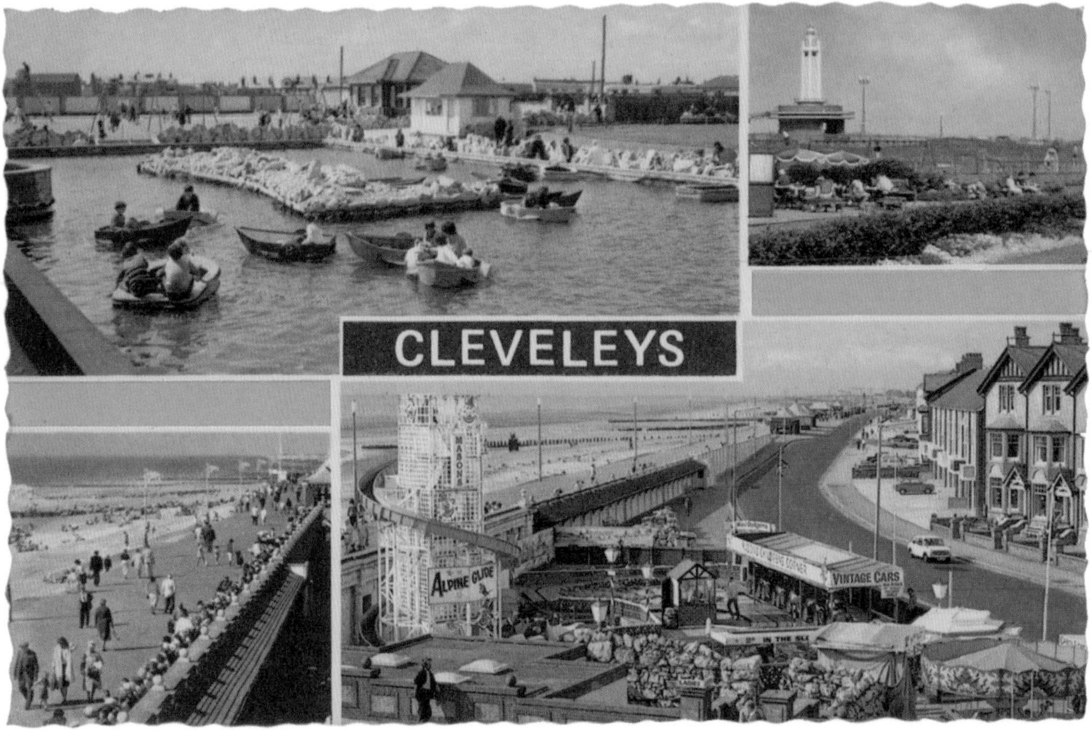
CLEVELEYS
ALPINE GLIDE
VINTAGE CARS

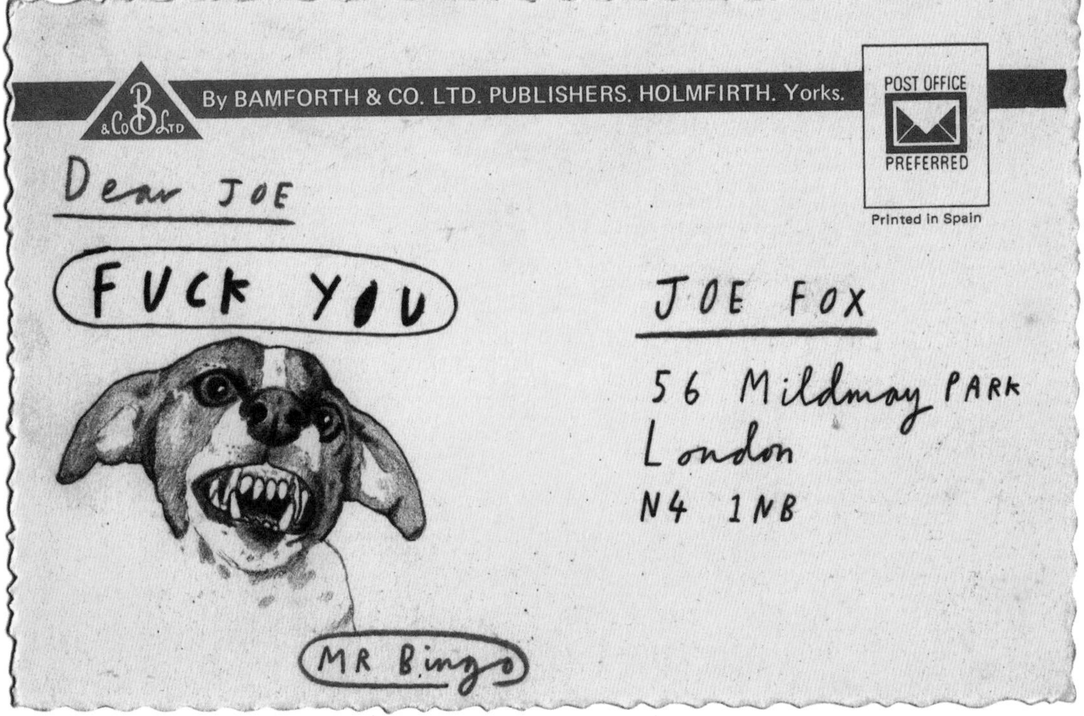
By BAMFORTH & CO. LTD. PUBLISHERS. HOLMFIRTH. Yorks.
POST OFFICE
PREFERRED
Printed in Spain
Dear JOE
FUCK YOU
JOE FOX
56 Mildmay PARK
London
N4 1NB
MR Bingo

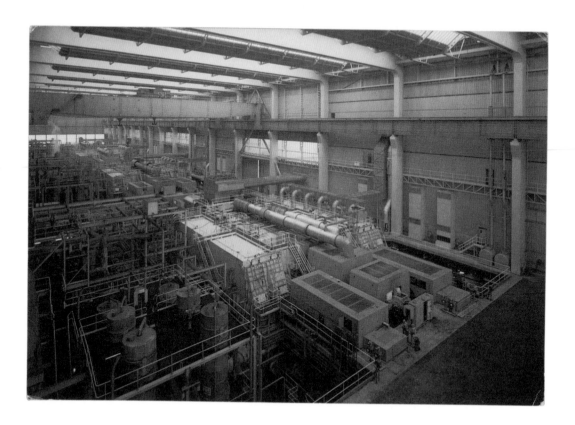

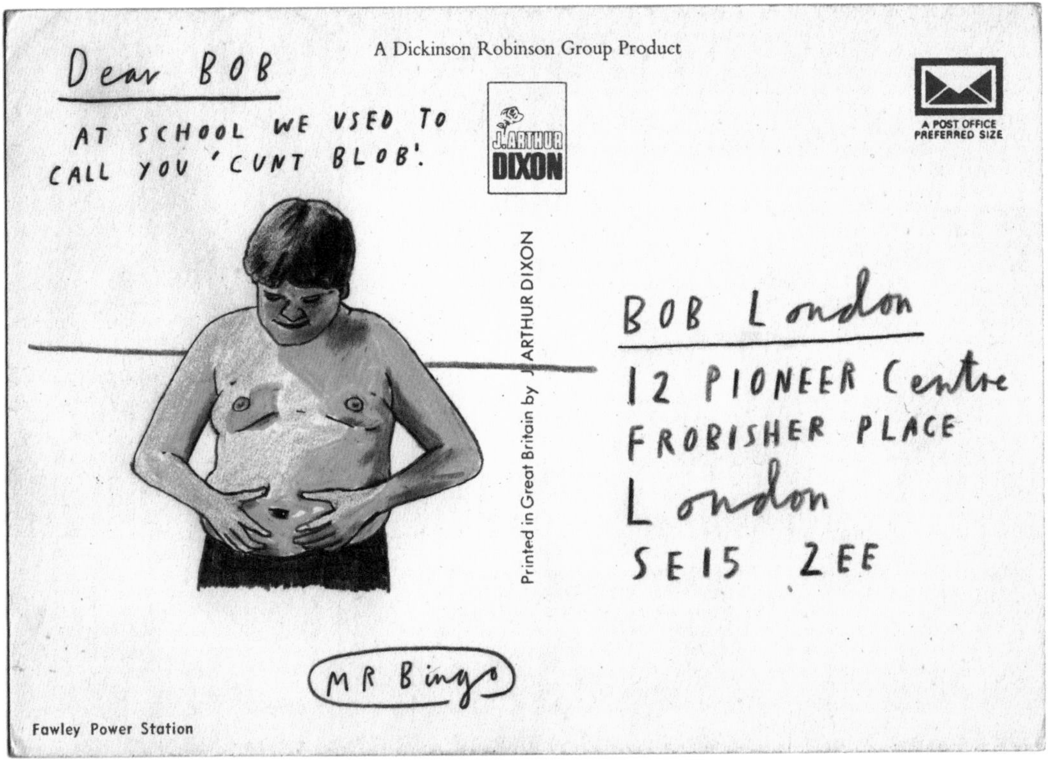

Dear BOB

AT SCHOOL WE USED TO
CALL YOU 'CUNT BLOB'.

A Dickinson Robinson Group Product

A POST OFFICE PREFERRED SIZE

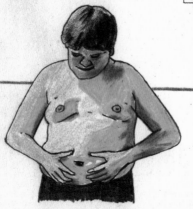

Printed in Great Britain by J ARTHUR DIXON

BOB London
12 PIONEER Centre
FROBISHER PLACE
London
SE15 2EE

MR Bingo

Fawley Power Station

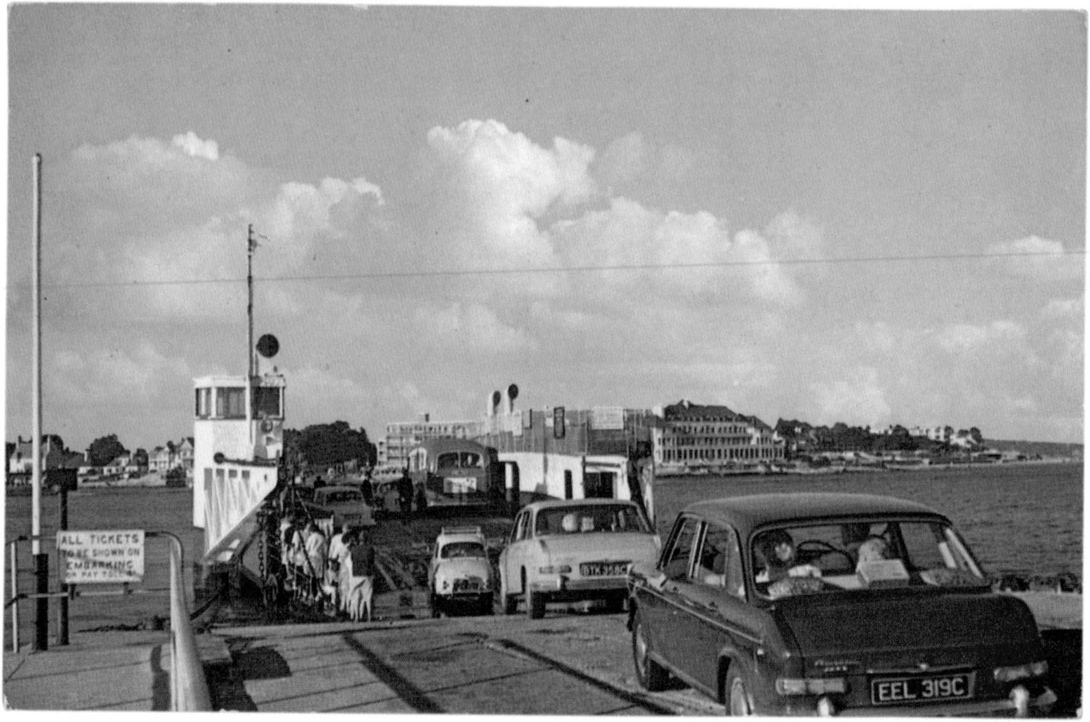
ALL TICKETS
TO BE SHOWN ON
EMBARKING
EEL 319C

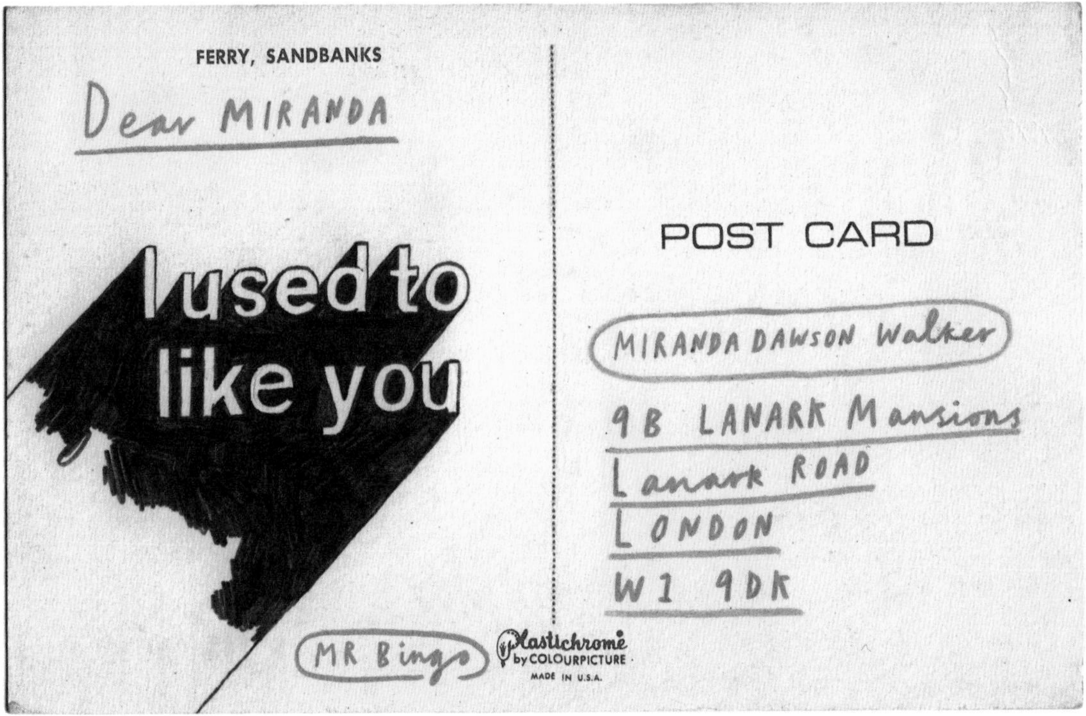
FERRY, SANDBANKS

Dear MIRANDA

I used to like you

MR Bingo

Plastichrome by COLOURPICTURE MADE IN U.S.A.

POST CARD

MIRANDA DAWSON Walker

9B LANARK Mansions

Lanark ROAD

LONDON

W1 9DK

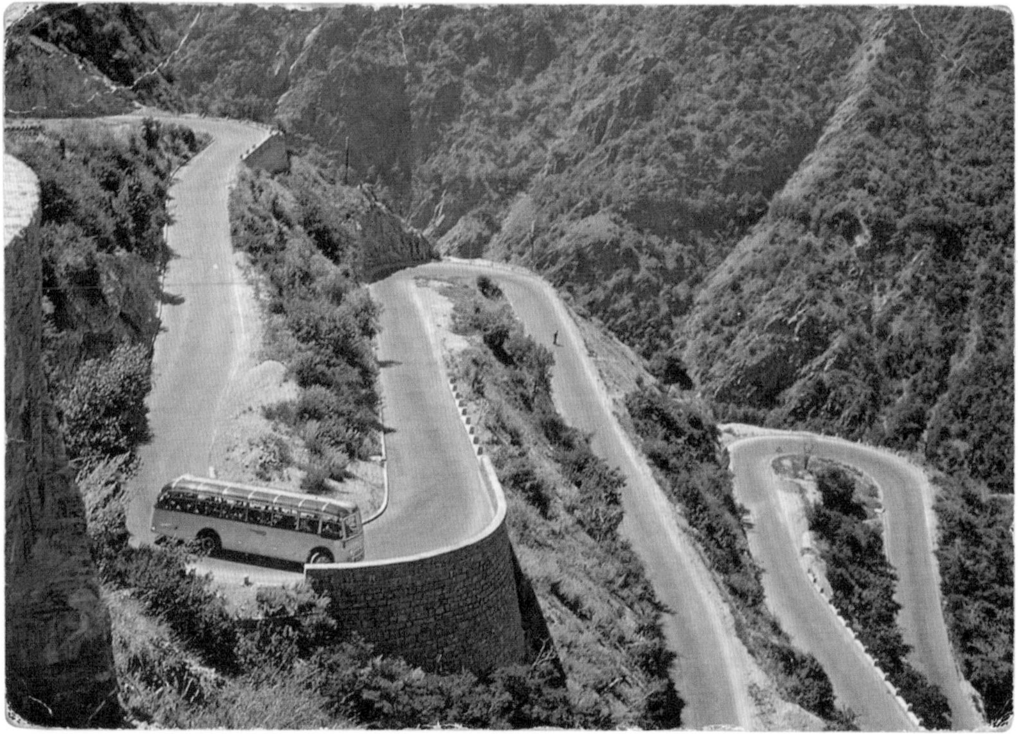

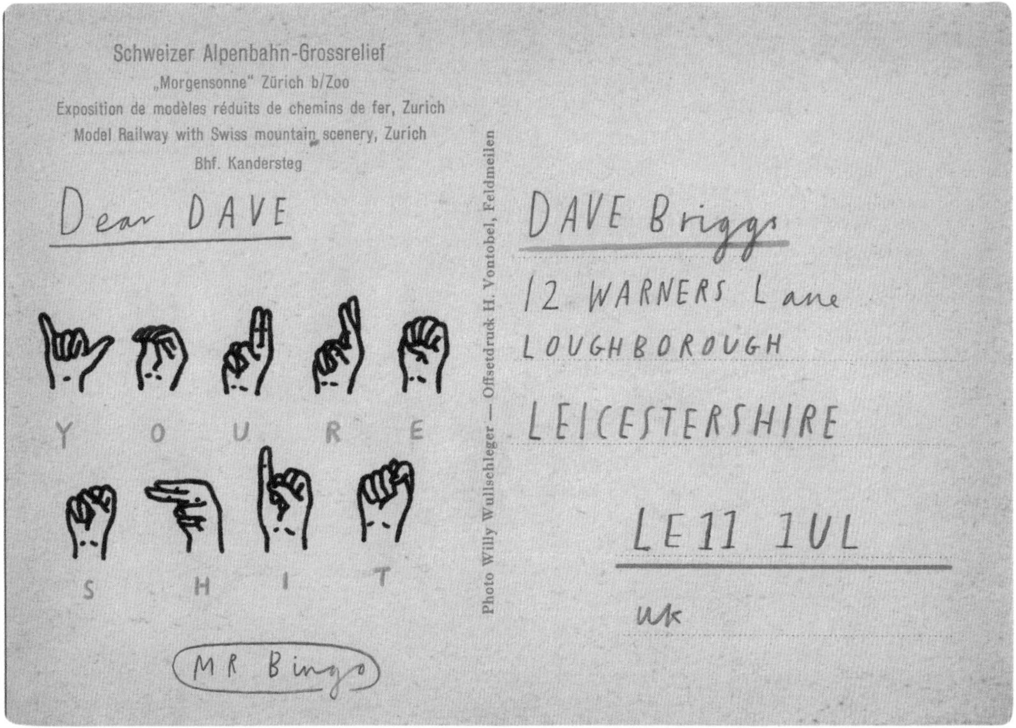
Schweizer Alpenbahn-Grossrelief
„Morgensonne" Zürich b/Zoo
Exposition de modèles réduits de chemins de fer, Zurich
Model Railway with Swiss mountain scenery, Zurich
Bhf. Kandersteg

Dear DAVE

Y O U R E

S H I T

MR Bingo

Photo Willy Wullschleger — Offsetdruck H. Vontobel, Feldmeilen

DAVE Briggs
12 WARNERS Lane
LOUGHBOROUGH
LEICESTERSHIRE
LE11 1UL
uk

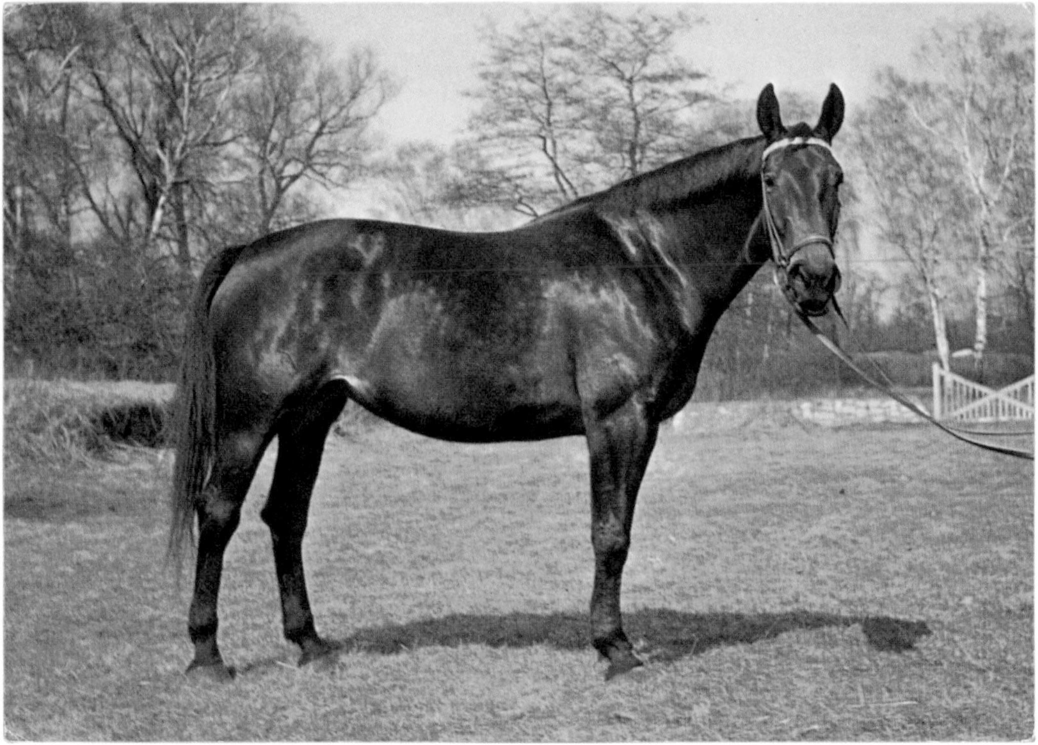

POST DENNIS Productions CARD

AFFIX STAMP HERE
POST OFFICE
PREFERRED

Dear KATE

YOUR BUM
LOOKS
BIG IN
EVERYTHING

Printed & Published by E. T. W. DENNIS & SONS LTD. SCARBOROUGH

KATE Jones

BRANDOPUS
The CHARLOTTE Building
17 GRESSE st
London
W1T 1QL

MR Bingo

D.200

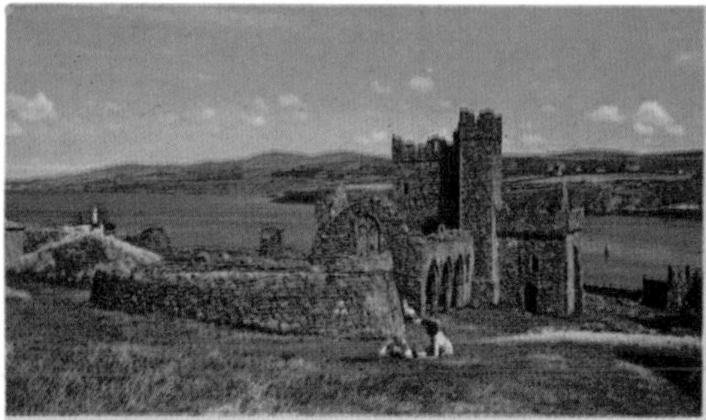

ST GERMAIN'S CATHEDRAL

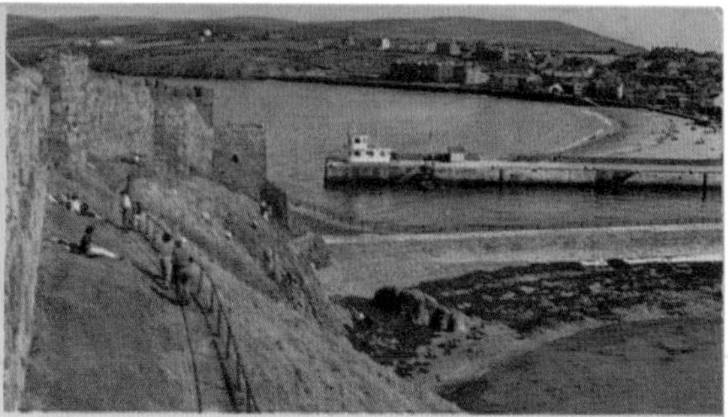

PEEL

PEEL

ST PATRICKS ISLAND

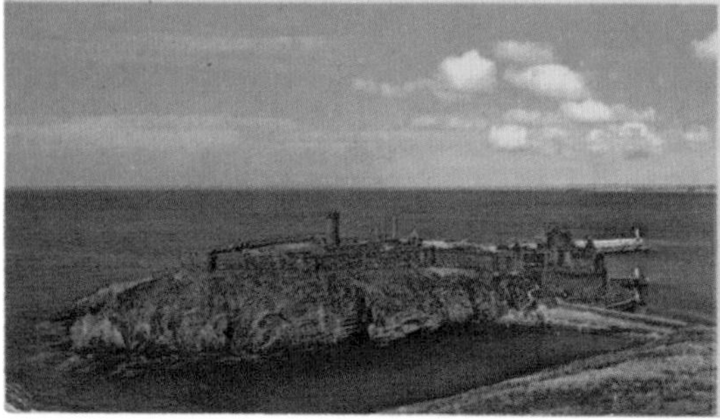

CASTLE AND BEACH

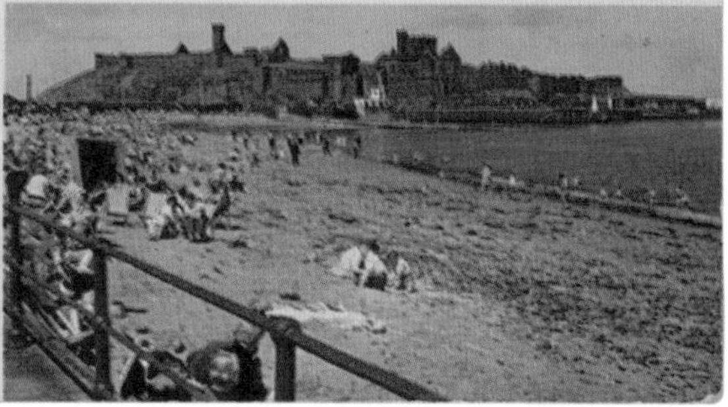

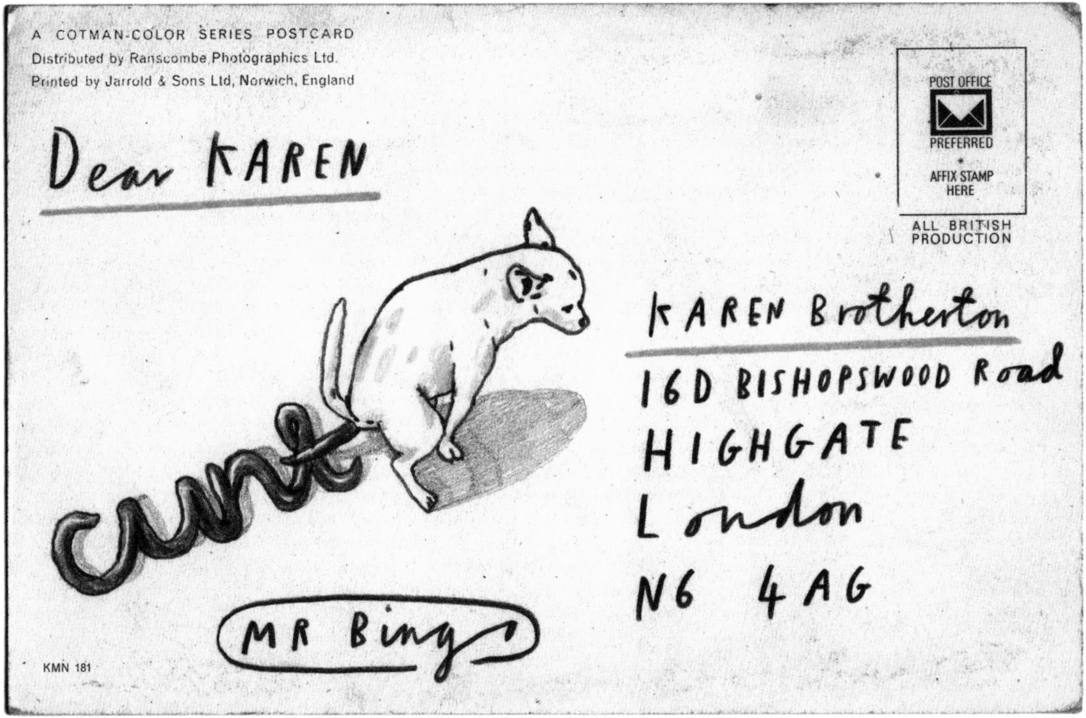
A COTMAN-COLOR SERIES POSTCARD
Distributed by Ranscombe Photographics Ltd.
Printed by Jarrold & Sons Ltd, Norwich, England
POST OFFICE
PREFERRED
AFFIX STAMP HERE
ALL BRITISH PRODUCTION
Dear KAREN
cunt
MR Bingo
KAREN Brotherton
16D BISHOPSWOOD Road
HIGHGATE
London
N6 4AG
KMN 181

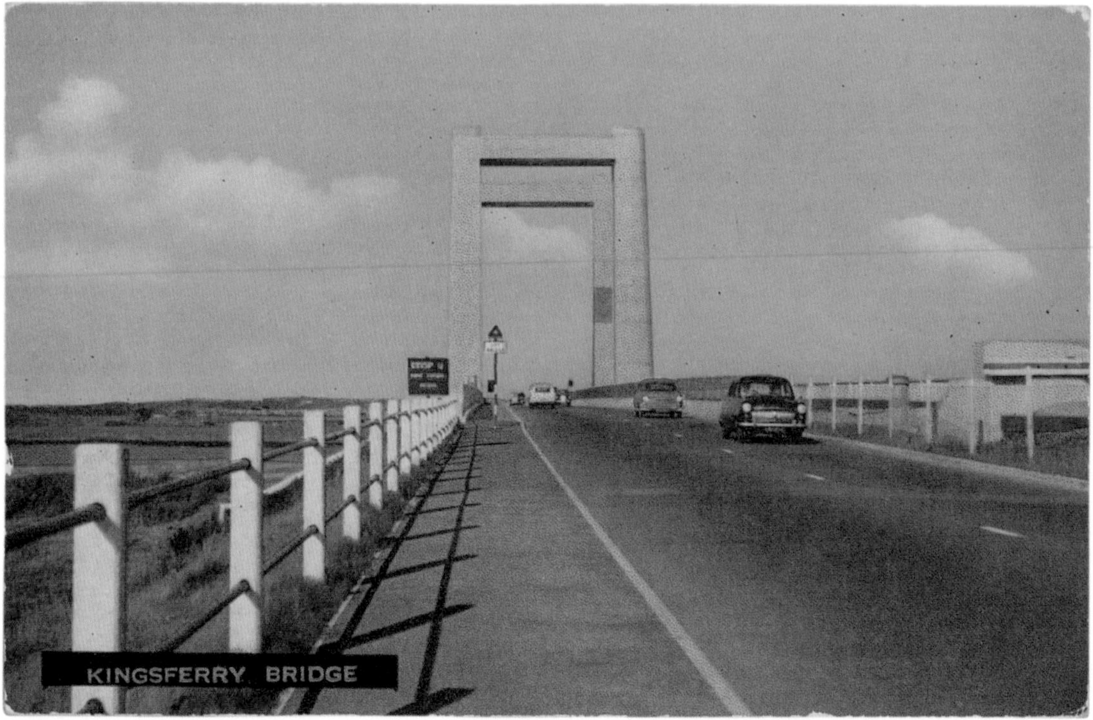

KINGSFERRY BRIDGE

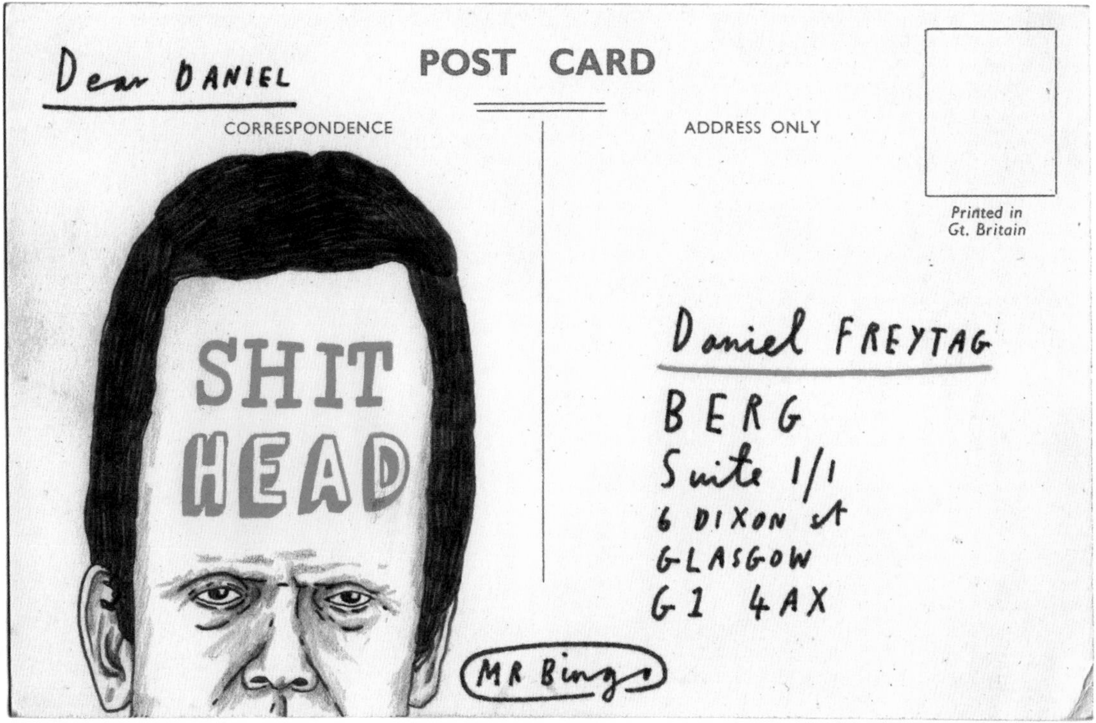
Dear DANIEL
POST CARD
CORRESPONDENCE
ADDRESS ONLY
Printed in Gt. Britain
SHIT HEAD
MR Bingo
Daniel FREYTAG
BERG
Suite 1/1
6 DIXON st
GLASGOW
G1 4AX

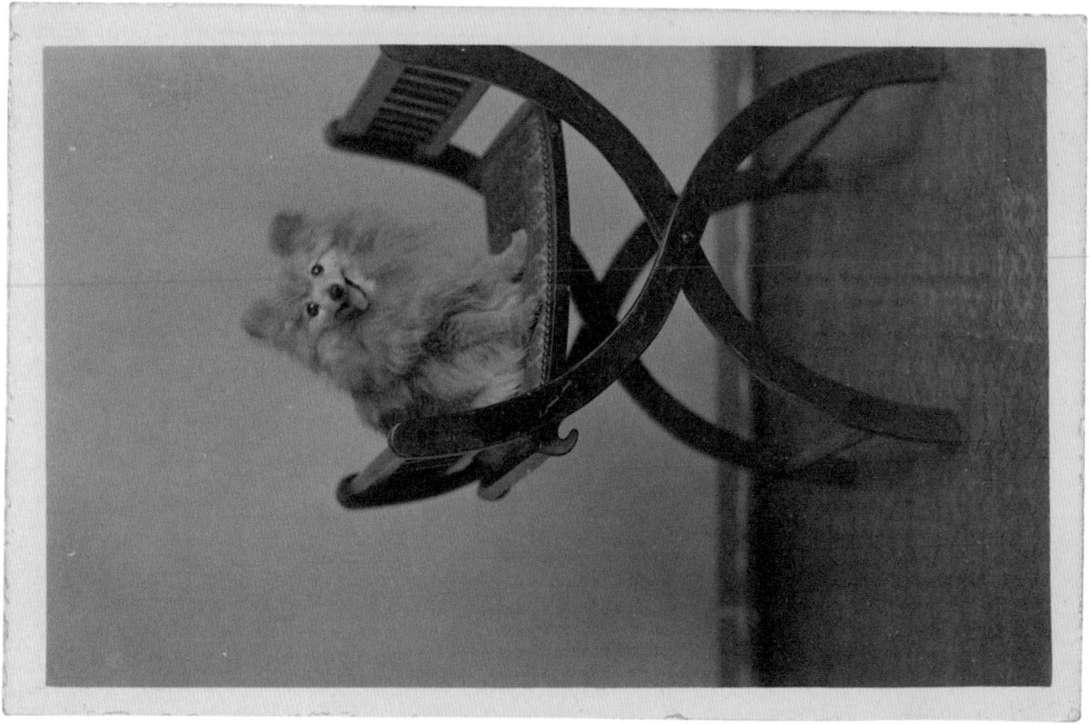

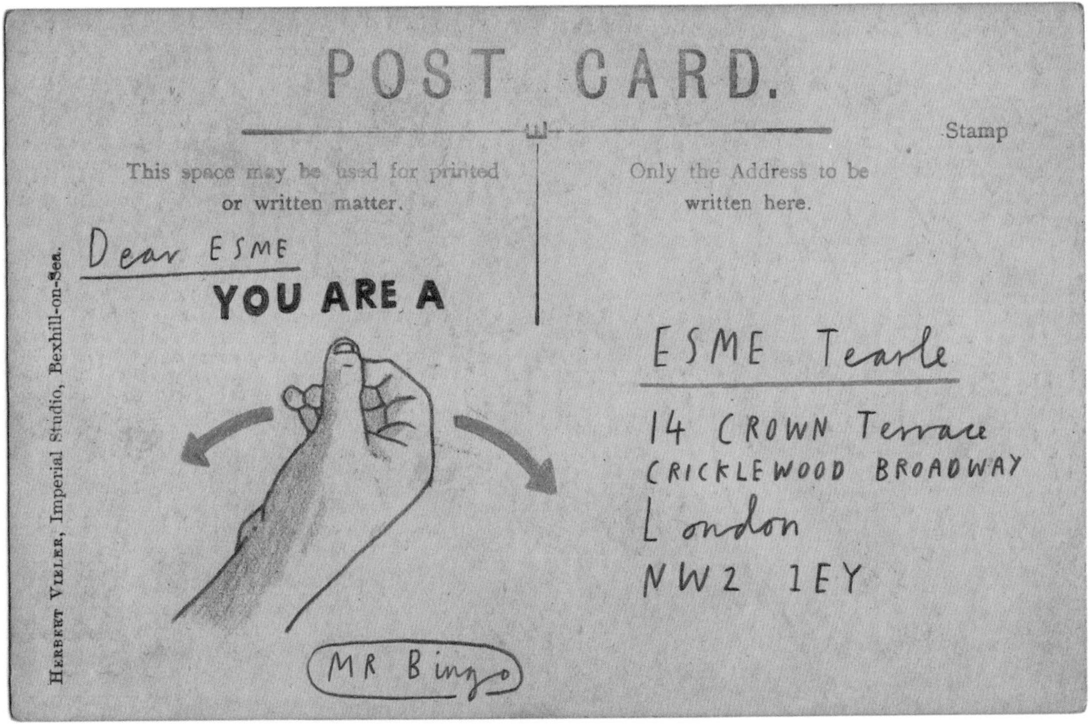
POST CARD.

Stamp

This space may be used for printed or written matter.

Only the Address to be written here.

Dear ESME

YOU ARE A

MR Bingo

ESME Tearle

14 CROWN Terrace

CRICKLEWOOD BROADWAY

London

NW2 1EY

HERBERT VIELER, Imperial Studio, Bexhill-on-Sea.

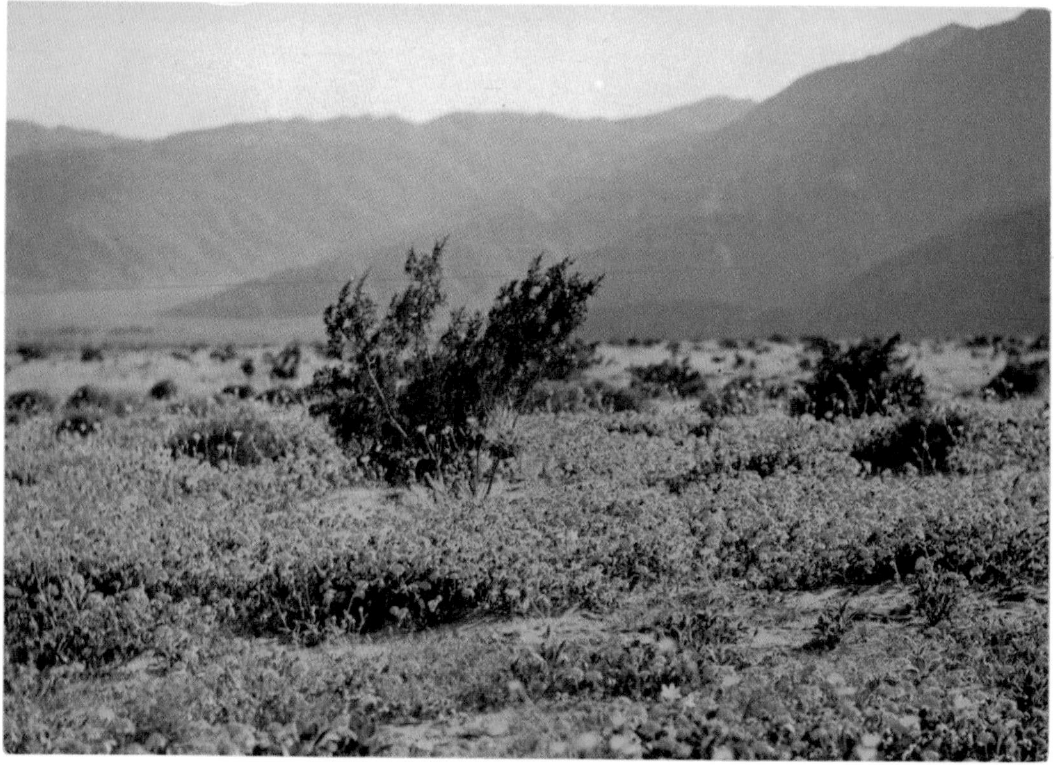

Lavender sand verbena carpets the desert in February, March and April.

MCG 411209

© KENDALL KARDS, 1217 11th Ave., Yuma, AZ 85364 (602) 783-8947

Photo by Charles P. Kendall

Dear ADELAIDE,

I HAD THE WEIRDEST DREAM LAST NIGHT. THERE WERE 3 OF YOU.

MR Bingo

Address

POST CARD RATE STAMP

ADELAIDE Fallon

82 FARM Hill

EXETER, Devon

EX4 2LJ

****

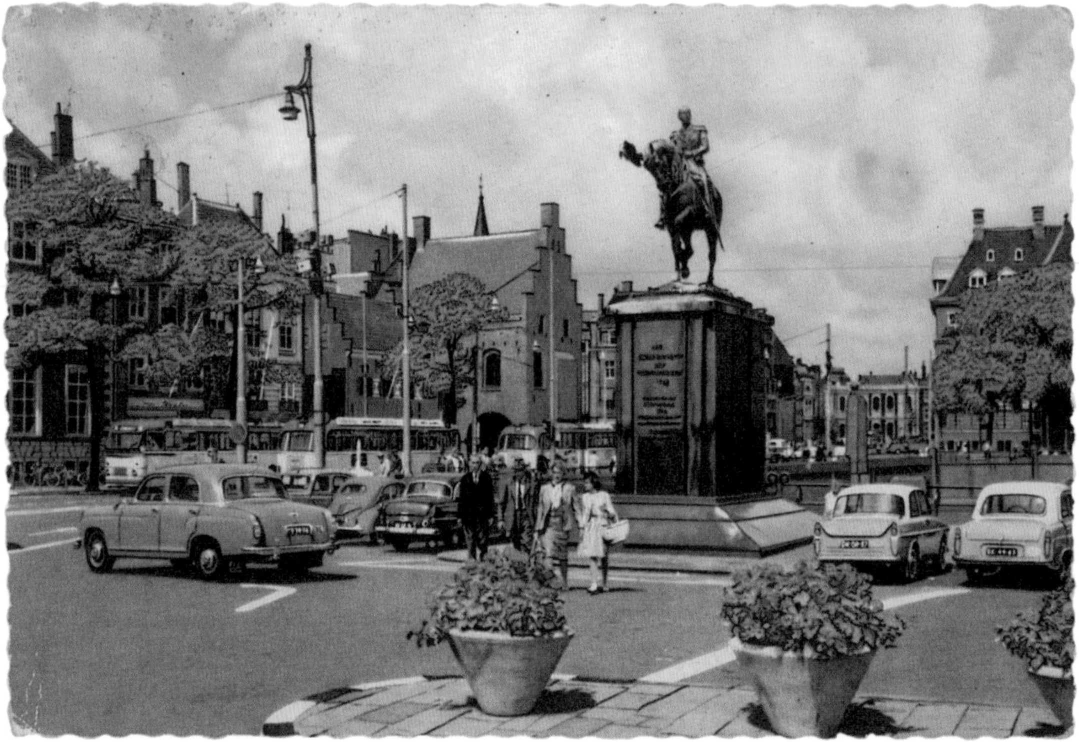

DEN HAAG
Buitenhof met Standbeeld Willem II

Dear LUKE

YOU'RE A

LUKE N Prowse
124 CHASE HILL ROAD
ARLESEY, BEDFORDSHIRE
SG15 6UF

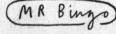

DE MUINCK & CO., AMSTERDAM · C

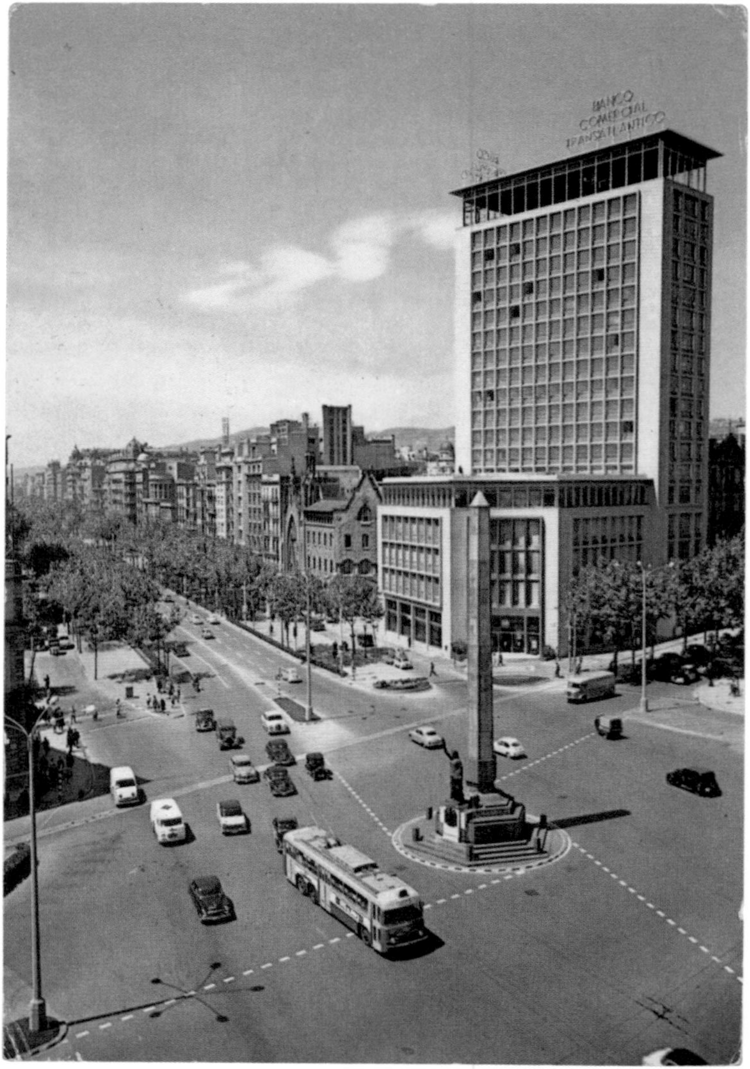
BANCO
COMERCIAL
TRANSATLANTICO

457-BARCELONA. Avda. Generalisimo Franco

Dear HARRY

YOU'RE A FUCKI
PRICK MATE

GARCIA GARRABELLA y Cia. S.R.C.
(Prohibida la reproducción).

HARRY Sprout
21 DOVE ROAD
CAMDEN Town

London

NW1 7AE

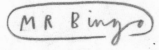

MR Bingo

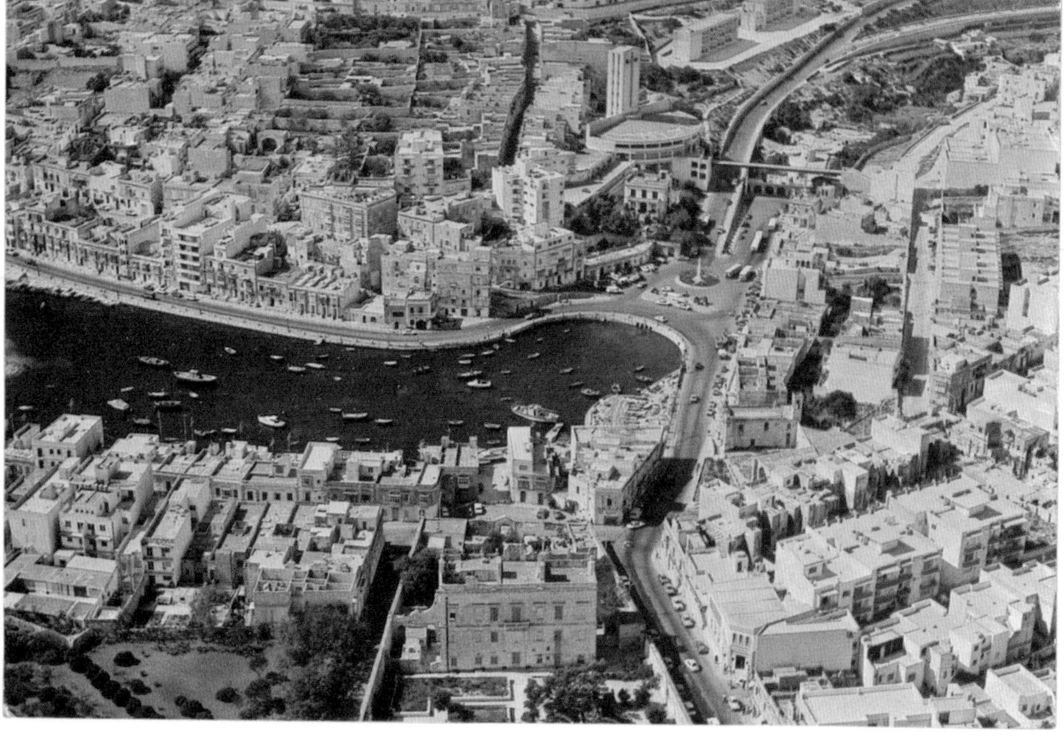

MMI-075B

Dear CARMEN

MALTA – Aerial View – Spinola Bay.

FUCK
NUT

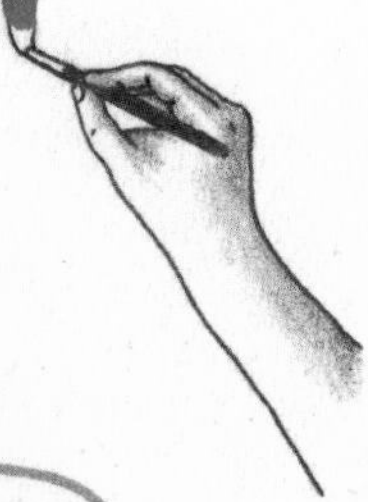

printed by Interprint Limited, Malta

CARMEN Mirelle

9 HAVERFIELD Road

BOW, London

E3 5BH

MR Bingo

G178

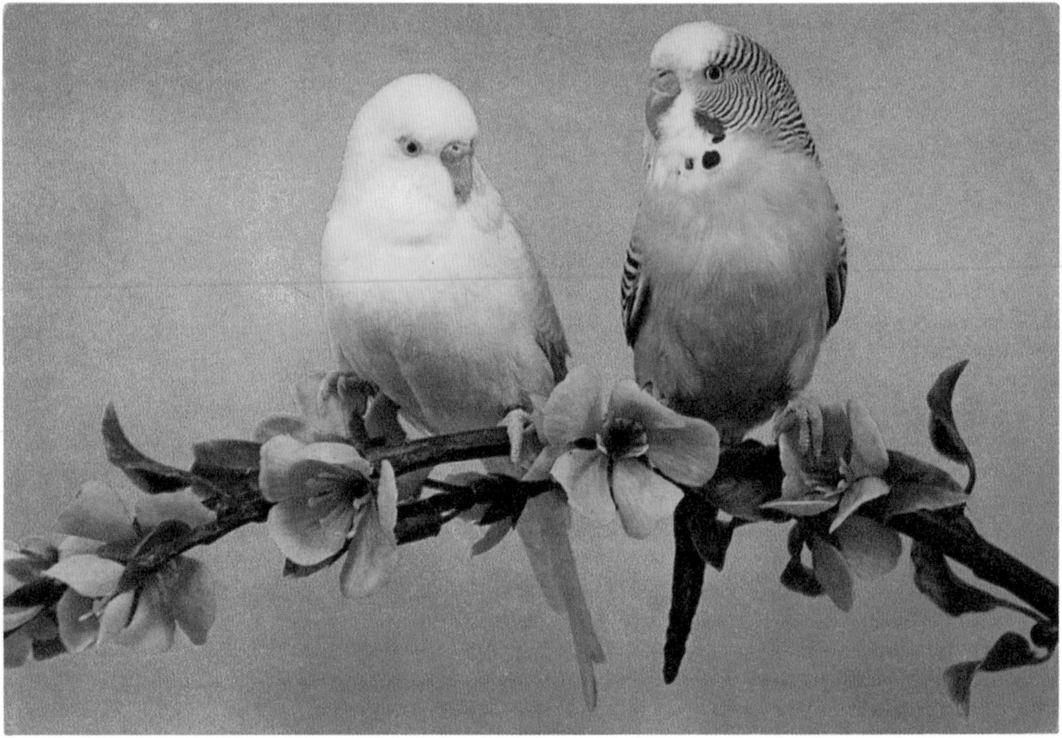

NATURAL COLOUR
J. Arthur Dixon
PHOTOGRAVURE
POST CARD

Dear JANE,
IF YOU WERE THE LAST PERSON ON EARTH,

I WOULD IGNORE YOU

MR Bingo

Budgerigars : Sky-blue Cock
and Albino Hen.

From a Colour Photograph by Harry V. Lacey

Printed and Published by J. Arthur Dixon, Ltd., Newport, I.W., England.

JANE Trustram
80 CANROBERT st
London

E2 6PX

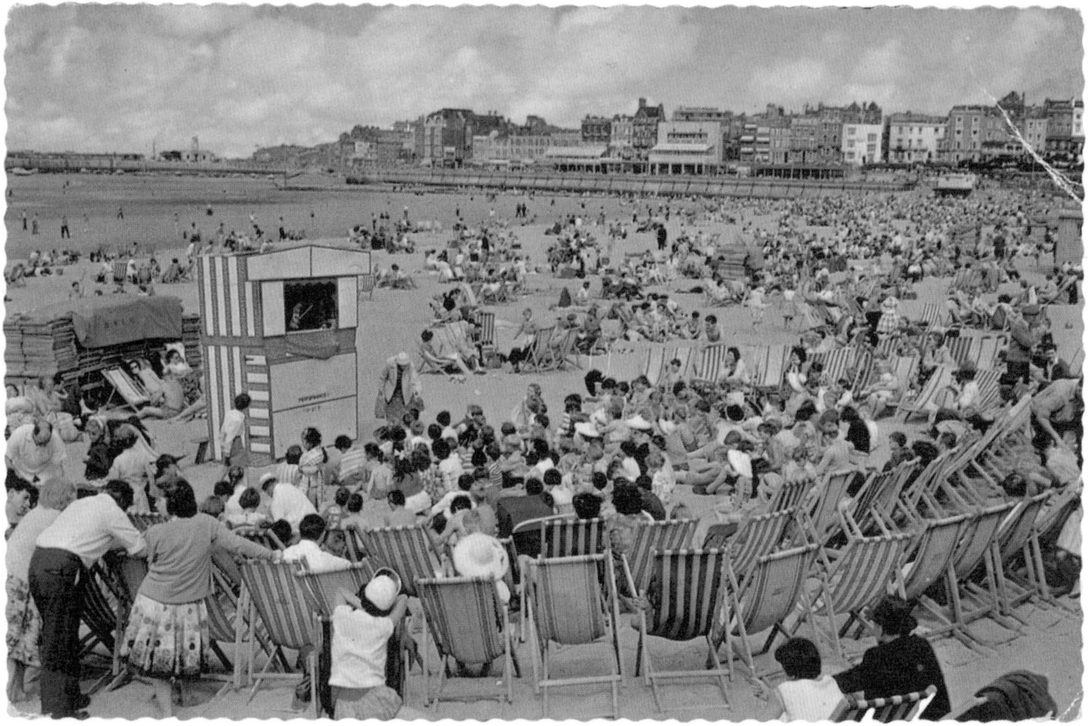

Punch and Judy Show, The Sands, Margate

NATURAL COLOUR SERIES
PHOTO
GREETINGS
CANADA

THE PHOTOGRAPHIC GREETING CARD CO. LTD.

C12548

Dear ALEX

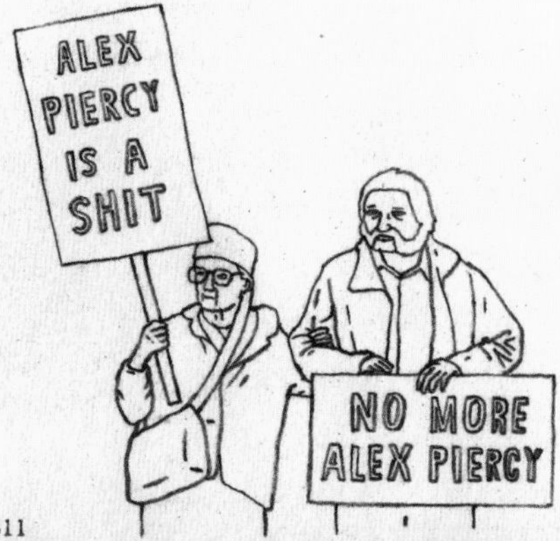
ALEX
PIERCY
IS A
SHIT
NO MORE
ALEX PIERCY

MR A Piercy

9 LEDBURY MEWS NORTH

Notting HILL

London W11 2AF

MR Bingo

811

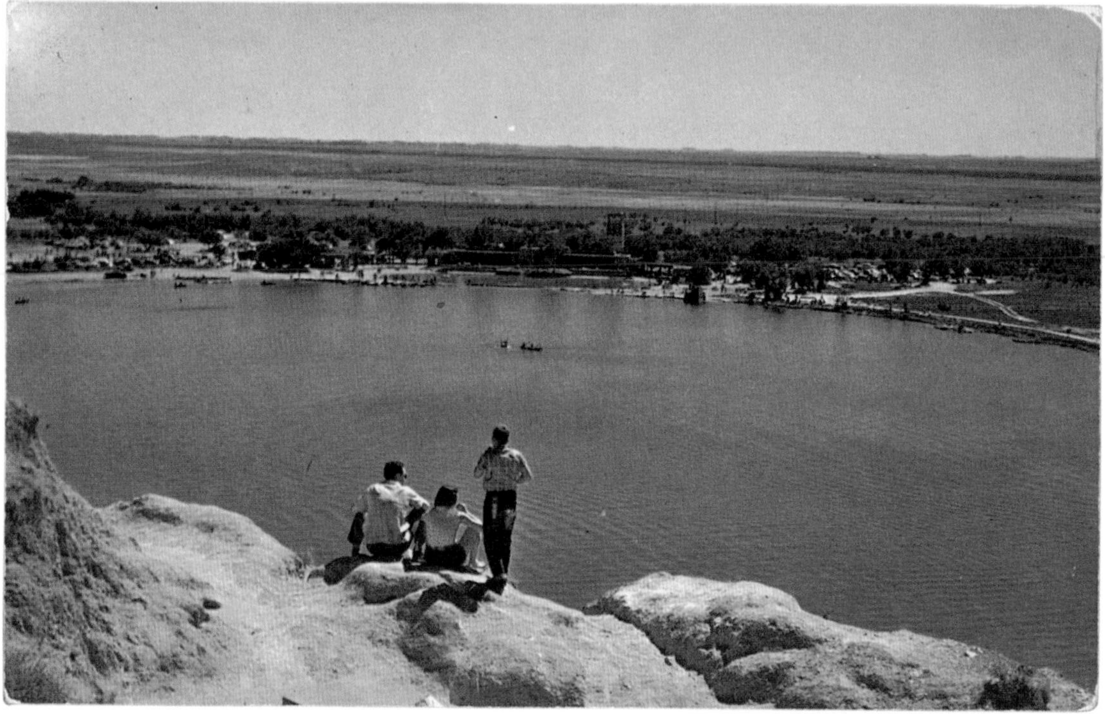

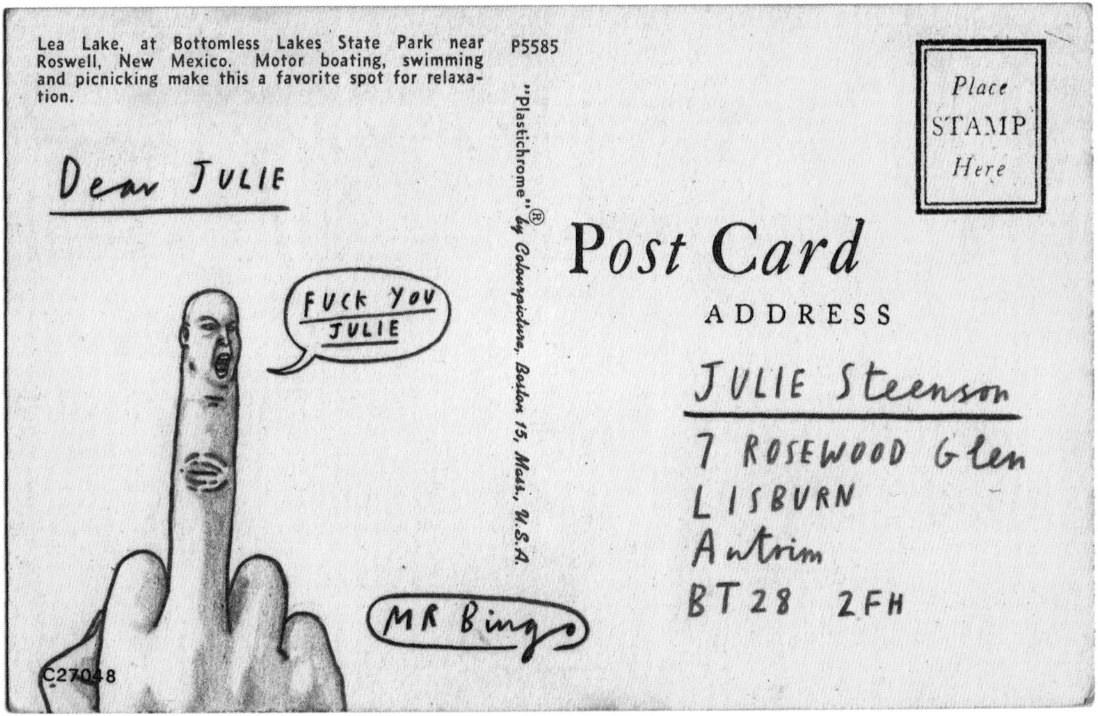
Lea Lake, at Bottomless Lakes State Park near Roswell, New Mexico. Motor boating, swimming and picnicking make this a favorite spot for relaxation.
P5585
"Plastichrome"® by Colourpicture, Boston 15, Mass., U.S.A.
Place STAMP Here
Post Card
ADDRESS
Dear JULIE
FUCK YOU JULIE
MR Bingo
JULIE Steenson
7 ROSEWOOD Glen
LISBURN
Antrim
BT28 2FH
C27048

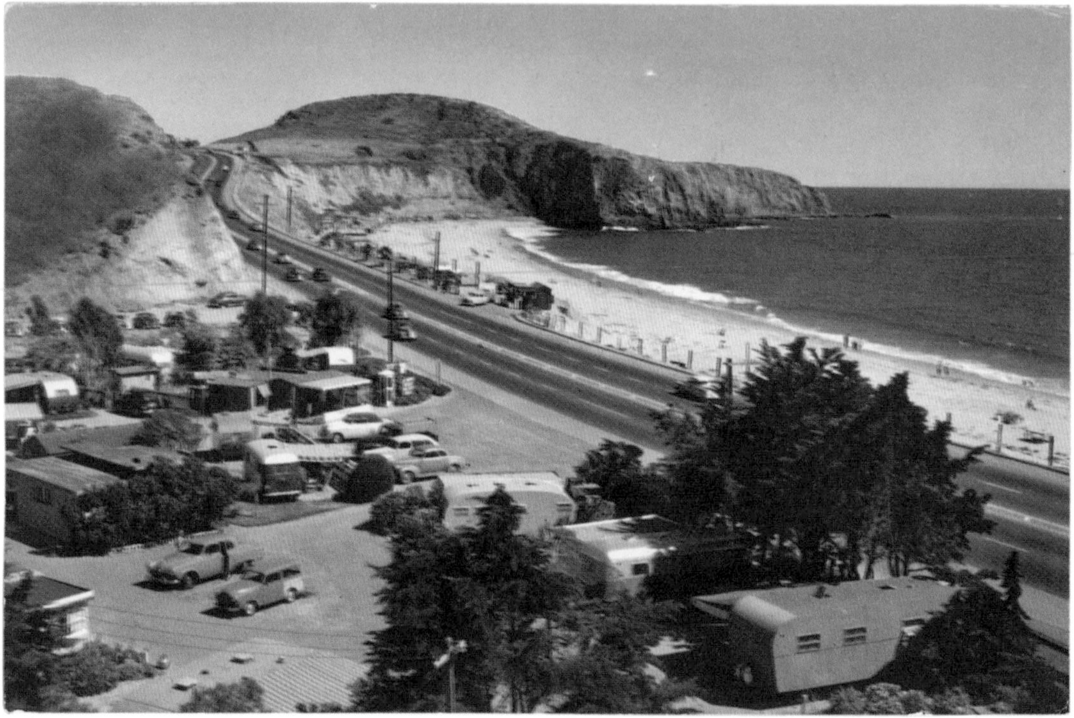

GW-129

U. S. HIGHWAY 101 (ALTERNATE)
Southern California

Trailering along a fine stretch of private beach between the communities of NEWPORT HARBOR and LAGUNA BEACH, on the highway from Long Beach to San Diego. Curious and uncommon "Devil's Postpile" rock formation appears in the cliff just offshore.

Dear CATHERINE

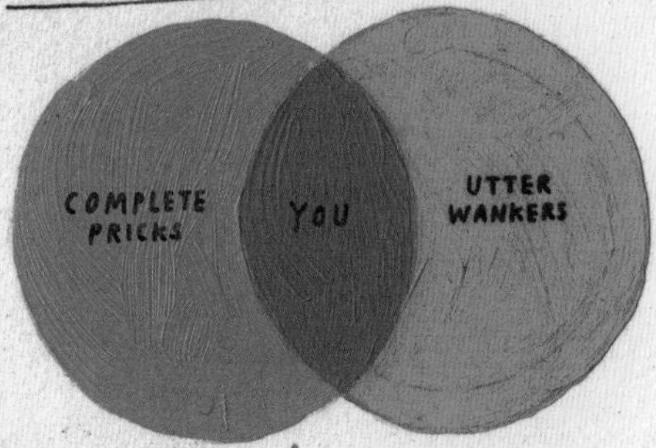
COMPLETE PRICKS
YOU
UTTER WANKERS

MR Bingo

Geo. E. Watson, Color Photographer

MIRRO-KROME ® CARD BY H. S. CROCKER CO., INC., LOS ANGELES 17, CALIF.
PUBL. & DISTR. BY "Golden West" ® COLOR CARD CO., 2583 MAINE AVE., L. B. 6, CALIF.

GW

PLACE STAMF HERE

ADDRESS ONLY

Catherine GARRETT

22 SHIPTON st
London
E2 7RU

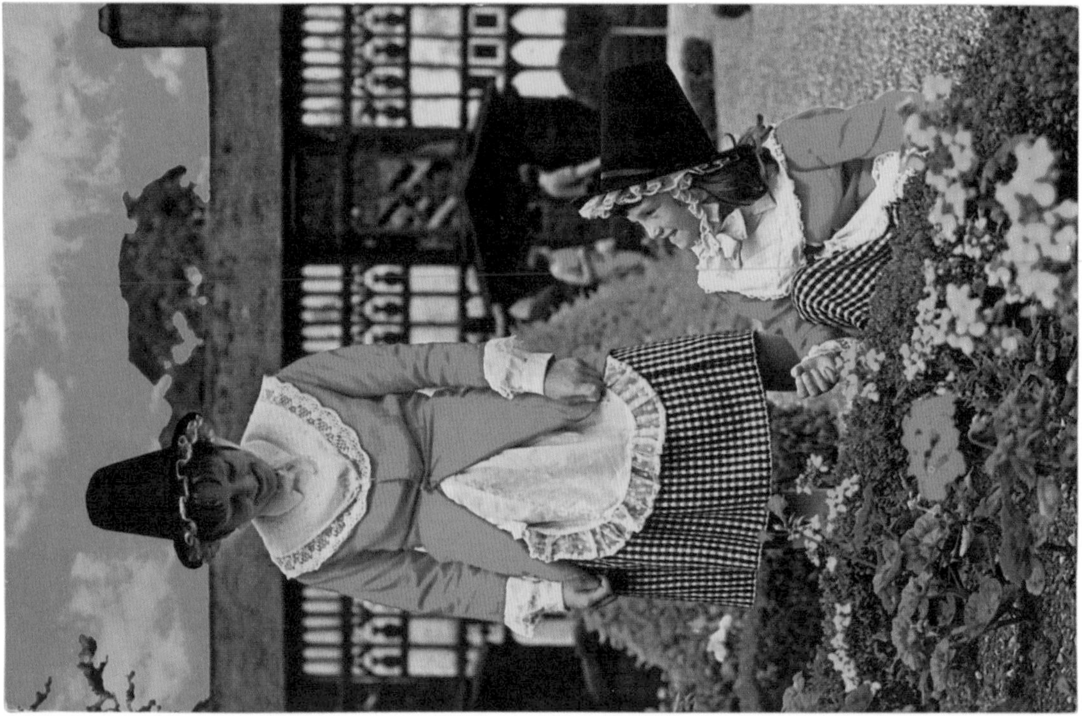

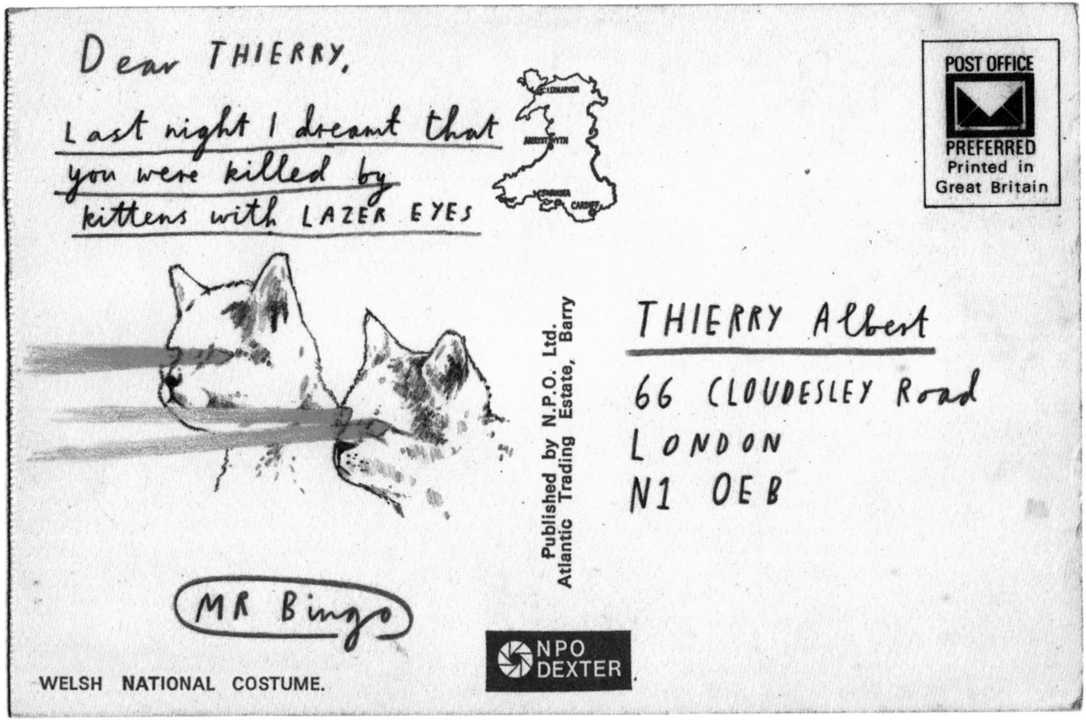
Dear THIERRY,

Last night I dreamt that you were killed by kittens with LAZER EYES

MR Bingo

WELSH NATIONAL COSTUME.

Published by N.P.O. Ltd. Atlantic Trading Estate, Barry

NPO DEXTER

POST OFFICE PREFERRED
Printed in Great Britain

THIERRY Albert
66 CLOUDESLEY Road
LONDON
N1 OEB

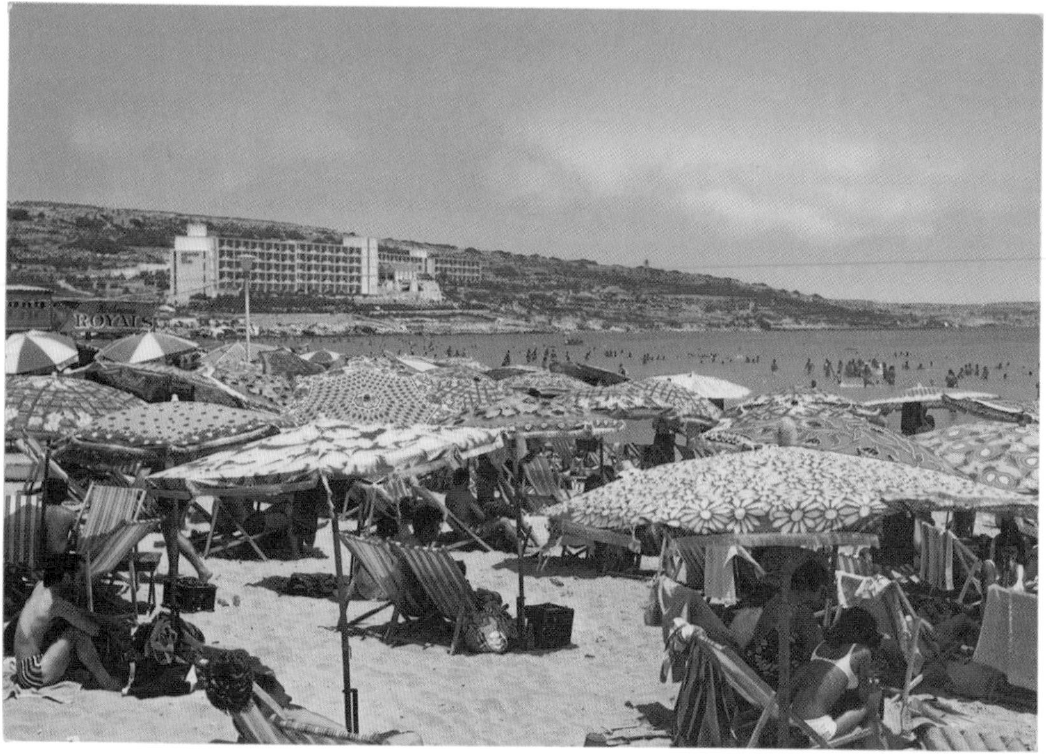
ROYALS

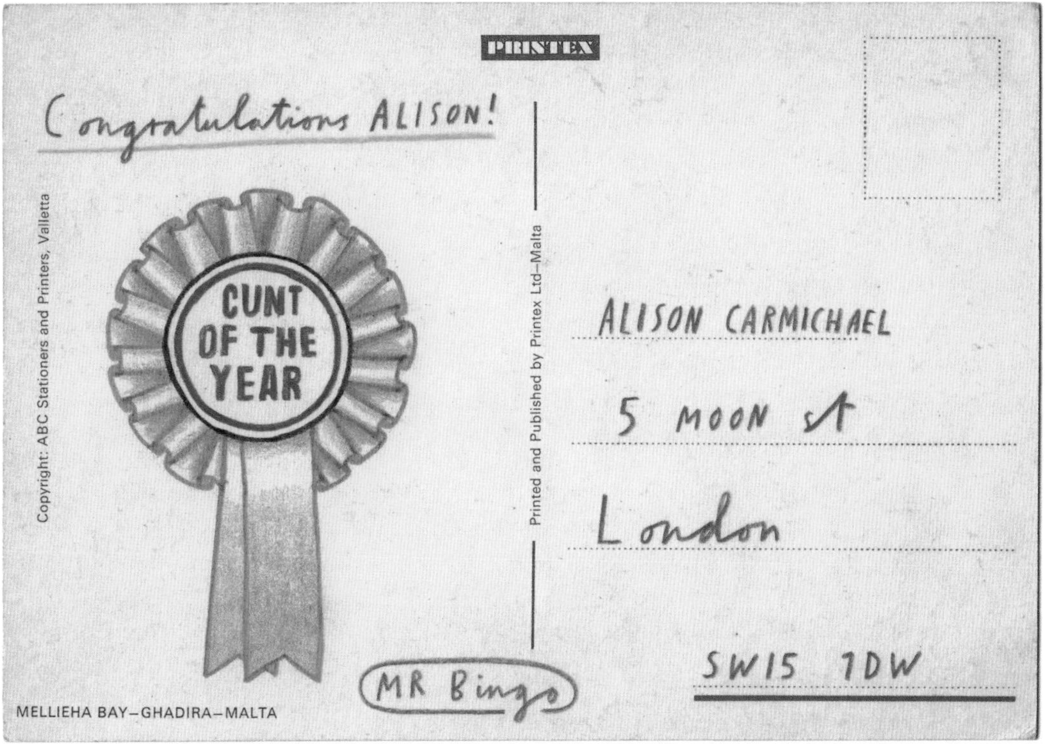

PRINTEX

Congratulations ALISON!

Copyright: ABC Stationers and Printers, Valletta

CUNT
OF THE
YEAR

Printed and Published by Printex Ltd–Malta

ALISON CARMICHAEL

5 MOON st

London

SW15 1DW

MR Bingo

MELLIEHA BAY–GHADIRA–MALTA

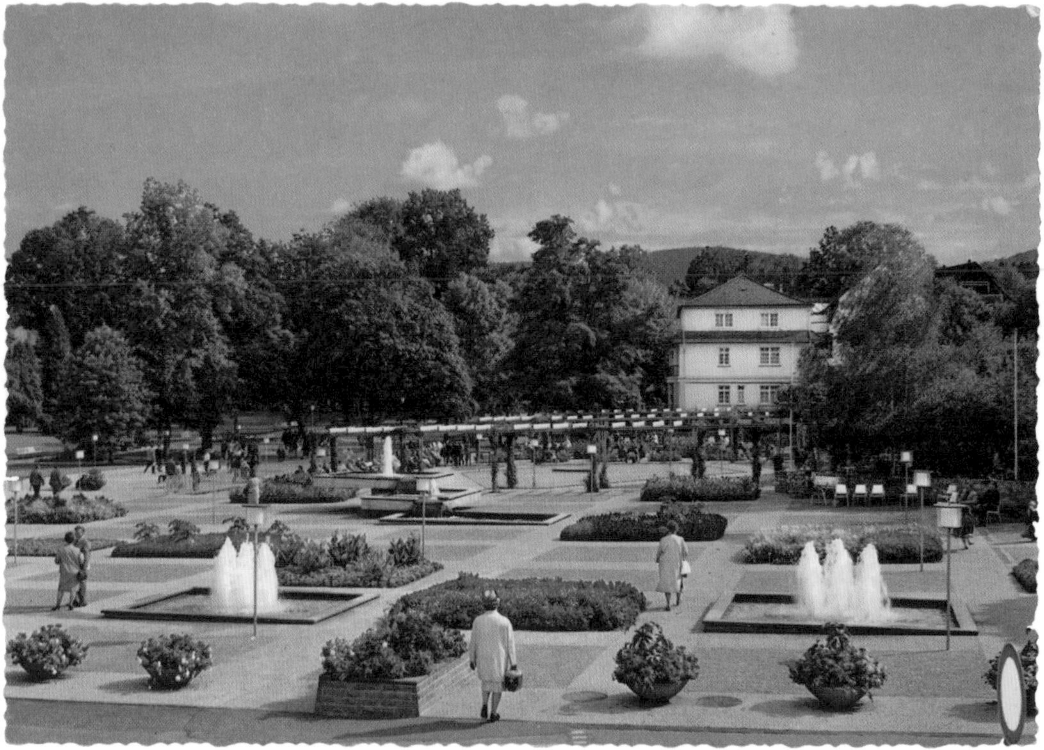

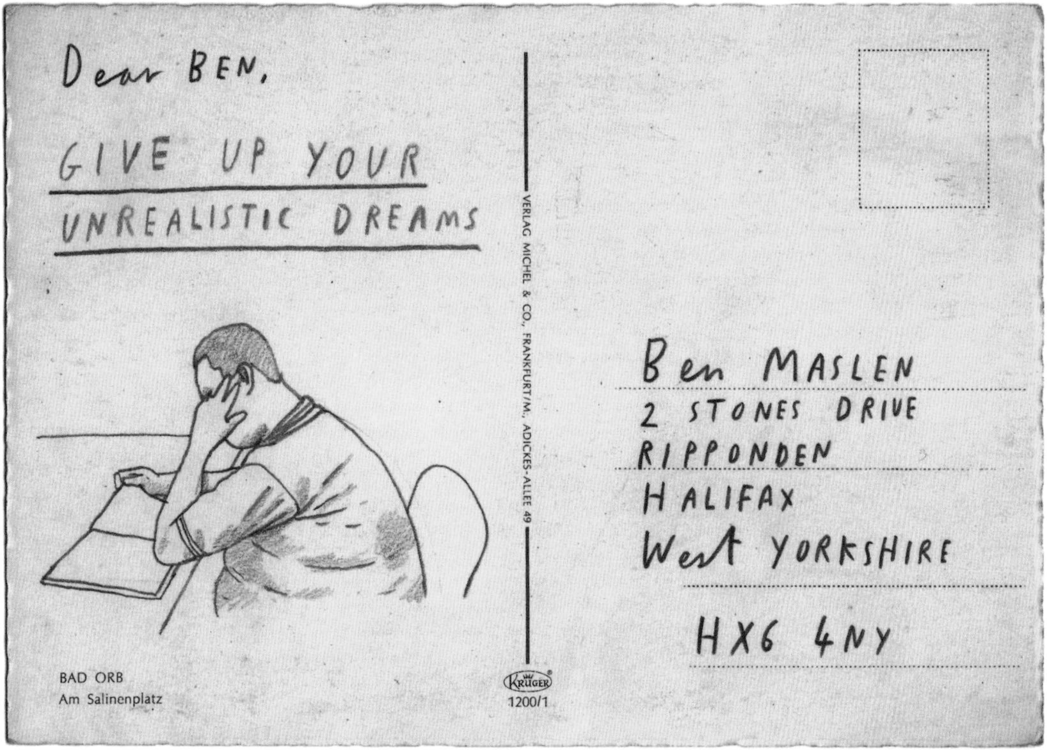
Dear BEN,
GIVE UP YOUR
UNREALISTIC DREAMS
VERLAG MICHEL & CO., FRANKFURT/M., ADICKES-ALLEE 49
Ben MASLEN
2 STONES DRIVE
RIPPONDEN
HALIFAX
West YORKSHIRE
HX6 4NY
BAD ORB
Am Salinenplatz
KRÜGER
1200/1